*To my wife, Aoife, and to Ann, Brian, Seamus
and Dolores, my parents and parents-in-law*

Contents

Acknowledgements

My first thanks go to my wife for her patience in tolerating my writing a second book within the first two years of our marriage! After that I have to thank Newstalk staff, in particular Chief Executive Frank Cronin and Editor Garrett Harte, for their flexibility in enabling me to structure my working week in a way that allowed this book to be finished on time. The contribution of the *Sunday Independent* – in particular Willie Kealy and Aengus Fanning for allowing me to work material in the book into my articles – is greatly appreciated, as is the contribution of many colleagues in both the fields of economics and journalism – print and broadcast – for their kindness in reading and commenting on both this and my last book.

Transworld Ireland, in particular Eoin McHugh, deserve thanks for their patience with me as well as their speed in what has necessarily been a stressful and condensed production process. Despite his own modesty, Patrick Arnold as usual provided excellent research assistance, and various economists of the ESRI provided helpful insights into the material covered in the book, as did Colm McCarthy and other non-ESRI economists.

Thanks are also due to Garrett Fitzgerald, Brian Lenihan,

Padraig White, Pat Cox, Martin Cronin, Alan Dukes, Ray MacSharry and many others too numerous to list (but whose contributions merit mentioning) for interview material and/or other assistance. Some people were of tremendous help to the book but, in their own interest, cannot be named. They know who they are and that I am grateful to them. So should those whom I – to my shame – may have forgotten to mention here, those whose contributions deserve acknowledgement as much as others here but who due to the time pressure on me were, I fear, looked over when writing this. I hope they will forgive that omission.

Preface

Writing an optimistic book on the Irish economy at the moment is a little like running backwards up a downward-moving escalator. Having written a book entitled *The Best is Yet to Come* on the cusp of Ireland's most severe decline in output, some advised me not to pursue a second book until the economy had fully recovered. On rereading that book, however, the recession that followed its publication has validated its core message, namely that the economy lost its senses in 2005 and needs to return to where it was in that year before Ireland's amazing longer-term demographic rebound can continue in a lasting way.

The title of that last book can only be criticized by those who never bothered to read the rest of it. A new book on the Irish economy is necessary. This is true for several reasons, the first of which is that economic growth is as much a matter of confidence as it is of fundamentals. Having been battered by negative comment, the economic morale of the nation is on the floor. It needn't be. Therefore the first task of this book is to show how the most recent economic data validates what was predicted in *The Best is Yet to Come*: that whether you look at GDP, GNP, employment or tax levels, the economy will – post-recession – settle back to where it was in the period between late 2004 and early 2005. That is the focus of Chapter 1.

Chapters 2 to 4 explain the international economic crisis of 2008 and 2009 and how it affected Ireland. Chapters 5 to 8 explain why Ireland suffered a more severe decline in output than the rest of the world, and how excessive government during the 'Inchidoney years' left state coffers bare at a time when they were needed to counter the effects of recession.

But the most important part of the book is contained in chapters 9 to 14: the practitioners of the backward-looking blame-game narrative on this crisis have had their say. If the country is to move forward, then we have to come up with ideas and solutions. And those ideas and solutions need to be organized and joined together. Part IV – chapters 9 to 12 – looks at the key pillars of recovery: restoring cost competitiveness and building the smart economy, a new approach to planning and spatial strategy and an overhaul of banking and finance; but they also look at the important ethical issues that have to be confronted if all, and not just some, of the lessons of the last two years are to be learned.

Part V brings the reader back to Ireland and, in two chapters, points out that we can't implement the right economic policies for the future unless we have a functioning political system. But with opinion polls showing unprecedented shifts in public support, that system is showing signs of collapsing with *nothing* new arising to replace it.

Ireland's economy is on the mend. But that process could be interrupted and quickly reversed unless there is a stable seven-year plan to implement all the necessary policies. And such a plan needs to be politically as well as economically competent: if it plunges the nation into a divisive and inconclusive election, a plan that is economically competent but politically stupid will be hugely damaging.

Finally – on the basis that a good crisis shouldn't be wasted –

the last chapter looks at the opportunity to build a new and reformed system of politics and government, one more suited to the prosperous high technology economy and a young, educated electorate that will emerge from this recession still largely intact. The glistening promise of the hundredth anniversary of the 1916 rising and the severity of Ireland's recession during 2009 are – respectively – positive and negative reminders that problems that have lingered in Ireland since the nineteenth and twentieth centuries must be finally confronted before Ireland can achieve its full exhilarating potential in the twenty-first.

Prologue

In March 2008 the Irish economy was teetering on the edge of a cliff. Two years earlier, in March 2006, that cliff edge was already visible and drawing closer. Ireland's prolonged boom was continuing. But as Economics Editor for the *Irish Times* I wasn't sure it should have been. In an article* that month I warned that a housing crash was possible. Then again, if prompt action was taken it was avoidable. Two years and no action later, I and others, to varying degrees, have been proven right.

By March 2008 house prices had been falling for a year – a healthy and welcome affair up to that point. That month I found myself in New York as a guest of the Bank of New York Mellon. It was the oldest bank in the US and the first one to lend to the US government. 'A big mistake!' I joked with the bank's vice president, Brian Ruane, when he showed me the first US government bond purchased by the bank's ancestor over two centuries earlier. That morning, Friday 14 March, I gave a breakfast talk to leading Irish Americans on Ireland's future, not just as an economy but as a society. The talk was given in the top-floor

---

* 'Housing Market Vulnerable to a Crash', *Irish Times*, 6 March 2006.

auditorium of the bank's stunning art deco headquarters at the prestigious address of 1 Wall Street. I and the other guests could, from a vantage point of two centuries and over a hundred stories, look down on the rest of Manhattan's financial district where that day a crisis would unfold that was to signal the start of the deepest recession since the 1930s. Our focus that Friday was not on the imminent downturn, though. Entitled 'The Best is Yet to Come', my talk, based on a book of the same name, was a look back at how far Ireland had come in the past two decades and a look forward at how far it could still go once the downturn had passed.

But the middle of March 2008 was a difficult time to look into the long-term future. The Romans had always regarded the month of March as a time of omens. In William Shakespeare's play, Julius Caesar is warned on the morning of his assassination[*] to 'Beware the ides of March'. There had been omens for Ireland's economy too, but they were avoidable if you chose to ignore them. By March 2008 that wasn't possible any more: credit in the economy had risen to near delinquent levels, the cost of doing business was too high, and Ireland's system of social partnership had become sclerotic and irrelevant. More to the point, Ireland had become a spatially retarded economy. From the top floor of the Bank of New York Mellon on that March day I was able to look out over a population greater than the entire Republic of Ireland clustered neatly within a bird's-eye view of Manhattan. Thanks to low-rise development during our boom, in Ireland a population of similar size was spread over an area the size of South Carolina. A US builder could fit ten thousand office workers or a thousand residents on an acre of land; an Irish builder could fit in only a tenth of that.

The significance of these numbers is now clear to us in the huge cost being paid by the National Asset Management Agency (NAMA) for development land, land whose potential value was

---

[*] 15 March 44 BC.

in many cases held back by a failure of planning and urbanization. The consequences of Ireland's failure to reap what I call the 'density dividend' – a failure to use land properly and urban space efficiently – was a key theme of my talk that day. It was, I said, preventing the country from growing efficiently, leading to high accommodation costs and long commutes. By trapping many of our citizens in housing estates with one shop, one pub and no public transport, it was also leading to rip-off prices. Not to mention distorting economic growth: instead of productive economic activity, growth was being driven by too much construction in the wrong places. On the other hand, I told my listeners, Ireland's strong population growth could drive a second wave of growth in the near future, once the downturn had passed. With appropriate government action, that can still happen. As a mighty recession shakes out the imbalances in the world economy and the Irish economy, the toxic results of a decade of loose monetary policy and looser regulation are exiting the global economy's digestive tract. As a country with the least dense population in western Europe,* Ireland's level of population and economic activity remains far below its long-term potential level, even after the boom. Fortunately, the message is still true. It is now over a year and a half since I gave that talk, and despite the ravages of a severe recession, in 2008 Ireland recorded its highest birth rate since 1896. Although likely to be temporarily blunted during 2010 and 2011 as the recession bites, so strong is Ireland's natural population growth that the twenty-six-county total is headed for five million by 2020, having already risen by a stunning half a million between 2002 and 2008.†

The tens of millions of Americans claiming Irish ancestry – some of whom were listening to me that day – are the mirror image of a potential still to be realized. They aren't just a sign of how Ireland's history could have been different. Once the

---

* Except for Nordic countries, where climate is a limiting factor.
† Census 2002 and Vital Statistics 4th Quarter 2008 (Central Statistics Office).

recession is over, they are a sign of the unfinished business to be completed. The crisis is not to be lamented. It is to be ruthlessly exploited as a catalyst for the changes needed to make the best possible future come true. Stunning population growth aside, a doubling of real incomes in under a generation, staggering change in infrastructure – still incomplete – and a transformation in attitudes are the first steps towards that future. As I told my audience that March morning, this recession is the end of a beginning, not the beginning of an end. And, at the time of writing, that recession is ending.

My audience needed to hear good news. A few days earlier the US Federal Reserve had extended to twenty-eight days the time it was giving banks to repay short-term loans from the Fed. A liquidity crisis was gripping US banks. Normally banks with temporary funds shortage would borrow and repay within twenty-four hours. But inter-bank lending – lending between commercial banks – was seizing up. The reason? It had been abused. A golden rule of finance is that you don't fund long-term lending with short-term borrowing. But, although originally designed as an emergency stopgap to meet day-to-day shortfall, overnight lending was becoming an essential part of the business model. Investment banks like Bear Stearns with no depositors' money to fund its investments found it could do so by borrowing in the overnight market, using its large stock of mortgage-backed securities. Those securities, described in more detail in chapters 2 and 3, were created by institutions that had bought up lots of individual mortgages and parcelled them together. Once parcelled, they were sold on at a discount to the likes of Bear Stearns, who profited from the revenue paid by the thousands of individual mortgage payments. For as long as confidence in America's massive mortgage security market prevailed, banks like Bear Stearns could get away with it. Financial regulators should have been doing something about this. But even the fact that they weren't might not have led to crisis, had an even bigger mistake not been made by another monetary institution: under Alan Greenspan, America's central bank, the Federal Reserve, had kept interest rates far too low between 2000 and 2005, inflating America's housing market in the process. As chapter 3 will explain, the lack of financial regulation and loose monetary policy formed a deadly combination.

By March 2008 this poison was doing its work, and on 14 March a point of no return was reached. Earlier that week speculation on Wall Street had grown about Bear Stearns' difficulties. A major international bank, its identity undisclosed, had refused to renew €2 billion in short-term credit to Bear Stearns. For a bank with Bear Stearns' level of capitalization it was, as one analyst described it, like your buddy refusing to lend you five dollars for a beer. At a time of nervousness, the effect was devastating. The main conclusion drawn was that a decision made some weeks earlier by the New York Federal Reserve Bank to pump in $200 billion to address liquidity pressures obviously wasn't working. Those doing the lending to investment banks like Bear Stearns didn't believe that the mortgage-backed collateral they were getting in return was worth the risk. Neither did they believe, it soon transpired, that Fed action could stave off an inevitable correction in the US housing market, with all the implications that had for banks whose funding activities were based on the idea that that market was sound.

On the night of Thursday the 13th, Bear Stearns' crisis escalated. With over $300 billion worth of debts, its fall would have terrible implications. Efforts to save the bank that night involved the then New York Federal Reserve chief (now Treasury Secretary) Tim Geithner, his predecessor then Treasury Secretary Hank Paulson, and even Fed chairman Ben Bernanke. I rose to the podium the following morning at around 7.45 a.m. to give my speech in front of bankers many of whom were aware of what was happening.

Just after the speech, at around nine, my wife and I were

invited by a member of the audience, Michael Brewster of Lehman Brothers, to attend an Irish American lunch at Bobby Van's on 52nd Street, a famous Italian American restaurant. With a few hours to spare before taking up the kind invitation, we chose to go back to our hotel to freshen up. En route we did some sightseeing. Ground Zero was a few short blocks from the Bank of New York Mellon headquarters. The collapse of two great financial institutions that year, Bear Stearns and Michael Brewster's own bank Lehman Brothers six months later, was a financial allegory of 9/11 – without, of course, the tragic loss of human life. The second landmark we passed was just a short walk away from Ground Zero, a beautiful monument commemorating the Irish famine in the form of an entire Irish potato field, complete with granite cottage, that had been transported sod by sod from Connemara. The co-existence of two surreal sights like this can only happen in New York. The connection between the monument and what I had been talking about – the release of Ireland's post-famine suppressed potential – wasn't lost on me. But time was pressing. It was 11.30, so we hailed a taxi for the hotel.

Before we got there, New York had one more surreal moment to offer. Our hotel was on 54th Street. Frustratingly, over forty minutes later we were still on 40th Street where, courtesy of George Bush, our taxi was stuck in traffic. A huge cordon of security surrounded the New York Hilton Hotel, where Bush was about to give a speech on the US economy to the Economic Club of New York. Trying to allay fears about the economy, he pointed to 'strong Fed action' the week before. Fed action had certainly given banks like Bear Stearns a breathing space. But the US housing market, on which banks and their capital ratios relied, was too far gone and about to crumble.

Among others, Bobby Van's had fed Frank Sinatra and Dean Martin. The lunch we were about to attend had a few famous guests: Tony Bennett's nextdoor neighbour William Flynn, ex-Governor of Arkansas and mentor to Bill Clinton, was in attendance, as was Gerry Adams and leading Irish American leader Tom Moran. I was seated beside John Brown, who currently works for Bank of America but at the time was working for Merrill Lynch, a creditor of Bear Stearns that had played a major role in what was about to happen to it by calling in, the previous summer, loans that Bear Stearns had used to leverage investments in sub-prime mortgages. Having heard Flynn and Adams speak at the lunch about the peace process in Northern Ireland; having seen Ground Zero and the famine memorial; having been embroiled that morning in the gridlock caused by Bush's keynote speech on the US economy; and thrilled as we were by the prospect of our first St Patrick's Day in New York the following Monday, the sense of history was inescapable. And it wasn't over yet. I was looking forward to a long post-lunch chat with my fellow guests when John Brown suddenly received a phone call. 'I'm sorry,' he said, 'you'll have to excuse me, I have to leave. It looks like Bear Stearns is finished.'

By the following Monday – St Patrick's Day 2008 – the greatest global financial crisis since the Second World War had begun.

I

Introduction

What doesn't kill you makes you stronger.

FRIEDRICH NIETZSCHE

If you stare into the abyss, the abyss will stare back at you.

FRIEDRICH NIETZSCHE

1

20–20 Vision: The Best is (Still) Yet to Come

> Whether you believe you're going to succeed or fail,
> you're probably right.
>
> JAPANESE SAYING

Ireland needs to start believing in itself again. Badly. We have swung wildly from excessive belief in our abilities just a few years ago to dejected despair. There is a middle ground. A strong and balanced centre that we need to find. And as we dust ourselves down from the shock of the last year and look around us, we will find that events are beginning to turn in our favour. On Tuesday, 18 August 2009, the International Monetary Fund (IMF) declared an end to the deepest world recession since the 1930s. On 24 September it was confirmed that Ireland's economy was bottoming out. Asian economies are rebounding strongly, some growing by 10 per cent or more. Recovery is gathering pace in the Euro Zone. In the US and UK this is also happening, but on more dubious foundations. There is little doubt, though, that the world's economy will be growing by 2010. The big question is, will Ireland's? To anyone who lived through them, the 1950s and the 1980s are a damning illustration of how incompetence and pessimism destroy a country. They could do so again. Then again, they might not. Two things will decide the matter: is our government brave enough to do the right thing, and are we brave enough to be confident about the future?

As the global recession ended, signs of a bottoming out in Ireland's recession came in August 2009 came when the Live Register recorded the smallest rise in the dole queue since March 2008, the month it all began. The 600 rise compares with a 5,400 rise in August 2009 and a 30,000 rise recorded in January. And in the second quarter of 2009 our economy stopped shrinking: after a 5.6 per cent fall in the first quarter, GNP fell by just 0.5 per cent.

Some believe our best days are behind us. If they convince us to think like them, then they are right. If, on the other hand, we can start talking about solutions and stop talking about despair, they will be wrong. A war is going on over the future of Ireland's economy. It is a war that may yet spill into the ballot boxes at an early general election. Or even worse, it might spill on to the streets. This book is a manifesto for those who want to fight in that war on the side of realistic and dynamic optimism.

For some, all that's left is to tell the tale of the hundred ways we died. With not a credible set of solutions to their name, many are nonetheless motivated by good intentions. But not all. For some megaphone commentators, promoting a media profile has been a strong additional motive, even if at a subconscious level. And while an honest belief in an underlying truth in what they say sustains them – underlying truths many of which I share – they have for reasons of courting publicity simplified and dramatized facts in a way that has done untold damage to the economy, and to the lives of those now on the dole or living in negative equity.

In the long term, such commentators have nothing to offer us

– and the only way we can solve our current problems is by thinking in the long term. Ireland and its economy are travelling on two journeys back to the future. One is an exhilarating journey of long-term and breathtaking proportions. A journey on which we've come a long way, before being rudely interrupted by recession, and on which there is still much further to go if the right choices are made. The other is a short-term and painful journey, a reversal of disastrous mistakes made since 2004. To resume the first journey, we must complete the second. And quickly.

Some commentators would like nothing more than to see Ireland's economy plunge vertically into oblivion like some kamikaze pilot. How pleasing it would be for the reputations they have built on the recession if it were to continue. And it wouldn't hurt them one little bit. Many are safely inside the walls of academia where no recession can touch them, afforded the luxury of sending confidence and spending into a nosedive while their generous salaries and pensions are paid for. Most of them are without a doubt well motivated. But is that good enough?

Are they right to keep stressing how far we've fallen since 2007? Ironically, those with PhDs – those whose patient years of study and research ought to have imbued them with an ability to consider the long term – are taking a short-term view of where we are. And this is precisely where they are so wrong. The heights we reached in 2007 should not have been reached in that year.

The fact that our Gross Domestic Product (GDP) per capita was a staggering 50 per cent above the EU average[*] ought to have given the game away. Better than Europe we were, but 50 per

---

[*] Eurostat Statistics in Focus 112/2008: GDP per capita, consumption per capita and comparative price levels in Europe (preliminary results for 2007). The GNI per capita figure put Ireland 5 per cent above the EU average. However, this was before the accession of Eastern European states, whose entry to the EU would make that 5 per cent a conservative estimate. In an enlarged EU, Ireland's GNI per capita post-recession will be – depending on what measure is used – between 10 and 20 per cent above the new EU average.

cent better than Europe we were most definitely not. Using the more modest Gross National Income (GNI) per capita in 2007 we were 27 per cent higher.* For headline seekers, comparing where we are now with where we were in 2007 is just too tempting to avoid, but like a racehorse on drugs, our position was so far ahead of the pack in that year as to be suspicious. Looking at forecasts from the global think-tank the Organization for Economic Cooperation and Development (OECD), it's certainly clear that we've fallen a few lengths behind where we were. But the real issue is whether after the recession we'll still be ahead of the EU average. The answer is a clear yes.

In terms of GDP per capita, the latest forecast by the EU Commission† says that Ireland will suffer a 16.3 per cent decline in the three years between 2008 and 2010. That compares to a decline of 4 per cent for the EU. So from 150 per cent of the EU GDP per capita, Ireland's GDP per capita will fall 12 per cent faster. Do the basic maths and it's clear that by 2011 Ireland's GDP per capita will still be in the region of 30 per cent greater than the EU average. Forecasts for GNI – the more reasonable measure of living standards – are not available on a per capita basis. With total GNI expected to fall almost 12 per cent faster in Ireland than in the EU, and with Ireland's population likely to rise faster than the EU, Ireland is heading for a decline in living standards. But that decline is still likely to leave us somewhere between 10 and 15 per cent better off than the EU. So, even after having experienced one of the most savage recessions in world history we'll still have blessings to count.

And how bad is the fall in GDP really, when all is considered? During the few years between 2007 and 2010, it certainly looks dramatic, as chart 1 shows.

*

* 'Measuring Ireland's Progress' (table 1.3), Central Statistics Office, 2008.
† EU Commission, 2009.

1. Ireland's GDP from 2007 to 2010 compared to Euro Area and OECD

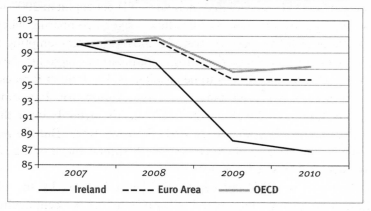

Source: OECD, June 2009, data rebased 2007=100

But the longer view – one few commentators are bothered to discuss – puts this in a staggering context. If we go back a few years before 2007, to 2005, we can see that the economy is forecast to return broadly to where it was in that year. Data published in September confirm GDP and GNP are returning to early 2005 levels.* Of course, this is in terms of GDP. In terms of GDP and GNI per capita – living standards – and their after-tax equivalents we have gone back even further in time. But this is thanks to tax increases. As chapter 5 argues, had the government focused on cutting spending instead of raising taxes, this outcome would have been avoidable. At least the government has reacted. And the tax increases of 2008 and 2009, like those of the 1980s, can be reversed once the public purse is brought under control. The corner is being turned. At the time of writing, for the third time in succession the European Central Bank (ECB) has forecast that 2010 is the year of recovery for Europe. In Asia, recovery is astonishing, which shows how much less vulnerable the world

* National Accounts for the second quarter of 2009, Central Statistics Office 2009.

2. Ireland's GDP at current market prices

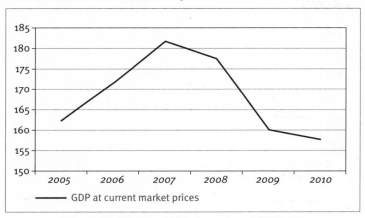

Source: OECD, June 2009, data rebased 2007=100

economy is to a US recession than was the case in the 1930s. The second quarter of 2009 saw China, Indonesia, South Korea and Singapore grow at over 10 per cent a year. With joint populations of nearly two billion, a small slice of this can work to make the following prediction by the Economic and Social Research Institute (ESRI) ring true: 'The Irish economy, as long as it regains competitiveness, can be expected to grow quite rapidly in the 2011–2015 period.' The ESRI also says that Ireland can return to full employment by 2015. This is, of course, conditional on world growth surviving the withdrawal of artificial stimulants that central banks must undertake in 2011.

Chart 2 shows how Ireland has wasted half a decade with a period of unsustainable boom and self-reversing bust. But Ireland's long-term performance is still mesmerizing. Far from being something to fear, a return to 2005 – a short-term journey backwards – is needed if the long-term journey is to resume. Chart 3 shows how astounding that long-term journey has been, how Ireland has pole-vaulted over its peers since 1994. So although the recession now is more severe than in the 1980s, the

3. Ireland's long-run economic performance compared to the Euro Area and OECD

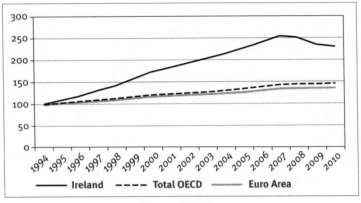

Source: OECD

economy is much stronger. In real terms GDP levels are over twice what they were in 1994; and if not all of that is true in per capita terms, it is because the state has done the right thing in growing its population. So the idea that the Celtic Tiger was a wasted period is nonsense. If competitiveness can be restored and the trend towards high taxes faced down and reversed, the fruits of its first decade can be secured. But a tactical retreat to a defensive position must occur first. Before advancing, the economy must regroup and reform. If it does so, by 2016 – just seven years away – it can be back in a position of healthy growth.

Even before then a majority of citizens will have survived the recession in reasonably good order. For Joe average, pre-tax income in 2010 will be one half higher than it was a decade earlier. Tax hikes have dented this, but, as chapter 6 will explain, this is a problem of politics, not the economy. But even with tax increases, most taxpayers in 2009 were taking home substantially more than they took home in 2002. Even after a savage April budget the likes of Sean, on €40,000 a year, with full PRSI,* was

---

* Pay-related social insurance.

paying 22 per cent of income in tax. It is one of the lowest shares in Europe[*] and is lower than the 26 per cent of income he paid in 2002. Sean's after-tax income is now back where it was between 2003 and 2004. The higher-paid have been hit harder, of course. Mary, on €60,000, pays 32 per cent in tax, the same as in 2002. For most Irish taxpayers the share of income paid in taxes is, depending on income and circumstances, back to where it was somewhere between 2002 and 2005.

And there are more positives: for someone repaying a typical mortgage of €250,000, the European Central Bank (ECB) rate cuts since late 2008 had put €4,600 back in their pocket. Even the budgets of October 2008 and April 2009 are not enough to offset that.[†] Of course interest rates will rise again. But this will happen slowly. Nonetheless, that makes it more important that we begin to implement a steady reversal of income levy hikes. Chapter 5 will argue that those levies, introduced in 2008 and doubled in 2009, have backfired badly, hurting government revenue and rattling consumer confidence.

With the case for tax increases now discredited,[‡] however, the climate for income tax reductions has improved. Consumer confidence is beginning to stabilize[§] and retail sales are slowly returning to growth. By the end of the recession, employment levels will be 1.8 million. Although down on over two million at

---

[*] The level of the average burden of income tax is not to be confused with the marginal rate of taxation – the amount of an additional euro earned in the top tax bracket. Marginal taxation in Ireland is high when various additional taxes are accounted for, such as the health levy, the income levy and PRSI. The low level of the average taxation relative to other EU countries is due to the very low burden of tax in Ireland on lower incomes.

[†] For a one-income family on €50,000 a year – an income level consistent with such an average mortgage – this exceeds by over €2,000 the impact of the budget tax rises on income (see Budget 2009 annex table A, example 2).

[‡] Over the summer of 2009, Finance Minister Brian Lenihan repeatedly stated that the December 2009 budget will avoid further increases in taxation.

[§] Various sentiment indicator surveys published by KBC (Krediet Bank Company) Ireland for late summer 2009 show this.

the height of an unsustainable boom, this is back to the levels prevailing in 2004 and half a million above 1997 levels. Tax receipts are also returning to 2004 levels, as are retail sales and house prices.

Some people would like to see the economy go further back in time. Since the late 1990s, when Irish house prices were well below EU norms, they argued that house prices were overvalued. Chapter 4 will take on their reasoning and demonstrate that there is no reason why – other than self-reinforcing comment – prices cannot stabilize at the levels prevailing before the credit boom of 2005.

Unfortunately, this sort of negativity isn't the only thing we have to combat. There are those who would argue that we should leave the euro. Strong and credible arguments for not entering the euro, or for waiting longer to do so, were advanced in the late 1990s by economists like Jim Power and Jim O'Leary. Chapters 5 and 11 of this book do acknowledge that Ireland should have done more to adjust its housing market and budgetary policies to the rigours of EMU before joining it. But as Jim Power has acknowledged, leaving the euro now would be madness.

Another destructive idea is the proposal that we should become a high-tax economy. The idea is factually stupid. Although average income taxes are modest by EU standards, Ireland's marginal income tax rates are among the highest in the world. Given our young demographic and consequent low inherent need for public spending, we are, due to inefficiency and the obstacles to public sector reform put in place by entrenched self-interest, spending too much on our public sector. And given our lack of indigenous productivity, the high average income taxes of countries like Germany and Sweden are something Ireland simply cannot afford.

Those who talk the economy down to promote their own media profile need to be confronted. And those who argue for higher taxes to promote their own or sectional interest as public servants also need to be challenged. Things in Ireland can get better. We can recover. But if left unchecked, destructive negativity and high taxation could still wreck the hopes and dreams of hundreds of thousands of Irish people. This book is about taking those two trends in the Irish economic narrative head on with a clear message: go sell crazy somewhere else.

A Tide on the Turn

Like grain through a goose, the recession is still working its way through the guts of the Irish economy. That will continue for some time. But as confidence grows that the worst of the recession is over, the challenge now is to limit the recession's effects to only what is necessary.

Although economic output is heading back to levels prevailing just before the credit boom – i.e. somewhere around the 2004 to 2005 mark – living standards are, due to higher population, heading back to levels prevailing a few years earlier than that, perhaps to 2002 levels. Is that so bad? Ireland's GNI per capita post-recession will be somewhere between 10 and 15 per cent above the new EU average. At the end of a decade during which the population will have grown by half a million people, that is an amazing achievement, even if most commentators don't want to recognize it.

As for the loss of what we had in 2007, good riddance to it. Economist Colm McCarthy has rightly described this idea that the loss of what we thought we had achieved that year as '07 nostalgia'. We could waste time looking back in anger. Or we could look forward. The fact that Ireland has western Europe's lowest population density and is the only EU country with a lower population than in Napoleonic times means there is huge future potential for growth. Chapters 4, 9 and 11 will look at how we can harness that by reaching a tipping point of population in city areas that will also make our economy more productive.

And let's not forget social objectives. Ireland might in the past decade have sustained a higher living standard compared to Europe by remaining stagnant population-wise, but which is better, an ageing nation of four million souls that are on average 30 per cent better off than the EU or a young and vibrant nation of 4.5 million souls with living standards that are 15 per cent above EU levels? In a world where population ageing is becoming a chronic problem, Ireland is in a far better position than wealthier countries in terms of demographic decline. No nation can take its wealth with it to the grave. Positives like this are important to focus on right now. This is especially true because the Irish economy will bump along the bottom until the summer of 2010 before the potential upturn later that year. During turning points like this, maintaining confidence is crucial.

Fortunately, that confidence needn't rely on long-term arguments about population. In June 2009, for the first time in two years, ESRI stopped downwardly revising its economic forecasts. Meanwhile, optimism about global recovery in 2010 is growing. The levels of cholesterol clogging the arteries of the world's lending markets are falling steadily. At levels not seen since July 2008 – before the global crisis became full-blown[*] – prices of so-called leveraged loan products are at the time of writing rising,[†] restoring confidence in the global banking system. A decline in the cost of servicing Irish government debt is further good news. That, too, is no thanks to negative commentators who chose to broadcast a gospel of despair about Ireland's economy far and wide. Despite high state borrowing, the confidence of international investors in the economy in Ireland's ability to pay its debts is being steadily restored as this book is being

---

[*] Anoushka Sakoui, 'Prices for Leveraged Loans Reach Year-high', *Financial Times*, 4 August 2009.

[†] This reflects a corresponding and inverse fall in the discount required for buying them, a discount the size of which is made bigger by the buyer's fear of default.

finalized. A successful bond auction in August raked €22.7 billion into the state's coffers – 90 per cent of its borrowing for the whole year. Whether they did so deliberately or unwittingly, those talking us down are losing the battle. But that battle is not over yet.

The Boys Who Cried Wolf

Untrained comment on our economy has been deeply damaging. Thanks to it, hundreds of millions of euros have been spent on higher-than-needed costs associated with national debt repayment. The worst appears to be over, but further comment at a crucial time could still damage domestic confidence. So could tax increases. The collapse in consumer confidence during 2008 and early 2009[*] was heavily influenced by negative commentary. So negative were some economists that I frequently encountered examples of people telling me how they had stopped watching television and reading newspapers. Even before they were implemented, calls for tax increases did as much damage. Often they came from the same source as those predicting disaster in our housing market.

There isn't a conspiracy to talk the Irish economy down. But sometimes you could be forgiven for thinking there was. Of course, when based on fact and perspective, negative comment on the economy is absolutely essential. Between 2005 and 2007 it became clear to trained commentators that the Irish economy was entering dangerous waters. By 2006, and in measured tones, the *Irish Times*,[†] the ESRI and the central banks were pointing to clear and quantifiable signs that something was going horribly wrong. Among other economists, I pointed to construction

[*] See KBC/ESRI consumer sentiment survey releases and related press releases between May 2008 and May 2009.
[†] See, for example, my article of 6 July in the *Irish Times* opinion page, and Brian Cowen's response of 13 July.

employment levels as a clear leading indicator of the danger signs, obvious to anyone looking closely at economic data since 2005. In an article in the *Irish Times* published on 3 March I warned that 'Acceleration is replacing moderation as debt rises . . . Stop the Economy, I want to get off,' and in *The Best is Yet to Come*, a book about Ireland's future post-2020, I spelled out that the economy would have to undergo a correction before that future could be realized: 'The construction industry employs one in seven of the workforce, double the EU average. From a peak of 280,000 employed in the construction industry, some 140,000 stand to lose their jobs as output and employment shares return to EU norms.' Over two years later, this process is drawing to an end.

But like warnings from elsewhere, no one was listening. Why was that? The seventeenth-century astronomer and mathematician Johannes Kepler once complained that in order to make a living from astronomy he had to pander to astronomy's 'silly little daughter' astrology. So it is three hundred years later with economic comment in Ireland. Economic astronomers use method and numbers to predict events; economic astrologers use emotion and sensationalism. Guess which pays better and gets more attention?

One of the first economists, a man with estates in Ireland, was Sir Thomas Gresham, famous for coming up with Gresham's law: bad money drives out good. The same could be said about economic comment. In 2007, Bertie Ahern could dismiss real warnings about the economy by pointing to previous warnings that had been wrong. From well-intentioned scepticism to sheer publicity generation, such warnings had often been devoid of fact. But they were fun to listen to. For a while at least. Not that the economy was perfect before 2004. It was developing proverbial love handles, losing its earlier lean and fit image. It wasn't in a crisis situation, but at the time of the 2007 election a leading opposition spokesperson confided in me that the opposition Fine Gael/Labour alternative was too scared to challenge the government's economic forecasts. Those forecasts had, nonsensically, said the economy would grow in real terms by 4.5 per cent a year between 2008 and 2012. In a Dutch auction for votes, both government and opposition competed to offer the electorate a mix of tax cuts and spending increases that assumed the economy would grow by 20 per cent over the term of government. As we now know, the economy will by 2010 have contracted by almost as much. A proper debate, challenging where our economy was headed based on facts and figures rather than emotion, might have averted the worst of this. But the astrologers had cried wolf too often and the public, now bored and disbelieving, had no time for those who had kept their powder dry.

If negative comment was needed between 2005 and 2007, when the boom had overreached itself, more sober comment is what we need now to pick ourselves up off the floor. Especially now that the world is watching us. By 2009, internationally respected economists such as Paul Krugman were dishing Ireland's reputation to anyone who'd listen; and they were being helped to do so by domestic commentators who couldn't find a good word to say about the place. In a *New York Times* article entitled 'Erin Go Broke', Krugman painted Ireland as a financial basket case. In Britain, the Labour government's Scottish Secretary Jim Murphy – ironically of Irish extraction – warned Scottish voters that following Ireland's example of independence from Britain would mean Scotland becoming part of an Arc of Instability. Like much other wrong-headed international comment, Krugman's article began with a pithy by-line, 'Krugman hopes we don't turn Irish'. It then began to quote facts about the Irish economy that, taken out of context, could only damage Ireland. 'The Irish government now predicts that this year GDP will fall more than 10 per cent from its peak' is a classic example, an example that ignored the point made above about Ireland still ending the recession way ahead of where it was a decade before and ahead of its key peer group. Krugman also got it wrong by arguing that 'the troubles of the banks are largely responsible for putting the Irish government in a policy straitjacket'. In the short-term turmoil of financial market panic – panic caused by comments of this nature – this was probably true.

A few weeks before Krugman's article, however, the EU Commission showed that by the end of our recession Ireland's debt would, as a share of GDP, remain below our Euro Area peers. For a country whose average age is around seven years lower, Ireland ought to have higher, not lower, levels of public debt. Taking that into account, even a worst-case National Asset Management Agency (NAMA) outcome[*] would not bring our debt to a level very far away from Euro Zone norms. But negative commentators aren't interested in facts.

For Murphy, for example, news hype about Ireland was a convenient opportunity to draw attention away from the fact that Ireland's living standards were and would remain, despite recession, around a third higher than those in Scotland. Britain's Labour government was in the embarrassing position of trailing the Scottish National Party (which wants independence for Scotland) in opinion polls and was desperate to discredit any good example that Ireland might offer in that regard. I pointed out this fact in a column in the *Scotsman*. BBC Scotland also organized a debate, but Mr Murphy was unable to take up the offer. Likewise, domestic negative commentators have refused to debate the facts in public.

Certainly the period of Irish government between 2005 and 2007 was not an example for Scotland to follow. But a longer-term view of Ireland's progress over the last two decades shows how for most of that period we were on many fronts an

---

* See chapter 11.

inspiration for Scotland; on others – prudence and disciplined regulation and thrift – the reverse is true. Of course progress must happen in years, not just decades.

No reversal of progress, however short, is welcome, but as chapters 13 and 14 will argue, our current reversal is a huge opportunity to deal with underlying and deep-seated problems that need tackling, recession or no recession. The position we'll tackle them from in 2010 won't be ideal, but it won't be disastrous either.

2010: Where We'll Stand

By the end of our recession, then, Ireland's debt level will be lower than the Euro Area average. NAMA is an imponderable here, but as already stated, even a worst-case outcome is unlikely to leave us with debt levels that, when the young age of the country's population is accounted for, are unbearable. Employment levels will be half a million higher than in 1997. For those with jobs, living standards will in terms of pre-tax income be roughly where they were in 2004. They will also be at least 10 per cent higher than the EU average, if not higher. Share prices have been sent reeling back to levels last seen in the 1990s. Here confidence is crucial, but so is diversifying our economy – an issue discussed in chapter 9 – so that we never again put all our eggs in one basket. Ireland's cost competitiveness and labour markets are the keys to what happens next (see chapter 7). If competitiveness is restored then the ESRI's prediction of a return to rapid growth in the 2011 to 2015 period is possible. At the very latest, Ireland's economy will be back on track by 2016.

The signs of a return to competitiveness so far are good. Price levels will fall by at least 5 per cent in 2009, and possibly by almost as much the following year. Wages must eventually follow. In parts of the private sector this is happening. But chapter 8 discusses how the failure of the same happening in the public sector could interact with the issue of immigration to produce a dangerous social and political situation. If we can restore competitiveness in a way that is effective and politically fair – with both public and private sectors contributing in proportion to how uncompetitive they are now[*] – then the potential for future growth is vast. If we can use the next seven years to complete the reversal of recent mistakes, we will be easily on course to becoming an all island economy of 7 million souls by 2020 and 8 million or more by 2040.

Back to the Future: Part I

When I wrote *The Best is Yet to Come* I knew that the economic events of the ensuing years would make that title seem strange. Even though I spent three chapters in that book explaining why a painful correction was inevitable, the title of the book was correctly chosen. A look at what happens to Ireland between 2020 and 2050, the work's central prediction was that Ireland's population is on a long-term trajectory of recovery from the famine and the century and a half of under-population that followed. Globalization and the increased mobility in labour and capital have increased that degree of under-population. Provided we could maintain our culture and restore our competitiveness, I argued, achieving a population of five million in the Republic (seven million on the island) by 2020, and six million in the Republic (eight million on the island) by 2050, was more than achievable. I thought the recession would delay this process, but I was wrong. In the book I cited population figures from the 2006 census that put the South's population at 4.2 million (5.9 million for the island). I thought that for a few years this level might remain steady or fall a little before resuming an upward trend in the middle of the second decade of the millennium. But in the

---

[*] See chapter 5.

less than three-year period since that census was taken the South's population has risen to 4.4 million. For the first time since 1857[*] – and exactly 150 years later – the island's population in 2007 passed the six million mark, and in 2008 stood at 6.2 million.

It wasn't surprising to me that Vital Statistics (Central Statistics Office, 2009) showing our population continuing to grow during 2008 – the figures from which the above numbers are derived – did not receive the kind of widespread media coverage that depressing economic stories did, or opportunistic predictions about house prices (chapter 4 takes this aspect on). What did surprise me though was the sheer momentum of that growth. By the start of 2009 there was already 4.5 million people in the Republic. Assuming that our forecasters are right in predicting an end to world recession in 2010 and Ireland's own by 2011, the population target of five million in the twenty-six counties remains more than achievable. With the right policies and long-range vision, by mid-century the Irish will outnumber the Austrians or Swedes. Net emigration in 2010 and 2011 will delay, but not destroy, this process.

But will we be able to provide all these people with jobs? And if so, what kind of jobs? Like Israel fifty years ago, Ireland is undergoing a process of historic proportions. The contrast is not just statistically relevant – Israel's population has surged from two million in 1948 to seven million today – but inspirationally too. Just a few short years after the Holocaust, the most devastating disaster to befall a nation in human history, the Israeli nation rebuilt itself in a way that puts our own problems in perspective. Ireland's troubles are not only far less serious: with political will they are just as solvable. Better still, they are a golden opportunity to reform the country from top to bottom as we continue the journey back to a prosperous, bigger and brighter future.

* Derived from a linear interpolation between census figures of 1851 and 1861.

4. Ireland's journey back to the future: population 1841–2041

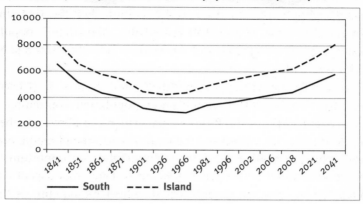

Of course, Irish scepticism and fatalism being what it is, it is difficult for many Irish economists to accept this prognosis from another Irish economist. Just as we believed our own guff about how great we were some years ago, we have now swung to the other extreme: self-flagellation. If we were never as good as we thought we were, neither are we as bad as we think we are now. It takes outsiders to make us believe the truth. On the day of his election as US President, one of Barack Obama's key campaign advisers, Robert Shapiro, was in Ireland to promote his book *Futurecast 2020: A Global Vision of Tomorrow*. For many countries, Shapiro's vision is anything but good. 'It's almost inevitable,' he states at one point, 'that over the next decade or so, the politics of these issues [demographics] will turn very nasty. Europe has a long tradition of divisive politics and unhappy experience with extreme popular movements. At a minimum, slow growth, high taxes and pressures on pension systems will force some governments to cut social services – and if recent experience is any guide, those whose services are cut will take their grievances to the streets. Some will blame immigrants, others will blame the generation of their parents or their children.' From a highly trained economist familiar with political campaigning, it's grim stuff. But what Shapiro says about Ireland's long-term potential (the book was published halfway into the first year of Ireland's recession) is anything but grim. 'Ireland is the one place in Europe likely to avoid these problems,' he writes. 'Most important, Ireland has resisted a large welfare state and avoided mortgaging its economic future.' He adds that 'the Celtic Tiger has finessed its demographic shifts by sustaining higher birthrates and attracting large numbers of educated immigrants'. Harnessing this demographic power means reducing costs so there are jobs for them to go to – an issue discussed in chapter 7. It also means addressing the apartheid of competitive conditions prevailing in the traded and non-traded sectors of the economy – an issue dealt with in chapter 8.

To complete the journey, the economy must first reverse out of the cul-de-sac it entered in 2004, and do it in a way that restores fairness to a private sector that has borne almost the entire brunt of adjustment. So, before the long-term journey back to the future can happen, the shorter one must be completed. To step forward, we must step back.

Stepping back is what the next chapter does, to examine how the US economy became increasingly built on sand building up to the greatest recession since the 1930s. Chapter 3 looks at how the authorities in the US failed to act, and even contributed to the insanity that followed. Chapter 4 connects Ireland's mistakes to those of the world monetary authorities influencing our economy, showing how we made things worse, and it also distinguishes Ireland from the US, taking on those who believe our housing market should suffer a similarly sized collapse. (Apart from the self-fulfilling negative commentary of those very sources, the only thing that can lead to a US-style situation is, of course, government.) Chapter 5 shows how the state has eaten away at the economy's vitals, upping prices faster than the private sector and stoking inflation with binge rises in state spending and stupid policies like Special Savings Incentivization Accounts (SSIAs). The state is still at it, raising taxes and charges instead of curbing hugely wasteful and excessive spending levels.

Politics is also failing us. Chapter 6 considers what are referred to as the Inchidoney years – the years 2005 to 2007 inclusive – and examines how, crucially, a chance to take corrective action in 2007 was defeated by the failure of our party political system to debate the economy in a general election. Chapter 7 charts Ireland's slide down the competitiveness rankings from a cost point of view, drawing a critical distinction between the role of the state sector and that of the private sector. Chapter 8 focuses on immigration and how it is not just an economic mirror of the divide between state and private sectors, but has the potential to blow our political system apart.

Then we enter the hopeful part of the book. Drawing important parallels with Denmark, chapter 9 asks how Ireland can become a modern competitive economy where indigenous as well as multinational companies drive productivity. Chapter 10 takes us back to our attitudes to land and space – things we must change to become really competitive. Chapter 11 argues that it is time to say goodbye to the 'yellow brick road' approach to banking and finance, not just in Ireland, but globally. Encompassing everything from the way central banks and regulators act and cooperate to internal recruitment and pay systems, change must occur if a crisis of this kind is to be averted in future. As far as timing allows – this book was written over the spring and summer of 2009 – the central issues facing NAMA and financial regulatory reform in Ireland are discussed. Chapter 12 bursts the illusion that only policy change is required to avert crisis again. At a very deep level, the current debacle has been coming for generations, if not centuries. Our current system of capitalism, with its short-term focus and lack of understanding of communal and long-term objectives, must change if the reforms suggested in chapter 11 are to have lasting effect.

The final part, Project 2016, concerns itself with the mission to bring out the best in our country by the 100th anniversary of the 1916 Rising. Chapter 13 looks at how the various changes we need to make can best be structured and sequenced to achieve this goal on time, in a politically feasible way. Last but not least, chapter 14 returns to some themes developed in chapter 6 and asks if we should continue with our current political system, arguing that within one or two general elections from now a decisive structural change in Irish politics is likely. Such a change, along with other suggested reforms, could help Ireland realize its full, exhilarating potential in this new millennium.

II

Yellow Brick Road Syndrome

More Americans should own their own homes.

DEMOCRAT PRESIDENT BILL CLINTON, 1994

We made a mistake as a society in promoting home-ownership as a universal achievable goal.

BARNEY FRANK, DEMOCRAT CHAIRMAN OF THE HOUSE
COMMITTEE ON BANKING AND FINANCE, 2008

In a market system based on trust, reputation has a significant economic value ... I am therefore distressed at how far we have let concerns for reputation slip in recent years.

ALAN GREENSPAN, 2004

2

Follow the Yellow Brick Road

And now, my beauties, something with poison in it, I
think. Something with poison in it, but attractive to
the eye.

THE WICKED WITCH OF THE WEST, *THE WIZARD OF OZ*

'And I,' said the Wizard, 'have been to Europe and
Ireland.'

THE WONDERFUL WIZARD OF OZ (CHAPTER 15),

FRANK L. BAUM

Warnings from History

From the confines of the US economy, the St Patrick's Day collapse of Bear Stearns was to hit Europe and Ireland extremely
hard and within just six months of its occurrence. Bear Stearns
had been the leading underwriter of mortgage-backed securities
in America. When someone in America took out a mortgage, the
chances were it was bundled up with thousands if not tens of
thousands of other mortgages of people they had never met

before. An investor who wanted a stream of income would buy the security that resulted from this bunching together. Bear Stearns' job was to make sure those investments were guaranteed. By underwriting the sale of these securities – guaranteeing to pay the income stream if all else failed – they allowed everyone to have faith in the system. The 'system' had doubled US house prices in just over a decade. By 2005 it drove growth in the US economy. But it was a yellow brick road of delusion.

In just the first five years of the third millennium, the world showed how quickly it could forget the hardest lessons of the first two. Since early times, the over-creation of money has ruined civilizations, overthrown governments and changed societies for ever. In the third century BC Roman emperors reduced the amount of silver in the coinage so they could print more money and convince the people they were more prosperous. Two millennia later banks would, with little or no intervention from the financial regulator, explode the amount of credit available for house purchase. The form of money might be different – relaxing the availability of credit for house purchase is an indirect way of allowing money to expand. But whether it was wages and bread prices in ancient Rome or house prices in modern Ireland, the result was the same: too much money chasing too few goods. We are re-learning that the relationship between growth in money and credit and growth in goods and services that people want to buy needs to be managed carefully. We'd already re-learned it in the 1930s. Just a few decades before that America had been gripped by a crisis that, although different, was just as serious as the 1930s recession.

In a successful economy, money increases at a rate neither too fast nor too slow for the rate of increase in goods and services. Having too little money growth is as damaging as having too much. Just over a century ago, the American economy proved the point as deflation, a fall in prices, hit America's Mid-west particularly hard (Rockoff, 1990). To many, Frank L. Baum's classic book *The Wonderful Wizard of Oz* (1900) is a commentary on those times. And its themes appear distinctly Irish in flavour:* an emerald city whose inhabitants wear green uniforms and hats straight out of a St Patrick's Day parade and leprechaun characters who form guilds – a comment, perhaps, on the huge Irish influence on organized labour in nineteenth-century America. The heroes of the story, however, represent rural America. Baum's exact intentions will never be known for sure, but few doubt that his work was aimed at adults, not children. Nor that its meaning was heavily influenced by a serious crisis in America in the 1890s (Littlefield, 1964). That meaning was lost in translation when the book became a Broadway play and, eventually, a film. But like the hurricane that hits Kansas at the start of the book, the US economy in 1893 was hit hard by deflation, and the yellow brick road that leads the characters along an eventually fruitless path stands as a metaphor for an economy facing disaster. From around 3 per cent in 1892, unemployment rocketed to over 18 per cent in 1894 (Rockoff, 1990). Like today's Ireland, prolonged rapid growth had left many people heavily in debt. Fears about the sustainability of the gold standard, even that the US might leave it, caused a withdrawal of gold deposits.

America's gold standard meant that from 1873 each dollar was fixed in value at one forty-third of an ounce of gold. It was part of a worldwide system that facilitated a wave of globalization, a wave much like the one that lifted Ireland out of relative poverty. Able to compare currencies with a common reference, gold, exporters and importers around the world had faith in the value of what they were trading with, and trade flourished. After decades of experimentation, and with some interruptions, modern

---

* The references are likely to be satirical and also influenced by the physical environment the author lived in. He resided for several years in Dakota. Himself of Scots-Irish descent, Baum's views on the Catholic Irish were ambiguous at best and sometimes derogatory, while his views on Native Americans bordered on genocidal hatred.

governments have learned to keep currencies relatively stable against one another. Today, faith in currencies is maintained by confidence, the belief that no matter what occurs, that currency will be accepted in payment. From a confidence point of view, the old gold system was even more reliable.

But its rigidity created a huge drawback. Since the Gold Rush of 1848, relatively little new gold had been found. When economic output rocketed after the civil war, the stock of dollars – tied as it was to the amount of gold – couldn't keep pace. Like a fixed amount of butter being spread over an increasing supply of bread, the price level started to thin. For those with assets – banks, professions and industrialists concentrated on America's East and West Coasts – this was a boon. Real output in the US economy doubled between 1873 and 1893, but the general price level had fallen by one quarter. For the winners, falling prices increased the real value of their wealth. But for the indebted, or those with no bargaining power over the price of what they sold, the result was misery. Small farmers from the Mid-west found that the prices of their produce were falling even faster than the general price level (Rockoff, 1990). With no savings to protect them they were wiped out as the real value of their debts soared above that of their income. It is no accident that the key character in Baum's book, Dorothy, is from a small farm in Kansas. She symbolized the rural Mid-westerners stricken by the plight of deflation, looking desperately towards the political and monetary wizards of Washington for a solution.

In 1896 they found their champion: Democrat presidential candidate William Jennings Bryan. New silver mines had been found in California, and by rebasing the dollar on a mix of silver and gold Bryan would, if elected, allow more dollars to be printed, in turn allowing prices and wages to rise and ease the burden of those in debt. In one of the most famous political speeches in American history, Bryan told the 1896 Democratic National Convention in Chicago, 'You shall not crucify Mankind on a cross of Gold.' Most (not all) commentators agree that when Baum wrote about a yellow brick road, he was talking about the role of gold in the US economy.* 'Oz' is, after all, the abbreviation for the 'ounce' in which gold is measured. The wizard represented the US Congress's power 'To coin Money, regulate the Value thereof, and of foreign Coin, and fix the Standard of Weights and Measures'; Dorothy and her slippers – ruby for the purposes of the film but originally silver in the book – reflected Bryan's view of how Congress could best solve deflation. The Wicked Witches of the East and West represented an establishment doing well out of the way things were. On account of abandoning his stance on bimetallism after losing to the Republicans, William Jennings Bryan is seen as being represented by the Lion, though this interpretation is disputed.[†/‡]

Three decades after Bryan's failure, his legacy returned to America's economy. Once again a hurricane gripped the country but this time the cause was loose, rather than tight, money. The chairman of the Federal Reserve during the mid-1920s was a man called Benjamin Strong. He was a close friend of Bank of England Governor Lord Montagu Norman. In a foreshadowing of what was to happen almost eight decades later, both men were determined to keep interest rates as low as possible to fuel growth. Their close collaboration also foreshadowed the unhealthy relationships that were to characterize America's

* One interpretation, by former *Business Week* editor Evan Schwartz, has it that the book is infused with experiences from the author's personal family life, and that it also reflects a dream sequence involving the search for a better world (see chapter 12).
† See Parker, David B., 'The Rise and Fall of *The Wonderful Wizard of Oz* as a "Parable on Populism" ', in the *Journal of the Georgia Association of Historians* 16 (1994), 49–63.
‡ The indebted farmers of the Mid-west are represented in the story by the Scarecrow, while America's hard-working industrial classes, whose working conditions were seen as turning them into soulless automatons, were represented by the Tin Man.

banking system in the 1980s, as described in chapter 3. Before dying in 1928, Strong kept the Fed funds rate at around 3 per cent, far too low for America's booming economy. By doing so, he allowed the US to absorb exports from the UK while the latter returned to Britain's gold standard. In what he later regarded as the worst mistake of his career, the then Chancellor of the Exchequer Winston Churchill failed to acknowledge how Britain's economy had been exhausted by World War One, and how the pre-war exchange rate of £1 to $4.86 – to which he was returning the pound – didn't reflect Britain's permanently weak-ened productivity.* But Norman and Strong agreed that if the US held its rates below that of London, demand from America might lift Britain out of recession. It couldn't. It didn't.

But it did lead to the Great Crash of 1929 and the ensuing depression. Within a decade of Strong's weak policies, the continent that gave the world democracy was overrun by dicta-torships, and a rearmament process that made war inevitable had begun.

In the US, Democrat President F. D. Roosevelt was elected by a coalition of the proverbial Scarecrows and Tin Men who had made up Bryan's support in 1896. His response, an economic 'New Deal' consisting of heavy investment in infrastructure as well as a regulatory overhaul of America's financial system, was questionable. Apart from some reform during the 1980s, banking reforms of 1933 were to dominate American banking into the twenty-first century. For four decades, they seemed to work reasonably well. But as the Vietnam War and oil crises of the 1970s pushed up American prices and wages, the gold standard came under pressure again. American exports became too expensive for foreign markets, and the Gold standard was finally abandoned in 1975. With the only discipline on US money growth abandoned, the path was set for an unprece-

---

* The role of productivity is discussed in chapter 7.

dented expansion in money and credit. But it didn't happen immediately.

As America's imports increasingly exceeded exports, Americans found they needed to borrow to fund their collective lifestyle. Like their Irish Celtic Tiger counterparts, they were big spenders and bad savers. The Japanese and Chinese save around a tenth of their income; Americans saved barely 1 per cent of theirs. And why would they save more? Over a century after Bryan tried to achieve a limited expansion of America's money supply, the wizard of the US Federal Reserve, Alan Greenspan, was overseeing one of the most aggressive lowerings of interest rates in US history. With US inflation, especially house price inflation, outstripping the rate of interest, borrowing money was a no-brainer. A buyer could either wait and save to buy a house, in which time its price would have risen faster than the interest rate, or borrow and repay the interest. To the individual facing such a choice, it was no contest. But from a collective macroeconomic point of view, it showed that the system had no brain: interest rates were so low that a self-reinforcing bubble of property prices was getting bigger and was destined to burst.

Unfortunately there was no shortage of willing lenders. Too far away to see the huge risks involved, Chinese investors were anxious to invest all the money China had been making since joining the world economy over a decade earlier. Instead of allowing its currency, the renminbi, to rise as more people demanded China's currency, it held it more or less steady.[*] With their currency held artificially low, China's exporters had become flush with cash. But global interest rates were low; where could it be invested? As they looked for high returns denominated in dollars, one market stood out. Thanks to Greenspan's weak monetary policy, house prices in the US had risen by one half during the 1990s. The

---

[*] Some limited appreciation of the renminbi was tolerated from late 2005 on.

shock of 9/11 caused the Fed to reduce rates even further, and between 2002 and 2005 they fell to lows not seen since the 1950s. Ambitions for house price growth went even higher. In their droves, Asian lenders offered money to American borrowers in return for collateral based largely on the American housing market.

It was a generation since confidence in the US dollar had been based on gold. It was seven decades after the great depression and just over a century since William Jenning Bryan had campaigned for abandoning the gold standard. America was going down a new yellow brick road. Only this time, the bricks were for real. Like the Wicked Witch of the West, America's property market had put something very attractive but poisonous into the world's financial system, allowing the rest of the world to join it on that road. On St Patrick's Day 2008, the journey down the yellow brick road came to an abrupt end.

The Crisis Begins in Earnest

Their joint passion for celebrating St Patrick's Day wasn't the only link between America and Ireland in the year 2008. Like few other economies in the developed world, both the Irish and US economies had been driven by property. In 2005, equity in the housing market was driving one tenth of US retail sales growth. In Ireland, one ninth of employment and one quarter of both economic growth and employment growth were driven by the sector. As in America, property prices had increased significantly. The causes were different and healthier in Ireland (as chapter 4 will explain), but, modestly at first then at increasingly dangerous levels, overvaluation in the housing market was from 2005 becoming serious. Up to 2006, prompt action might have averted a   disaster. But by early 2008 the extent of overvaluation in Ireland's property market had gone beyond a soft landing. In a different way, the same was true for the US economy.

But 17 March 2008 wasn't just St Patrick's Day. It wasn't just the day on which the collapse of Bear Stearns finally sank in. It was also a month to the day since UK Chancellor of the Exchequer Alistair Darling had announced the nationalization of the Northern Rock bank. For a few weeks, that seemed to be the symptom of something that would go away. Like stock market falls of a few years earlier, it was an isolated event. A largely self-fulfilling panic had caused a run on deposits, pushing the bank to the point of insolvency. In Ireland, the major stock index, the Iseq, fell during February and March, but this was part of a process that had begun in late 2007, a necessary correction of previous excess: the Iseq was back where it had been in the late summer of 2005, before Ireland's credit boom exploded. To the stoics, this wasn't a bad place to be. But within a few weeks, the Irish and US stock markets would begin a journey back to levels unseen since the mid 1990s.

As the bands marched down 5th Avenue in New York, Bear Stearns was preparing to sell itself to J. P. Morgan Chase for $2 a share. Noticed by financiers and leading economists the world over, it still didn't quite register as an event of major economic importance with the world's media. But this was the first American bank to bite the dust over property investment since the 1990s. When US banks failed in the 1980s and 1990s, the ramifications usually stopped at the economic borders of the US. Sub-prime mortgages were to change all that.

The Sub-prime Mortgage Phenomenon

The roots of sub-prime mortgages go back to the 1930s and the great depression. As unemployment rose to new heights and with many unable to afford housing, Roosevelt created the Federal National Mortgage Association. Its mission was to help America's new poor to obtain mortgages. By pooling low-income mortgages, banks could obtain lower interest rates from the Fed.

Affectionately known as Fannie Mae, the FNMA guaranteed the ultimate lenders that in the event of default it would make sure investors got their money back.

For decades the system worked well. Perhaps that was because not too much strain was put on it. In 1968 the Government National Mortgage Association was created. FNMA guaranteed securities invested in directly by financial institutions, GNMA guaranteed them to anyone who wished to purchase these securities. A secondary market – a market for those who were neither mortgage borrowers nor mortgage lenders – was born. Thanks to GNMA, now the state would guarantee against default any speculator who wanted in on America's housing boom. In testimony before the House and Senate Banking Committee in 2004, Alan Greenspan acknowledged that it was this belief that kept investors piling into the market.

But in the 1970s, volatile interest rates – themselves caused by America's currency turbulence and inflation – prevented investors from getting too comfortable. Heavy borrowing to finance the Vietnam War increased inflation and prompted the Fed to raise interest rates. Banks found that the funding of fixed-rate mortgages was becoming expensive, if not prohibitive. In the year America left the gold standard, 1975, variable-rate mortgages were introduced in California and soon spread around the country. These were to make America's housing market jump like a marionette a quarter of a century later, when interest rates fell to record lows.

But the real poison had yet to enter the system. For the best of motives, US President Jimmy Carter signed the Community Reinvestment Act (CRA), forcing banks to open branches in the most deprived parts of America's cities. The goal was improved access to housing finance. But not enough was done at the same time to improve the earning potential of those to whom finance was being given. The young population of ghettoized America was rising. But traditional structures of family and kinship, and the impact they had on income stability, were breaking down. American city centres were becoming increasingly unattractive places to live. A flight to the suburbs was beginning, a flight that investment in urban centres, better education and collaboration with religious and community leaders might have stemmed. Thirty years later, a black President is implementing these policies. But in 1977, the focus was on sticky-tape solutions. Banks were told that without a CRA rating – a statement that they were issuing a minimum share of loans to the underprivileged – their profitability could be severely impaired. Sub-prime mortgages had not only been born, they had become the favoured child of government.

In the generally high interest rate climate of the 1970s and 1980s, it didn't matter so much. House price growth was out of control. In 1999 another Democrat President was to give the CRA another, fateful, push, only this time he did it a few years before interest rates fell to their lowest levels in half a century. As Bill Clinton increased the amount that banks had to lend to those who couldn't afford to repay, he also lowered the reserves that FNMA and its new competitor the Federal Home Loan Mortgage Corporation (FHLMC, or Freddie Mac for short) had to keep on their balance sheets. Normal banks needed to keep 10 per cent of their deposits on reserve. For those lending to the riskiest borrowers of all, this was lowered to 2.5 per cent.

By 1999 even the Democrat-leaning *New York Times* was worried. 'Fannie Mae is taking on significantly more risk, which may not pose any difficulties during flush economic times. But the government-subsidized corporation may run into trouble in an economic downturn, prompting a government rescue similar to that of the savings and loan industry in the 1980s,' it wrote in one editorial. Republican George W. Bush, who replaced Clinton in 2000, was listening. In 2003 he attempted to put Fannie Mae and Freddie Mac under more stringent supervision, but in vain. Opposition from Democrat politician Barney Frank was passionate.

To him, house ownership was a right to be supported by government. In the absence of a proper system of public housing he had a point, but perhaps the point should have been directed against the lack of public housing. Instead of arguing for a fundamental approach to the housing crisis, Frank defended the sticky-tape approach of sub-prime mortgages against Bush's attempt to reform it: 'These two entities – Fannie Mae and Freddie Mac – are not facing any kind of financial crisis . . . The more people exaggerate these problems, the more pressure there is on these companies, the less we will see in terms of affordable housing.' Within five years Frank would eat his words. 'We made a mistake as a society in promoting homeownership as a universal achievable goal,' he stated.

Of course, the sub-prime phenomenon was not confined to the urban poor. All of America was travelling down a yellow brick road. But the sub-prime problem in the ghettos illustrated how the yellow brick road syndrome was something deeper than just an economic problem. A lack of social cohesion, planning and long-term thinking in America's approach to doing business – the flip side of its wonderful dynamism and creativity (where it often left Europe in the halfpenny place) – were real contributors to its current crisis. America could soar to heights Europe could never imagine; it could also fall to great depths. And when it did plummet, the consequences were devastating.

The half-empty streets of New Orleans are testament to the problems besetting America's housing market. They are also, as I explore in chapter 4, reasons why America's property cycle should not be seen as a template for us to follow in Ireland. With far greater worker mobility and less housing stock, America is a place where whole communities can disappear quite quickly. And no matter how cheap, no one wants to be the first to move back into what remains in many of its suburbs a ghost town. Without government coordination to move people in phases, tens of thousands of dwellings in this city will remain worthless. But

Americans don't do coordination. Like its hurricane-free weather system, most of Europe's housing market is less prone to such lasting damage. If it didn't reach the same dizzy heights as in America, nor did it fall as sharply. At their peak in July 2007, America's house prices were almost two thirds higher than they had been at the start of 2000. By contrast, German house prices had risen by just 11 per cent over the same period. In Ireland, bad planning, land management and poor urbanization have created problems of a different kind. And although not the problems of America, they were to be aggravated by them.

Ireland's fall in property prices actually started a few months earlier than the US fall, in late 2006. But when on 11 July 2008 the Independent National Mortgage Corporation collapsed – the largest mortgage lender in the Los Angeles region and the seventh largest in the US – the pace at which developments in the US began to spill over into the global economy picked up. By September, the crisis was a full-blown one.

On 8 September, US Treasury Secretary Hank Paulson announced that the Federal National Mortgage Association (Fannie Mae) and the Federal Home Loan Mortgage Corporation (Freddie Mac) were bust. They were to be put under the conservatorship of the Federal Housing Finance Agency – a belated recognition that their assets were hopelessly overvalued. In an unfortunate coincidence, the bad timing of this was underlined the day after when a deal Lehman Brothers chief Dick Fulman was trying to conclude with the Korean Development Bank fell through. Aimed at shoring up Lehman's equity, the psychological blow of the two pieces of news sent Lehman's share price plunging by 37 per cent.

Events now span out of control. On the evening of Sunday 14 September Lehman's bankruptcy was officially announced. The lie was now given to the assumption that the US government would stand by any bank exposed to these instruments, or to sub-prime mortgage securities. In the case of a much larger player, however, the US government was to step in. By mid-2007, insurance giant AIG was carrying over half a trillion US dollars in so-called super senior risk debt (Tett, 2009). Like Bear Stearns, its problems came to light in February 2008 when it was discovered that it had insufficient reserves to meet a spurt of claims that might occur. In that self-fulfilling way in which panics operate, the growing fear of AIG's insolvency created such a spurt. By 16 September panic gripped the markets, which feared AIG would lose its treble A rating. Downgrading would force it to find more collateral to boost its balance sheet, collateral it just didn't have. Another Lehman, but much bigger, was about to fall. Or so the markets thought. In little more than a day, half a trillion US dollars was wiped off the face of global stock markets.

A loan of $85 billion to AIG by the Federal Reserve on 16 September was, on the face of it, an embarrassing U-turn by an institution. Although separated by forty-eight hours, the collapse of Lehman and AIG might have been separated by an era. On the morning of 14 September the market had been worried, but fundamentally rational. The opening days of the week beginning on the 15th saw the first signs of the sort of panic not seen since the Great Crash of 1929. That Tuesday, the Dow Jones fell by 504 points, more than on 9/11. It was still only the sixth largest fall in its history. Moreover the Dow had fallen precipitously since reaching a high in the late spring of 2007.

But this time a pernicious loss of confidence was at work: a loss of confidence by banks in one another. On 9 August a different but related crisis had begun in the inter-bank lending market. In late July, President Bush had signed the Housing and Economic Recovery Act into law, guaranteeing up to $300 billion in new thirty-year fixed-rate mortgages for sub-prime borrowers. The act also established the Federal Housing Finance Agency. It was as good an admission that Fannie Mae and Freddie Mac had failed. But they had also polluted the world's banking system with toxic assets. From 9 August banks lost faith in one another's ability to repay loans.

Prior to that, if a bank wanted to borrow money for three months from another bank without security – as it often needed to do – it would pay between five and twenty basis points[*] over what it would pay with security. At less than a quarter of a percentage point, the narrowness of that spread was a symbol of trust between banks – a trust that was about to evaporate. US spreads rocketed to five times their former levels. Previously, the problem might have stayed in the US, but sub-prime mortgages had spread around the world's financial system like Mad Cow beef. No one knew just how widely or how far these instruments had travelled. Or what banks were fatally exposed to them. If they couldn't lend to one another, the banks would stop lending to consumers and investors. For a moment it looked as if the world's entire economic system could fall down dead. Within days, businesses would no longer have access to vital working capital that kept their operations going. Bank customers would find themselves staring in disbelief at ATM screens telling them a withdrawal was not possible. The world was staring into the abyss. And the abyss was staring back.

Some people were keeping their heads. Swiftly and decisively, on 22 August, the world's most important central banks began to inject hundreds of billions of euros in lending into the world's financial system. Like surgeons pumping blood into the victim of an awful accident, they kept the banking system on life support. The side effects – excess liquidity and inflation – will doubtless confront us very soon, but at the time it was the only thing to do. If we look back in the future and are able to say that the day was saved, it was this action that probably did it.

*

[*] A basis point is one hundredth of a percentage point.

When share prices fell on Wall Street on St Patrick's Day 2008, the shares of one Irish bank fell by 15 per cent as if in sympathy with the US economy. That bank was Anglo-Irish Bank. By 29 September Anglo-Irish Bank's share prices had fallen again, this time halving in value. The US had started with a banking crisis that became a recession. Ireland's recession had already begun early in 2008, but its banking crisis was just getting started. With the financial hurricane let loose on the world economy making itself felt on our shores, an internal crisis of our own making, very different to the US banking crisis even though property-based, was stirring.

In *The Wizard of Oz*, Dorothy's wooden house is lifted up from its roots and carried skyward. America's housing market, too, was carried away as the two things that should have rooted it to the ground – prudent bank management and good regulation – failed. That failure had two common causes. As IMF managing director Dominique Strauss Kahn observed, 'The financial sector not only in the US but in the rest of the world at the end of the crisis is going to be smaller than the financial sector today.' Simply put, the system collapsed because it became too large. The second cause was the trigger: a collapse in the most precious commodity underlying any economic and financial system. Trust.

3

Lax Americana

The low-hanging fruit, idiots whose parents paid for prep school, Yale and then Harvard MBA, was there for the taking. All of this only ended up making it easier for me to find people stupid enough to take the other side of my trades. God bless America.

ANDREW LAHDE, COMMENTING ON HOW HIS HEDGE FUND MADE AN 866 PER CENT RETURN IN 2007 BY BETTING THAT THE US SUB-PRIME MARKET WOULD COLLAPSE

Alan Greenspan was a great Fed chairman in the 1990s. His regime in the last four years of his term as chairman of the Fed was a failure.

ROBERT SHAPIRO, ECONOMIC ADVISER TO BARACK OBAMA DURING THE 2008 PRESIDENTIAL ELECTION CAMPAIGN

Few predicted precisely when the global economy would enter recession.* If they did, none said how hard the fall would be. But

---

* At the Irish Small and Medium-sized Enterprises (ISME) annual conference on 10 October 2006 I predicted that the downturn would come in 2008, but did not specify its magnitude.

in hindsight it is easy to see how the fall had been coming for several years. Like the Pax Romana in the fourth century, America's military and political pre-eminence in the world was the guarantor of a global peace of sorts. Some called it 'Pax Americana'. But also like Rome, that might disguised an internal weakness, something that no empire, no matter how powerful, can defeat. In the very deepest sense, the quality of America's money has suffered an erosion of trust, an erosion that many think reflects a broader decline in western values.

Despite having the most advanced military technology in the world, America entered the third millennium with a system of banking regulation that belongs to the nineteenth century. Despite its impressive unity in matters of foreign policy and military action, America's banking regulation remains fragmented and confused. When Dorothy finally meets the Wizard of Oz, the booming and awesome voice turns out to belong to a powerless weakling behind a flimsy curtain. As Barack Obama discovered the state of US financial regulation in the first months of his administration, he must have felt like Dorothy.

But America's money wasn't just plagued by its bank regulation. The sheer number of US banks – around 7,500 commercial banks – would boggle the mind of any regulator. The fact of having a different regulator in each state competing with several regulatory bodies at federal level suggests that whatever its impact on the state's rights in relation to abolishing slavery, the outcome of the American Civil War had a limited effect on US banking regulation. America also shared with the rest of the world systemic problems in how bankers were rewarded (issues dealt with in chapter 11). And if Alan Greenspan was right, the last line of protection – the power of individuals to behave ethically – was in decline as traditional American virtues of thrift and trust – celebrated by sociologists such as Max Weber and modern historians such as Francis Fukuyama – went by the wayside. But if there was a core weakness in America's financial affairs that brought all of these into focus and laid the foundation for the current crisis it was one Greenspan himself was arguably responsible for: the extreme looseness of US monetary policy.

(Loose) Money is the Root of All Evil

By 2007, both the Irish and US economies were narcotically dependent on their housing markets. In Ireland the dependency had become chronic in 2006. In the US, the addiction began earlier, in the year 1987.

1987 was an important year for both economies. Ireland was embarking on a tough period of fiscal tightening and monetary discipline. The Fianna Fáil government – with opposition backing – began a seven-year slog that would culminate in the birth of the Celtic Tiger in 1994. In America, the reverse was about to happen. Having spent seven years with relatively high interest rates, the US Fed was about to get loose. Too loose. On 11 August 1987 Alan Greenspan replaced Paul Volcker as chairman of the Federal Reserve system. His qualities were soon to be tested when the Dow Jones fell 22 per cent in value two months later. Unlike recent falls, the events of Black Monday reflected a combination of uncertainty about Greenspan's intentions as well as the impact of deregulation and new technology on world stock markets, such as program trading.* Markets were finding their feet in a brave new world, and although it took until 1989 to regain its pre-October 2007 heights, the Dow still ended trading that year at a level higher than it had begun it.†

And unlike recent times, interest rates had been high. Volcker

---

* Program trading involves programming a computer to automatically buy or sell share prices if they pass a certain price threshold – an approach which, if followed by too many investors, could result in a self-reinforcing fall in share prices.

† The Dow Jones recorded a reading of 1,897 points on 1 January 1987 and closed on 31 December at 1,939.

never allowed rates to fall much lower than 7 per cent. He had been hired by Jimmy Carter to tame inflation and that is exactly what he had done, never flinching from raising rates when inflationary pressures reared their head. Greenspan's challenge was more modest. After calming markets in October and November, he raised rates over 1989 and 1990. Although he never reached Volcker's highs of 17 per cent, he was nonetheless to be blamed by many Republicans for the defeat of George Bush by Bill Clinton. To many of them, Greenspan, a Reagan appointee, had let the side down badly. It was something that would be remembered a decade later. Under Clinton, US interest rates ranged between levels that might be considered reasonably normal, staying in a broad band between 3 per cent and 6 per cent. Greenspan was reappointed by Clinton, but in 2001 George W. Bush became President. Bush junior was strongly of the view that his father had been robbed of victory in 1992, and that Greenspan had played an unwitting role in this.

Two years before Bush's election, the European Central Bank (ECB) was born as eleven EU member states decided to join their currencies. Widely regarded as being more independent than the Fed, the ECB's president is chosen by a gruelling and independent process that involves all Euro Area governments, and the EU parliament. It is beyond the influence of any one EU political leader. Neither has it a mandate to boost the Euro Area economy. As legally defined, its sole mission is to maintain price stability. Even if it did follow the Fed's dash to cut rates in a crisis, Europe's housing market is such that interest rate changes have a more modest impact.

America is different. At such low interest rates it's easy to understand why a typical American saves around 1 per cent of his or her income and why investment in real estate appears to make sense. In a housing culture where public housing and tenant security are not readily available, money spent on rent might as well go on a mortgage. But America's fondness for variable-rate mortgages since the mid-1970s was amplifying the impact that interest rate policy had on house prices. And American interest rates were not just lower than in Europe. They also fluctuated more. So as well as being more sensitive to interest rates to begin with, America's housing market was subject to bigger swings. The power of the Fed to influence the lives of ordinary Americans by making them believe they were wealthy simply by lowering rates was huge, a power that European central bankers have never had, and probably wouldn't want.

In May 2004, George W. Bush reappointed Greenspan to his final term as chairman of the Fed. In 2000, Bob Woodward – who with Carl Bernstein reported on the Watergate crisis that led to the resignation of Richard Nixon – had written a biographical account of Greenspan's relationship with politicians entitled *Maestro* (an allusion to Greenspan's musical skills). The main argument was that in the cut-throat world of monetary politics, Greenspan was a man who knew how to survive. If Woodward is right, then Greenspan would have known at the very least that the President who under the American constitution had the power to reappoint or disappoint him was facing an election in 2004. Whether he intended it or not, historically low interest rates – often less than the rate of inflation – created a feelgood factor among the American electorate. As US voters headed for the polls in November 2004, house prices were 9 per cent higher than a year before. If it wasn't aimed at helping Bush to get re-elected, it wasn't hurting either. But at what cost? Between 1994 and 2006, US house prices doubled in nominal value. This rise was mainly concentrated in the three years between 2002 and 2004.

On the very day Barack Obama was elected[*] I interviewed one of his key economic advisers, Robert Shapiro, and asked him to comment on Greenspan's legacy. Shapiro was damning:

---

[*] 4 November 2008.

The real mistake by Alan Greenspan was that he said as a matter of policy that the Federal Reserve should ignore bubbles . . . well, frankly, everyone knew that we were in a housing bubble . . . The Fed could have taken measures. They also in particular could and should have taken measures to require capital requirements for the securitization of the mortgages based on that housing bubble and the derivatives which came on top of those. Volcker called for that, I called for it, many others called for it, Alan Greenspan rejected it. Alan Greenspan was a great Fed chairman in the 1990s. His regime in the last four years of his term as chairman of the Fed was a failure.

It is hard to disagree. US interest rates went through a decisive shift downwards on Greenspan's initial appointment, and again on George W. Bush's re-election. The first was a benign one. As Shapiro commented, rates were, for the late 1980s and most of the 1990s, appropriate. But the turn of the following decade saw another, unjustified, shift downward, a shift that during a period of strong economic growth was to lead the US and world econ-

5. US Federal Reserve interest rates 1979–2009

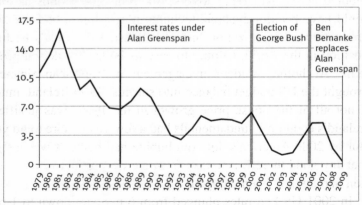

Source: Federal Funds effective rate, www.federalreserve.gov

6. US interest rates and house prices

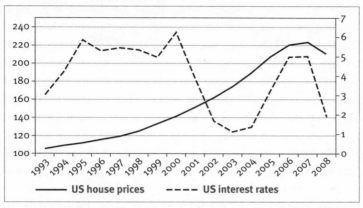

Source: Federal Reserve effective rate, www.federalreserve.gov. Monthly House Price Indices for Census Divisions, 1991=100, Federal Housing Finance Agency.

omy to the precipice. It would be pushed over it by events between March and September 2008.

Through the 1990s the increase in house prices – of the order of 40 per cent – had mostly been justified by new fundamentals in the US economy. Even if the benefits weren't as widely distributed across America's diverse socio-income groups as they could have been, a dynamic technology revolution had boosted productivity. Globalization had also boosted America's trading position in the world, helping to ease its budgetary deficit problems. At home, prudent management of American finances brought the US budget balance into surplus. As in Ireland, much if not all of the house price growth in the 1990s was justified. Ireland's economic fundamentals had a few years more to go yet. But by 2000 America's dot-com bubble had burst. It was a sign that any good there was to take from the US productivity revolution had already been enjoyed.

In 2001 US Fed rates plunged from 6 per cent down to 1 per cent. Only half a per cent of this precipitous drop was prompted by 9/11. As it became clear that 9/11 was a human tragedy rather than an economic disaster, it also became clear that this emergency half a percentage point interest rate cut should have been reversed. In fact the Fed went further down, bringing real rates into negative territory, and the US housing market went further up, only this time the fundamentals were not at play. This isn't to say that all of the US house price growth in the 2000s was fool's gold. Had interest rates followed a sober course some more moderate growth would perhaps have been justified. But whereas in the 1990s house prices took ten years to climb by 40 per cent, between 2001 and 2006 they achieved the same growth in half that time. Had Americans been the only ones betting on this, it mightn't have been disastrous. But like Barack Obama's election some years later, America's housing bubble was something the whole world took an interest in.

Regulation and Innovation: Another Contributor

If weak monetary policy tells us what we can do, it doesn't force us to do it. Investors have the option to exercise self-interested caution before betting the house on property. Neither do banks have to expose their loan books to dangerous property investment. And when greed and incompetence tempt investors into risky behaviour, regulators are supposed to protect them, and us from such temptation.

America's legislative framework has the stamp of history on it. Prior to reform by Barack Obama, a motley collection of bodies stood guard over the most powerful financial market in the world. With approximately 7,500 commercial banks in the US, America is one of the world's most over-banked nations. The McFadden Act of 1927 aimed to protect state banks from competition from their federal competitors. But it ended up fragmenting America's banking system to smithereens and undermining precisely the advantages that allow large banks to bring stability to financial markets: the size and scale to invest in expertise and knowledge about the financial products and markets being invested in.

The Office of the Comptroller of the currency oversees banks that are chartered at federal level,[*] examining their books and restricting the type of products they can invest in. The State Banking and Insurance Commission monitors banks chartered at state level. The Federal Reserve System examines books and sets reserves for all banks (although Fannie Mae and Freddie Mac were granted much looser reserve requirements). Finally, the Office of Thrift Supervision oversees the Savings and Loan industry.

The system itself is bad enough (some reforms[†] have made it a little more organized), but recent innovation has put it under even more strain. Since the 1970s a barrage of change – sub-prime mortgages, variable interest rate mortgages, credit derivatives based on sub-prime mortgages – has complicated the job of the regulator. The process known as disintermediation has also played a huge part. Once upon a time someone with a mortgage probably lived in the same town or region as the lender, and between them was a banker familiar with them both. Sub-prime mortgages broke that link, and as the number of players between lenders and borrowers grew bigger, the role of trust and faith – that the person on the other side of the transaction was worthy – became more critical to sustaining the system. The trend didn't just affect the housing market. In the 1970s, legislation setting minimum fees for brokerage services was repealed. Commission fees fell drastically and brokering firms began competing to sell the cheapest stock indices possible. At the same time computer technology made it easier to aggregate bundles of stocks. Instead

---

[*] Chartering a bank is a way of ensuring that its operators are trustworthy from a depositor point of view by giving it a stamp of state approval.
[†] The Riegle-Neal Interstate Banking and Branching Efficiency Act of 1994 overturns McFadden and has assisted recent consolidation within the US banking system.

of good-quality research and person-to-person advice, investment in the stock became a one-night-stand affair, with a high potential for risk of infection.

Another innovation was the creation of Bank Holding Companies. To get around the McFadden Act these entities allowed banks to get active in neighbouring states indirectly, by owning rather than being the bank in that state. Being outside the remit of the fragmented US regulatory system, they found that they could also lend more than if they were simply ordinary banks. Another innovation that facilitated this was the growth in Eurodollars. Since the 1950s, when the Soviet Union, fearing the confiscation of its dollar assets held in the US during the Cold War, placed those assets in Europe, dollars held outside the US had been growing significantly.

Perhaps the most deadly innovation, however, was Credit Default Swaps. These were private contracts between two parties traded over the counter on margin. This meant that only a fraction of the contract's value needed to be put up front. Holders of outstanding loans might seek insurance or guarantee that loans are repaid. But these derivatives were bought by speculators who wanted exposure to sub-prime mortgages. George Soros has called CDSs 'instruments of mass destruction'. Outside the regulatory framework, as they were, these instruments were allowed to grow to the extent that by 2008 they were 'worth' some $62 trillion.

Ethics: The Case of the Lincoln Savings and Loan Association

Before this bubble, banking crises were common in the US. The collapse of the Lincoln Savings and Loan Association is a typical example. It pre-dated the fall of the Berlin Wall by nearly a year and the Fed's supersize-me interest rate policies by over a decade. Sub-prime mortgages were still a limited affair then.

Globalization had connected America's mortgage market to the world, but thanks to the legacy of Paul Volcker's toughness, any overheating in the US property market was localized. But even if it had no implications for the US economy, the Lincoln case illustrated the chronic weaknesses of financial regulation in the US. And in a fateful twist, one of the key characters in that story nearly became the most powerful man in the world.

The story goes something like this. In 1984, a man named Charles Keating acquired Lincoln. Some four years earlier he had been the subject of an investigation into fraud by the Securities and Exchange Commission. He was cleared, but there remained doubts over how suitable he was to own a Savings and Loan association. The proud owner of construction firm American Continental, Keating planned to build large real-estate developments in Arizona, one of America's riskiest real-estate markets. Arguably it created too much temptation for Keating to resist. Access to cheap funding would allow Keating to invest in his projects without another banker scrutinizing the risks involved. Somehow, Keating convinced the Federal Home Loan Bank Board (FHLBB) – one of the US's many and overlapping regulatory bodies – that he would play by the rules. The bank's generally conservative auditors would, he promised, be retained and be allowed to work in their usual prudent manner. He was granted permission to take hold of the institution.

Within weeks he broke his promises, firing auditors he didn't like, before proceeding to invest in junk bonds, risky financial futures and large swathes of Arizona desert. It took nearly two years before the FHLBB sent in examiners to find out what was happening. Horrified, they recommended the seizure of the bank and its assets. But Keating was not about to lie down. He approached five US Senators and asked them to intervene. They were subsequently named the Keating Five, because they had all received financial donations from him. Those donations were about to pay off.

In a meeting with FHLBB chairman Edwin Gray, they urged the regulators to back off. Not only did they do so, but Gray was removed from the investigation and replaced with a man called Danny Wall, head of the Office of Thrift Supervision. The OTS was yet another one of the regulatory authorities fighting for turf. Wall stalled the examination process and removed the examiners from the case.

For another ten months Keating was left alone until eventually his institution collapsed under the weight of reckless investments. The cost of the bail in 1989 prices was $2.5 billion (it would be considerably more in today's money). Among other misdeeds, Keating had used the bank to pay his family members a total of $34 million, for which he went to jail. Danny Wall was forced to resign from his position due to the scandal. But it was the treatment of the Keating Five that was most interesting. All of them were subjected to a Congressional ethics investigation but none was punished in any substantive way and they continued to pursue mediocre careers. Until, that is, nineteen years later, when one of them, a Republican Senator from Arizona, achieved a global political prominence given to few people in the world. His name was John McCain.

Stages of Crisis

Looking back, it's clear that loose monetary policy, bad regulation and poor ethics laid the foundations of the current crisis. But how did that crisis unfold?

That interest rates had reached historic lows in the US, and in Ireland, was bad enough. In real terms, interest rates were negative in Ireland and the US for significant periods of time. When he stood down as Fed chairman in 2006, Alan Greenspan was replaced by Ben Bernanke. In the eyes of many, Bernanke's suitability for the job was (ominously) that he had done his PhD on why the Federal Reserve and Treasury had failed to stop the 1929 stock market crash becoming a depression. In the anatomy of a financial crisis, a steep rise in interest rates is always the first thing that happens. But this rise needs to be measured in relative terms. By raising rates to 5.25 – even though these rates were low by Volcker's standards – Bernanke increased the price of money fourfold since the record lows of between 2002 and 2004. To top this, mortgage lending increased greatly during those three years as more and more borrowers entered the market at record low interest rates. For those who had taken out their mortgages during the 1990s, the increases were annoying; for the huge numbers who had joined the frenzied speculation or house-buying mania of the 2002–2004 period, it was excruciating. Like an elderly person with high cholesterol being taken out of a hot bath and plunged into ice-cold water, the extreme change in monetary temperature was to cause the financial equivalent of a heart attack.

As this increase was happening, another bubble of sorts was being burst. The huge rally in stock markets during the 1990s and the first half of the following decade had been based on a simple presumption that was about to be revealed as very mistaken: the idea that nothing stood in the way of globalization. Sure, even the most hardline dictatorships were open to trade. But even if since the collapse of communism politics no longer stood in the way of global victory for capitalism, the investors who drove share values to new and dizzying heights – investors who assumed that what America and Europe had achieved could be replicated in China, Russia, Brazil and India – were forgetting just one thing: you might be able to quadruple the number of capitalist economies in the world, but you can't quadruple the world's oil reserves.

When in February 2007 at the World Economic Forum in Davos Exxon boss Rex Tillerson admitted as much, the penny began to drop. Over the course of 2007, oil price futures rose to $144 a barrel. This verdict on what declining peak production would do to future prices might have been overdoing it, but even if it wasn't $144 a barrel, the realization that oil prices higher than $30 or $40 a barrel were going to be a fact of life brought share prices down with a bump.

In a way this is positive. Share prices should fully reflect all information available to investors. In their frenzied rush to meet margin calls and make profits, not all investors have time to think about the resource constraints that will face us in the future. That share price levels now reflect this reality is a positive step. But that this trend kicked in when another factor, rapid rises in interest rates, was also forcing share prices to be discounted was bad timing. The adjustment to reality ought to have taken place some years earlier, during times of plenty, when the system could absorb the shock. In 2007, the combination of higher interest rates and oil prices was a double whammy the world economy didn't need.

When along came a third factor – the deterioration in confidence – the stage was set for recession. Before it reaches panic proportions, declining confidence can be a welcome unwinding of the irrational exuberance that preceded it. Unless that irrational exuberance has gone too far, a progression to panic is not inevitable. If asset prices decline early enough in an orderly fashion, it can be averted. That means maintaining a tough monetary policy so that asset prices do not climb to stratospheric heights to begin with (making a plunge thereafter less likely). After peaking in June 2007, US house prices fell gradually for a few months in what seemed to many to be a soft landing. But as the year ended it became clear that the US housing market was in for a hard landing. Things had gone too far before then. Rates had been too low for too long and house prices had risen too high. Although only down 5 per cent on peak levels in March 2008, prices would fall a further 10 per cent in the following fifteen months.

Once panic sets in, all of these factors begin to interact in a vicious circle. Higher interest rates frighten away good investment opportunities that are more prudent and creditworthy. As they stare at the possibility of insolvency, financial desperadoes realize they have nothing to lose and everything to gain from borrowing even more. And banks know this. Under panic conditions they have even less time than before to screen out good lending from bad, a process that not even the most modern technology can make easy. The result is an unwillingness to lend to even the best of borrowers. Stock market falls also worsen company balance sheets, by reducing their net worth, making it even harder for those companies to convince banks that they are worth the risk. And as prices fall, the cure for that decline in net worth – profitability – becomes harder to attain. Falling profits force share prices down further. Falling asset prices also make it harder for companies to get ready cash by selling property they don't need. The financial panic of 2008 was exactly this toxic cocktail of mutually reinforcing events.

Thankfully, prompt action by central banks and the stimulus package of a new US administration may have saved the day. At least it has stopped the vicious circle. In the autumn of 2009 it was too early to say that America's banking crisis was fully over, only that the pace of job losses and house price falls moderated as the summer drew to a close. In the UK, house prices even started rising. But the 'recovery' is happening with interest rates even lower than those under Greenspan. At 0.25 per cent, the Fed funds rate is virtually zeroed. Put simply, America's economy needs to return to medium- to long-term interest rates that are consistent with stability – that is, not negative in real terms. Only when that return to sanity occurs will we be able to judge whether recovery is real and based on fundamentals or whether it is the illusory product of loose money.

On their own, none of the individual causes of the crisis would have created it. Low interest rates on their own might tempt investors to take risks (and would also disincentivize savers to invest in more long-haul investments), but without an opportunity to invest in risky assets this would remain a temptation. Had interest rates never been lowered to the levels they fell to, the sub-prime mortgage phenomenon might have been confined to the most needy ghettos instead of becoming a global financial phenomenon. But perhaps the dominant factor operating behind these factors was the growing willingness of investors to take huge risks with dangerous investments. The human appetite for profit was growing. As efforts to re-regulate financial markets in both America and Ireland may yet show, government alone can't stop it without changes in ethics on the part of market participants. Andrew Lahde's quotation at the head of this chapter is a frightening comment on how greed and an appetite for risk was pursued to the point of reckless disregard for the stability of the entire financial system.

The sub-prime mortgage market put poison in the US financial system, but it was just one ingredient in the toxic cocktail of loose monetary policy, rampant unregulated growth in borrowing and explosive derivatives that by 2008 was primed for release into the atmosphere. The damage to the economy will take a decade to clean up. What is being done to ensure disasters like this don't afflict us in the future? That is the subject of chapters 11 and 12. First we must discover how this crisis affected Ireland.

4

The Revenge of Bull McCabe

The ghost of Bull McCabe still haunts the Irish
psyche.

AUTHOR, *IRISH TIMES*, 5 AUGUST 2005

The Irish property market will, we hope, never again play a role
in driving our economy. But with the Irish taxpayer committed to
the tune of tens of billions of euros to NAMA, its future is still of
make-or-break significance. If, as some predict, the market is
heading for further meltdown, then the Irish taxpayer is going to
be robbed blind by any purchase of bank property assets paid at
or above current market prices. If, on the other hand, the market
is set to stabilize at levels prevailing around 2005, then NAMA
can work appreciably well and the economy can stabilize in 2011.
Either way, we need to know what the government thinks.

But, as this chapter will show, there is a glaring lack of clarity
and consistency coming from officialdom about where the property market has come from and where it is going. This chapter
will argue that with the right policy action, stabilization at 2005

prices for the bulk of the residential market is possible. But some in government do not believe this. For one reason only, this is a huge problem. They have foisted on us a bail-out of our banking system that is based on the presumption that such a stabilization will happen. If they don't really believe it, then they're taking us down a path of disaster. These issues are explored in chapter 11, which also looks at the changes we need to contemplate to make sure of it.

In the meantime, we need to understand the parallels between America's crisis and our own, and, even more importantly, the many differences. Both countries have travelled down the proverbial yellow brick road, but Ireland's journey was made for different, more justifiable reasons. Much of America's subprime-ridden property, residential property especially, is beyond rescue. In Ireland, the same can be said for significant amounts of commercial and development property loans, but the residential property market is a different affair. In 2009, predictions of a housing collapse were being justified by pointing to the prices being attained for sections of the housing market where any price inference was a questionable affair. Under conditions of extreme banking distress, the rollercoaster gyrations of house prices in the upmarket area of Dublin 4 were no guide as to where the market would end up after recession. In fact, large tracts of the Irish market – the market for trophy houses especially – had effectively ceased to exist. With buying volumes down by two thirds and often a seller – usually desperate to sell for personal reasons – spending months being negotiated down by a sole buyer desperate to sell, the prices being fetched in Ireland's property market in late 2009 are no indication of what could happen once sanity is restored. Restoring that sanity means abolishing stamp duty and steering the market towards a realistic confidence based on long-term thinking.

And that means bringing an end to schizoid, panic-driven comment – the shift from exuberance to despair – and replacing it with sane and stable comment. We need to stop hectoring the property market, either into overdrive or collapse. We need to understand how it is changing and where it is going. Huge changes are affecting the market. Deep flaws warp its operation. Despite these, and in many senses because of them, for the broad bulk of residential properties a return to price levels prevailing in 2005 is possible. Provided, that is, the kamikaze commentators stop killing confidence and stamp duty is abolished. Negative commentators have a reputational incentive to continue wrecking market confidence. So self-fulfilling are their comments – many buyers are now refraining from purchasing because they are listening to 'experts' telling them how much further prices will fall – that they can in effect prove themselves to be right simply by keeping up their message. What they are doing is the opposite of what the other villains in Ireland's housing market story did, those who from self-interest talked up the market, forcing the gullible or desperate to buy overpriced housing for fear that if they waited prices would rise even further.

We need to stop listening to both camps. Instead we need to understand what went wrong, and why. Understanding the 'what' should help us to see why, given the way we do things in Ireland, property price levels prevailing in 2005 could constitute a stable equilibrium. Understanding the 'why' should help us to see why we have to change those ways of doing things, so that in the long term we stabilize the market for good. And we have to do that gradually so that the market isn't destabilized further.

We don't ever again want Ireland's property market to drive growth. But we can't ignore the way housing construction and employment will pan out: over the next few years it could have a crucial impact on the pace of our recovery. Once that recovery is secure, we need to plan a brave new world where our property market is transformed (the subject of chapter 9); then we can begin to implement reforms recommended decades ago. This is one part of our economy that needs to be guided not by big-mouths, but by clear heads and steady hands.

The Lure of the Land

The roots of Ireland's property conundrum are as deep as the roots of the land itself. When in 1957 the future president Erskine Childers issued the following warning, he couldn't have known that years later his prophecy would come true, and in a way he would never have imagined: 'It is not too much to say that our entire economy will stand or fall by the use made of the land.' Back in 1957, the idea of a booming economy was a pipe dream. Ireland's economy and society were dying a slow death of emigration and population decline. The idea that one day immigration and population growth would push Ireland's land prices up to the highest in the world was fanciful.

Some eight years later, Ireland's famous obsession with land was celebrated in John B. Keane's new play *The Field*, whose main character, The Bull McCabe, was obsessed with a plot of land to the point where he ended up killing another man and destroying his family. If Irish people didn't kill for land, they could come close. There was huge controversy over the way the Land Commission reversed the legacy of centuries of confiscation by the British and gave it back to the native Irish. Combined with the brutal psychological trauma of the famine, it reinforced a sense that the ownership of land was not just essential to economic and social survival, but that owning it, developing it and trading it was the most important source of economic endeavour. The fact that property developers and land owners – people who did little or nothing and often harmed Ireland's international competitiveness and trading position – were fêted in Ireland as exemplars of successful business is the clearest sign of the collective delusion that gripped the nation. A delusion with strong cultural roots.

In the late 1960s Ireland found itself enjoying a few years of prosperity. A government report was commissioned on how best to price and control the use of land in cities around the country that were witnessing something unseen in Ireland since the famine: population growth. When the so-called Kenny report was published, however, no action was taken to follow it up. By the 1970s the original motive behind Childers' quote – the impact that agricultural land holding patterns might have on agricultural productivity – was on its way to being out of date. As a share of the economy and employment, agriculture was declining relative to the rest of the economy. But in another respect Childers's words were becoming too crucial to ignore.

Ireland's amazing rebound in population and its sprawled low-density development were putting an enormous strain on the country's political system. In the absence of a nationally struc-tured way of regulating land pricing and usage, local authorities were zoning land in ways that drove up land prices to astronom-ical levels. Having failed to moderate land prices, as Kenny had suggested, those who owned land zoned for development found they could use their effective monopoly to charge almost what they liked. Instead of rewarding productive economic activity, Ireland's culture of land and property rewarded speculation and development. As well as being least helpful to the economy's competitiveness, these activities poisoned our body politic at local level, and ultimately, as a result, at national level. They also reflected a mentality deeply rooted in Ireland's culture of inherit-ing wealth, a mentality reinforced by the Land Commission and by political clientelism, a mentality that said you didn't really have to work to become wealthy. You could speculate or inherit your way to the top or have privileges given to you in the form of re-zoning or development rights that would make you wealthy. Like a ghost unseen for generations, the powerful drive to acquire property burst forth under conditions of unprecedented prosper-ity to show us that the stereotype portrayed in *The Field* was still a reality. That ghost needs to be exorcised from the national consciousness for ever.

Before that, though, we have to settle the Irish housing market at sustainable levels. But just what is sustainable?

This is not America

If someone can prove that property prices will fall by 50 per cent using analysis of Irish rather than US fundamentals, then they have a duty to say so. But in 2009 an argument was being advanced that, because prices in the US could fall from peak to trough by 50 per cent, the same must happen here. Forecasts based on Irish fundamentals – such as one published in August 2009 – have predicted that house prices have still further to fall. With one proviso, these Irish-based forecasts deserve respect and attention. The proviso is that similar forecasts failed spectacularly in the past to identify overvaluation. It is equally likely that they are now overstating it.

A comparison with the US is certainly needed in one respect: house prices have grown faster here than in the US, as chart 7 shows. But there are good reasons why this is far less a cause for alarm than many believe.

When in the *Irish Times* on 29 January Alan Ahearne, a respected academic, suggested that Ireland could follow US trends with property price falls of 50 per cent, he was engaging in something that is a highly respectable practice. As a theoretical exercise, comparisons between international property markets can establish useful insights. The trouble starts when they are generalized without considering how crucial differences between markets can affect price behaviour. Just because both a cat and a dog have four legs and fur doesn't make them the same animal.

In very clear and tangible ways, Ireland's property market is, under normal circumstances, subject to more moderate weather than the hurricane-swept United States. The ultimate weather god of our system, the European Central Bank, is more temperate. Peak to trough, the US Federal Reserve has seen its interest rate range by a full five percentage points between early 2007 and early 2009. In Euro Land, the range is 3.25 percentage points (and this is a relatively high range for the ECB, reflecting its reaction to the current crisis). The share of state spending and availability of social welfare support – critical to blunting the impact on the housing market of rising dole queues – is also a lot stronger here than in the US.

In the US, labour mobility is also much higher. Workers laid off in Minnesota will up stakes and move across the country to California, putting their houses on the market in the process. Buffered by a welfare state and constrained by language barriers, Europeans are more likely to sit tight beside kith, kin and hearth (Pagano, 1999).* In Ireland (and England) one's home is one's castle, a badge of identity. In the US, property is certainly important, but a more accepted tradition of renting prevails, and a more practical and less emotional relationship with where one lives makes it more substitutable. The very American term 'condominium' reflects this degree of emotional detachment.

If anything captures this difference in emotion, it is the difference between the character Bull McCabe and the American in *The Field*. McCabe's passion for a particular field drives him to put his entire life's savings into buying it. For the American, the project is also a high-commitment one, but not a life and death affair.

As Irish property economist Derek Brawn has pointed out, there are similarities between Ireland's property market and its American cousins (Brawn, 2009). Ireland's period of house price growth has been an extended one. And like Ireland, US home

---

* The implications of the mobility of migrant workers to Ireland, a different matter, are discussed later in the chapter.

7. US and Irish average house prices since March 1996 (indexed with common value set in March 1996)

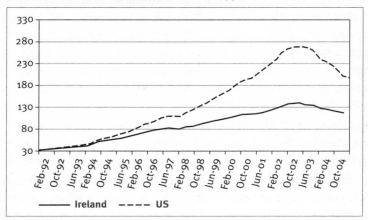

Source: Monthly House Price Indices for Census Divisions (rebased), Federal Housing Finance Agency (US); Permanent TSB/ESRI House Price Index (Ireland)

builders overreacted to the increase in demand. But compared to US population and employment, growth in Ireland has been in an entirely different universe. Between 1996 and 2008 the twenty-six-county population rose by almost one million* – a rise of over one quarter; at the same time the numbers at work rose by 700,000. Equivalent rises in the US would have seen America's population and labour force grow respectively by sixty and forty million in just over a decade! These figures are far greater than the degree of overbuilding in the US. Had such a population explosion occurred in America, house price growth would have rested on stronger fundamentals. Even the recession will not push employment levels in Ireland significantly below their 2005 levels. And America's property price falls are not caused by artificial state-created handicaps like a 7 per cent basis rate of stamp

* Source: Budget and Economic Statistics 2008 (Department of Finance, 2008); Vital Statistics (Central Statistics Office, 2009).

duty which, if abolished, would lift the market by a comparable percentage once confidence is restored.

There is another, more subtle, difference. Dramatic changes occurred in urban location in the US in the twentieth century, ones going far beyond Ireland's oozing suburban sprawl. As shown in a leading study of American ghettos (Cutler, 1999), the trend away from the ghettoization of ethnic minorities in the US since 1970, although welcome in itself, was still incomplete by the 1990s. In 1970 African Americans were on average living in neighbourhoods 68 per cent of whose other residents were also African American; by 1990 this number had gone down, but only to 56 per cent. Many were left behind in neighbourhoods that were being made uninhabitable by crime, drugs and a breakdown in urban civic society. And it was a vicious circle: as those with better prospects moved out, the quality of life deteriorated, laying the foundations for the sub-prime crisis. Addressing the long-term issues in these trends is, among other issues, the subject of chapter 12. For now we need to know that there is in the US a force driving down property prices that does not yet exist in Ireland, at least not to any similar degree.

Neighbourhoods in the US with high levels of joblessness have experienced higher crime, gang violence and drug trafficking (Wilson, 1996). Although this problem exists in milder form in urban Ireland (but as chapter 9 discusses, Ireland is relatively under-urbanized), the impact on the US housing market is far greater. As economists Christopher Mayer and Karen Pence have shown (Pence, 2008), sub-prime mortgages were all the rage in these communities.

In Ireland as in Europe, the greater availability of social housing and social welfare blunts the impact of these trends on the housing market. Instead of dealing with the root causes of ghettoization – the lack of opportunity and the breakdown in social order and traditional family structures and values – successive US administrations used sub-prime mortgages to buy peace of mind for America's conscience. The current crisis in the US housing market is the revenge of ghettoized America for decades of sticky-tape solutions.

In Ireland's case, the property story certainly is also a story of revenge. But revenge of a different kind, for the decades if not centuries of flawed and backward thinking about how we use, price and plan one of our most precious economic assets: land. The rupture in Ireland's property market, and all the financial headaches that stem from it, is nothing less than the Revenge of Bull McCabe.

A Real Cadbury's Fruit & Nut Case

There is another difference between Ireland and the US worth mentioning, one that, unlike others, doesn't work to our advantage. In the short term, it keeps land and house prices higher in Ireland compared to our peers, and damages our competitiveness. It is something we are going to have to deal with. But we'll have to deal with it carefully, over time and in a planned way (see chapter 10).

Seeing as both Ireland and the US are self-proclaimed Republics, the difference in question is particularly ironic and shows how little we have done to live up to the core principles of Republican government. Unlike America, and like monarchist Britain, town planning in Ireland is largely determined by the attitude of the Royal Institute for Town Planners. A UK-based body, the Institute has a huge influence on the way in which our towns and cities grow. Drawing much of its inspiration from the work of the nineteenth-century Quaker and social reformer George Cadbury, it is a benign institution with the best of intentions. But it is hopelessly and laughably out of date.

Appalled by the cramped conditions in which Britain's working classes were forced to live, chocolate manufacturer Cadbury advocated that workers had a right to live in houses that had no more than seven other dwellings in the same acre of land. His gospel of eight houses per acre soon became holy writ for every local authority in Britain and Ireland. It still is, and in twenty-first-century Ireland it became significantly responsible for our hugely destructive sprawled pattern of suburban development. The failure or inertia of our politicians to grasp the need to urbanize and build high-quality apartments – building cities up rather than out – is a major contributor to high house prices and for much of the loans on NAMA's books.

To make matters more ironic, two centuries before Cadbury another Quaker, Irish-born Republican William Penn, developed a grid-iron plan for the city of Philadelphia, the first American city to be so designed. With equal concern for the living standard of his town's dwellers, Penn was also interested in organizing a city that was productive, not just a city of 'brotherly love' but fraternal and efficient commercial activity as well. Three centuries later, his vision has stood the test of time. Los Angeles is an example of a US city that does not follow this pattern, which shows that we have adapted the worst of what America has to offer. Somewhere between that sprawl and Manhattan's claustrophobia, cities like Philadelphia offer Ireland inspiration on how it could structure its future growth.

Notwithstanding the high quality of his firm's chocolate, Cadbury's vision has melted into a sticky mess, staining everything from our property market to our quality of life. Had we adopted our native son William Penn's vision years ago, the property crisis needn't have happened. Building up would also have allowed younger citizens to live nearer their places of work at far cheaper prices: it would have allowed builders to extract more value from the huge land prices they were forced to pay in Ireland's badly regulated land market.

The failure of Dublin City Council to grant planning permission to Sean Dunne for a proposed thirty-two-storey building in Dublin's Ballsbridge was one of the main dominoes in the fall of

BACK FROM THE BRINK

Ireland's property market. Certainly 2008 was a bad time to be building such a structure. And Ballsbridge was not the place to be building it; the city's quays were arguably better suited. But the fact that Ireland's land regime made a developer pay €59 million an acre without allowing him to build up shows how ludicrous our system is. If we spent half as much time thinking about this as we do vilifying the likes of Dunne, we might not be in this mess. Certainly property developers should not profit from being able to stack 'em high on just any piece of land. But, as argued in chapter 10, in the right central locations, the economic benefits of high-rise development are ones we can no longer do without. Even if American cityscapes are not to our taste, comparisons with Copenhagen show that even modest densification could benefit us hugely.

Even attempts to prove the opposite point actually end up proving this. As a table in Derek Brawn's *Ireland House Party** shows, the more productive of Dublin's competitor cities – Paris, Seoul, Tokyo, Singapore and Beijing – all have substantially higher population densities. Dublin, in contrast, languishes at the bottom of the league with the likes of Karachi, Los Angeles (sub-prime city), Lahore and Bogotá. Of course high density does not mean having high-rise buildings everywhere: cities like Frankfurt and Berlin show how a limited and targeted use of high-rise can cluster population in cost-effective ways that make for a good quality of life. Dublin's situation – around 135,000[†] work between Dublin's Royal and Grand canals but only 15,619 live there – is the ludicrous opposite extreme of Manhattan. It is also heinous. For want of modest high-rise development, and the lower prices they bring, hundreds of thousands of people who could live in Dublin near where they work must currently

---

* Table 28 (chapter 24).
† ESRI, *Ex Ante Evaluation of the Investment Priorities for the National Development Plan 2007–2013*, 2006.

endure the misery of long commutes, negative equity and social exile.

A radical alteration in our approach to high-rise should, of course, have occurred before the boom in demand for housing. Had it happened, we would have got higher skylines and lower prices. Now that the reverse has occurred, we need to target change over the medium to long term. With demand for property currently weak, building high-rise developments now would flood the market. But not planning now to build in the future would be inexcusable. We need to look at Central Statistics Office population targets for 2020, take the most realistic of them, and roll out the needed changes in planning and densification to channel it into city centres, not sprawled commuter towns. High-rise buildings need not come on stream before 2016, by which time they will be needed. But even if they do, it will be a long time before they approach the extent of high-rise buildings in US cities. This – the absence of a dense supply of identical high-rise dwellings with neither gardens nor green public space – is another reason why the value of Ireland's stock of green and spacious properties should stabilize in the medium term.

Actually, thanks to a unique feature of the Irish property market, there is no option here, at least not until we change our land pricing regime. Not only does our dislike of urban living militate against productivity in our economy and property market, this factor – bad enough already – is made worse by the fact that the most essential raw ingredient in the property creation process, land, is more expensive in Ireland than anywhere in Europe.

When the Minister for Finance outlined plans to rescue our banking system in the form of the National Asset Management Agency, he gave an approximate breakdown of the assets underlying the €68 billion worth of loans the agency would have to purchase. One third of the assets was land, another third was building projects that were work-in-progress, and the remainder comprised completed commercial properties. The drastic escalation in the price of land has already been alluded to: the €59 million per acre paid by Sean Dunne for the site of the Berkeley Court Hotel. There are many other examples of exorbitant land prices,* but this one deserves a repeat mention because of the subsequent decision by Dublin County Council to deny high-rise planning permission. If those prices are to be paid, we must allow builders to build up to realize the revenues needed to justify them. If we are not to build up, there is only one alternative: we must do what practically every other European country including our nearest neighbour does, and prevent the cost of building land from escalating out of control.

The multi-million-euro deals, ranging from several million euros an acre in outer Dublin to up to €100 million for land on the Burlington Road bought by Bernard McNamara,† might grab the headlines. They are also main contributors to the mess NAMA will spend over a decade trying to clean up. But from the point of view of those on negative equity, the real culprit for Ireland's house prices – and a reason they are unlikely to resume once a recovery gets under way – is the unique regime for pricing of building land in Ireland, as it affects the acquisitions – more modest in price but far more numerous – made for the purposes of residential building. As Derek Brawn has pointed out (Brawn and Ashmore in IFA 2007, taken from Brawn, 2009), from a point of parity with the UK in 1999, Irish farmland prices per hectare had risen to five times UK levels by 2004 – a fivefold increase in five years. How on earth had this happened?

---

* Soon after that, developer Ray Grehan paid up to €81 million per acre for the nearby Veterinary College on the Shelbourne Road.
† As cited in Derek Brawn's *Ireland's House Party*.

Who Killed Kenny?

Brawn explores an interesting debate on whether land prices drive house prices (as he argues) or whether high house prices drive high land prices (as many estate agents argue). The argument misses the real point about our property market. The most central and fundamental source of failure in Irish land policy is not the developers or land owners, it is planning policy. Moreover, this failure was identified and signalled to the government a whole quarter of a century before the explosion in land prices that started in 1999.

In 1973, the Committee on the Price of Building Land Report to the Minister for Local Government – the so-called Kenny report, after its main author Justice J. Kenny – proposed radical changes to the control of land prices. It recommended that in cases where a local authority had zoned land for building purposes, a High Court judge of standing should be appointed and given the power to ensure that a builder undertaking the work could buy the land cheaply. It also pointed out that laws governing the arbitration of prices for land compulsorily acquired by the state to provide local schools, roads or other utilities were fleecing the taxpayer. By forcing the state to pay prices based on the land's 'building potential', the 1919 legislation made courts award ridiculously high sums to land owners with good lawyers – land owners who before the state wanted to buy it had no intention of doing anything with it.

In June 2009, Fine Gael rejected the idea of reforming the Kenny report on the basis that its contents were 'thirty years old'. But despite its vintage, the report recognizes a central truth that almost every government in the EU accepts: land zoned for development is a monopoly good the value of which has been created by the state. Far from being a Stalinist interference in private property rights, controlling land prices ensures that real economic activity – creating goods and services – can occur in competitive conditions. Even Tom Parlon, former head of the Irish Farmers Association and stalwart opponent of price control in the past, now accepts that land pricing needs to be changed. 'I do accept that this is something that has to be looked at in the future,' he told me in interview.

The reasons for this go beyond economics. Studies have found that where energy resources are a huge input into the economy, corruption and political instability can result (Torvik, December 2006). Energy resources require huge outlays (and therefore deep pockets), as well as permission from the state. Unlike real value creation, where the genius and graft of the entrepreneur is the key ingredient, the mix of money and politics makes energy production a highly corrupting activity. Without a good zoning and pricing regime, land use is exactly the same, as the recent history of Irish politics proves.

On 5 July 2006, the then Taoiseach Bertie Ahern made a promise to implement the Kenny report[*], saying he would hold a referendum if necessary. A day later Green Party TD Trevor Sargent welcomed the move. Eleven months later the implementation of the report became part of the Green Party election manifesto. But despite entering government, and in spite of a Green Party TD being Minister for the Environment with responsibility for land reform, no efforts have been made to change the law. Even the existing opposition, as we know, has no appetite for reform: it was Fine Gael's new TD George Lee who dismissed its relevance by saying that he had no interest in implementing a 'thirty-year-old report'.[†]

Apart from being the source of huge corruption at local authority level – which thanks to the strong links between local and national politics (an issue addressed in chapter 13) has seeped into national governance – the failure to implement the Kenny

[*] Michael O'Regan, 'Referendum on Building Land Prices not Ruled Out', *Irish Times*, 5 July 2006.
[†] *Nightly News with Vincent Browne*, TV3, 8 June 2009.

report's findings constitutes perhaps the single biggest reason for the escalation in property prices. Of course the timing of that escalation between 1999 and 2004 shows that in reality the chain of causality is complex; land prices don't just cause high house prices, nor is the reverse true. But, depending on the regime for zoning land and pricing it, both interact. Again, depending on the regime for planning, zoning and pricing, that interaction can produce high-quality, low-priced accommodation in well-planned urban areas. Or it can do what it did in Ireland: produce the highest prices for farmland in Europe, and a banking crisis that could cost billions of euros and take possibly decades to clean up.

The implications spread to those suffering negative equity, as well as to taxpayers charged with cleaning up the banks. There are other impacts as well.

One of the key figures in Ireland's economic success during the late 1980s and 1990s was Padraig White. As chairman of the Industrial Development Authority during the 1980s, he stewarded Ireland's stunning success in attracting foreign direct investment, a foundation stone of the later boom. But between 2002 and 2007, as chairman of the Rail Procurement Agency, he was in a less enviable position. This is what he told me about his experience of acquiring land: 'When I was chairman of the RPA we were acquiring strips of land and one of the extraordinary experiences was that because the residents along the old Harcourt Street line had been allowed to encroach on the sections of the old Harcourt Street line they had established squatters' rights and the state ended up having to acquire parts of that land and some other sections to accommodate that line.' This cost the state millions of euro. It also delayed the roll-out of infrastructure critical to the economy and to the lives of hundreds of thousands of citizens and commuters. Just like the authors of the Kenny report thirty-six years ago, White pointed to outdated legislation as the cause of high land prices.

One of the most unsatisfactory aspects in my view was the long-established almost secretive rules and procedures governing arbitration in relation to disputes over the price of property. If somebody had a strip of land they got a team of estate agents and architects to design a building on that strip of land and then claimed they had a commercial potential on that strip of land, even though they had no planning permission nor probably even the remotest possibility of obtaining planning permission. Invariably the arbitration price was struck at an extraordinarily high level and I regarded the whole process as completely outdated and completely biased in favour of the highest price where the state was trying to acquire the land. The RPA made various submissions in the public interest calling for radical change in this outdated system which had an in-built system to push up the prices but there was no appetite for dealing with this and the system remains as obscure today as ever.

Fine Gael's lack of interest in implementing the Kenny report demonstrates two things about Irish politics. Firstly, it is incredibly difficult to change stupid policies. Secondly, that however tempting it is, Fianna Fáil cannot be solely blamed for our current situation, for Fine Gael would have done no different. Under pressure from its councillors around the country, Fine Gael's position on land pricing, zoning issues and high-rise development has been virtually identical to Fianna Fáil's. Nor has the Labour Party (which ought to do so) insisted on land reform as a non-negotiable price for entering government.

Why the Pessimists are Wrong

These are vital issues we must tackle in the long term. But the questions facing us in the short term are equally pressing. Where is the housing market going? Back to 2002, when an average house cost less than €200,000, or back to 2005 levels, where it currently stands? Pointing to historical falls of around 50 per cent[*] in real house price values in the US, some commentators believe Ireland is due for a similar collapse. To bolster that belief they point to 'on the ground' evidence of house prices being fetched around the country. To the untrained eye their argument is convincing.

But if it is, then from around €311,000 (ESRI, 2009) at the start of 2007, the average national house price should fall by around 45 per cent by the end of 2010,[†] leaving a national average house price of approximately €170,000. Assuming a required deposit of around one tenth, this figure suggests an average mortgage of just €153,000. In a country where the average earnings as of 2007 were around €37,726 (CSO, 2009) and where, rightly or wrongly, family ownership is sustained by two incomes, this means that for most families the price of an average house would be just over twice the level of joint annual income. Even allowing for some reduction in the excessive multiples of loans to incomes, it still seems implausible.

Since September 2008, affordability in mortgages has improved by two fifths. The increase in mortgage rates by Irish Life and Permanent in July 2009 of half a per cent does presage higher margins between the ECB's main refinancing rate and those accessible by Irish borrowers. But a reversal or even a significant reversal of the 3.25 percentage point fall in base rates since September 2008 looks highly unlikely. As for earnings levels, evidence is cited in chapter 5 of falls in nominal incomes of perhaps 5 per cent in the private sector. But when negative

---

[*] Adjusting for inflation, in this case Harmonised Index of Consumer Price inflation which excludes the impact of changes in the cost of servicing a mortgage due to changes in interest rates.
[†] According to the summer 2009 ESRI Quarterly Economic Commentary HICP price increases from the start of 2007 to the end of 2010 should accumulate to around 5 per cent.

inflation in 2009 is taken into account – offsetting positive inflation in 2008 – average real pre-tax incomes (on which mortgage approvals are based) would be only fractionally lower at the start of 2010 than they were in 2007. The ESRI still forecasts employment levels to return to between 1.8 and 1.9 million persons by the end of the recession – i.e. 2004 levels. As for unemployment, the Live Register – which measures the number of dole claimants rather than the number of unemployed – has been widely quoted to suggest that it will reach 400,000 or even 500,000. But thanks to the wide availability of the dole in Ireland compared to most other EU countries, the Live Register includes both part-time and temporary workers and exceeds the unemployment level by around 60 per cent (Grubb, 2009). At just over one quarter of a million, the level of unemployment in mid 2009 was certainly high, but it was well below the Live Register count of over 400,000.

Finally, much has been made of the argument that between 2003 and 2007 400,000 dwellings were built, constituting an alleged huge oversupply (Brawn, 2009). Here is where we really need to put on our thinking caps.

As *The Best is Yet to Come* forecast, and as events since then have proved, the prospects for population growth to continue well into the next decade will soon put that number into perspective. As Derek Brawn states, between 2002 and 2006 the population 'only' increased by 8 per cent, from 3.9 million to 4.2 million. He contrasts this with the 20 per cent rise over the 2003 to 2007 period in the stock of property. What his analysis was not updated for is the fact that between April 2006 and November 2008 the Republic's population increased by another 200,000 or so persons and at the time of writing is 4.5 million. In other words, Ireland's population has increased by over half a million since 2002.

The influence of population is, as you would expect, a subtle matter. In June 2000 the third and final report into the Irish property market (Associates, June 2000) identified the twenty-five to thirty-five age group as the most important one for the housing market. Latest figures suggest that this age group is growing substantially, from 723,000 in 2006 to 763,000 in 2007. It takes a few years for this rise to travel through the property market to influence prices. Such trends on their own won't lift the market, but they will help. And in a country where employment will end the recession still half a million above 1997 levels, they create a latent demand bolstering the impact of lower interest rates.

Of course Ireland's population was swollen by migration. With rising dole queues, that might reverse. But migration aside, natural population increase in 2008 – live births minus deaths – was 47,000 persons.* The Quarterly National Household Survey suggests the labour force fell by 18,000 during that period (CSO, 2009). If this is any guide to net emigration, it suggests that natural population growth was still far exceeding any net emigration by around 30,000 persons. Even if, as is likely, emigration rises and natural population slackens, it's unlikely that the population will fall hugely between now and the end of recession.

A more valid point relates to excess supply in the market. The number of vacant dwellings in the state in 2006 had reached 266,000.† There are two extreme positions on this, and both are invalid. One says that all of these were investment properties or holiday homes whose vacancy means nothing for the overall residential market. The other view is that all of them are about to flood the market. The latter view ignores the high number of people absent from their dwellings at any one time. In 2006 Dublin airport had one of the highest turnovers of any airport in

* My full-year calculation is based on full data for the first three quarters of the year and assumes that natural population increase in the final quarter will have the same annual percentage increase as in the third quarter.
† Department of the Environment, Housing Statistics Bulletin, 2006.

Europe, showing that the Irish propensity to travel – and hence to be 'not at home' – is relatively high.

In one way, though, the argument is academic. Despite a large building spree, Ireland has one of the highest number of persons per dwelling in the Organization for Economic Cooperation and Development, suggesting significant underhousing (OECD, 2008). The latest trends show that a steady decline in average household size is underway, correcting this gap. The number of persons per private household dwelling continues to fall drastically. It's a point ignored by most of the pessimistic commentators, but it's a point that is unavoidable in any cogent analysis of the market, as a basic analysis will prove. From an average of 3.14 persons in 1996[*] to 2.81 in 2006 and, extrapolating that trend forward, to around 2.64 by 2012 this seemingly small change actually has no profound implications. Whereas in 1996 the 'typical' 1,000,000 persons would require 318,470 dwellings to keep them housed, by 2012 that won't be enough: the same 1,000,000 persons will require 378,780 dwellings – an increase of over 60,000. This means that without any population increase at all – and the population by 2012 is likely to have increased since 1996 by around a million (Central Statistics Office, 2008) – the number of dwellings required by the population for the state's 1996 population level of just under four million would by 2012 have increased by 240,000 dwellings! But as we know, that 4 million has become 4.5 million.

This assumption, by the way, is conservative. In Denmark, 2.5 million dwellings house 5.2 million people – an average of

---

[*] Table 21.1 of the *Statistical Yearbook of Ireland, 2008*, Central Statistics Office, 2008. Note that figures are given for census years 1996, 2002 and 2006 only. The extrapolation assumes that the rate of reduction between 1996 and 2006 will continue until 2012. Given the rising rate of urbanization and the fact that average household size is lower in urban areas, this assumption seems defensible if not cautious.

2.1 persons per dwelling (Department of Planning and Urban Affairs, 1999). But then Denmark has a highly competent approach to planning housing development on a nationwide basis. Unlike Ireland, where house building went totally out of control thanks to crazy and mutually inconsistent decisions by a myriad of local authorities, in Denmark a central national planning unit coordinates the zoning activities of all regional and local authorities. Rents are policed; the standard of rented accommodation is among the highest in Europe, the price of land is regulated and cities are dense enough to be highly economically productive while still being the most habitable in the world.

An equally tempting argument on the pessimistic side relates to rental yields. Here the argument is highly valid for that part of the market where investors dominate. But there are qualifications: monthly rents are not as directly comparable to mortgage payments as they are in other countries. This is principally because in Ireland tenants have security of tenure for up to a maximum of four years. In Germany, by contrast, rental contracts are usually unspecified by term and in effect give more or less permanent security of tenure. Even when a landlord's legitimate interests lie in turfing the tenant out, the tenant can frustrate the landlord by claiming that unjustified hardship would result from this.

It is reasons like this that make rental yield analysis to the Irish market in the context of international comparisons hugely flawed. Macroeconomists who attempt to make such comparisons do not understand the importance of complementing this approach with microeconomics. A key concept in microeconomics is the substitutability of a good. On a sunny day, for instance, an ice cream might be a good substitute for a cold beer in terms of its cooling-down effect; on a winter's night in a pub with friends, however, an ice cream is definitely not a substitute for a cold beer. Substitutability affects the extent to which price changes can occur without changing behaviour. Raise the price of a bottle of beer from five to seven euros on a hot day by the beach and someone might opt for ice cream instead; do the same in a crowded pub and the punter will grumble but stick with beer all the same. To some economists, the security of Irish rented property is a substitute for freehold property. This is so to only a limited extent. The extent of substitutability in Ireland is less than in many other countries due to the relative insecurity of tenant rights.

A Changed Market

In the decade since the Bacon report was published, the Irish housing market has changed drastically. That report, commissioned by the Irish government and published in 1998 and 1999, examined almost every aspect of the housing market and housing policy. But as its author, economist Peter Bacon, acknowledges on his website, 'time progresses and traditions change'. The population has risen since the first report by two thirds of a million. The median age has fallen by five years, right into the middle of the key demographic identified by Bacon as most important in the market. Despite recession, real after-tax incomes will end 2009 significantly higher than they were during 2009. Consequently the amount of income individuals are willing to spend on their houses is likely to be higher. Another notable change is that the average number of persons living in a single dwelling has fallen over the last ten years. This trend, which shows no sign of abating, will have a significant impact on demand as Ireland converges towards OECD norms of average household size.

Despite some useful studies of the housing market post-Bacon[*] there is a strong case for revisiting the Irish housing

---

[*] See, for instance, 'A Descriptive Analysis of the Irish Housing Market' by David Duffy in the ESRI's summer 2002 Quarterly Economic Commentary.

market to create a more up-to-date understanding of how it works now. The fact that the government is considering how to alter the taxation system as it applies to the property market is just one reason. Avoiding the stupid mistakes of the past and guiding proper regulation of the banking system is another. But perhaps the most pressing reason is to avoid the superficial, highly damaging and mutually inconsistent chorus of pessimism from different commentators who are using entirely different models and systems of analysis. Whatever conclusions are to be drawn about the property market, let them be drawn from the cleanest and clearest well possible.

As creating such a model was beyond the scope of this book, and in the absence of such a comprehensive model that is completely up to date in terms of the factors discussed above, in order to answer the question on everyone's mind 'Where is the property market headed now?' I must commit that cardinal sin of economics. I must rely on common sense.

Putting all of the above trends into the mix it seems that if the government abolishes stamp duty – as the Commission on Taxation has recommended – and as NAMA* restores capital adequacy to banks' balance sheets, allowing credit growth to continue, house price levels should return to levels prevailing in 2005. Given the foregoing assessment of real incomes, interest rates, employment levels and other factors, an average house price of around €250,000 – summer 2005 levels according to the Permanent TSB/ESRI house price index – seems to make sense. Of course that particular measure of house prices has its strenuous objectors. It does, as they rightly point out, lag developments in the market by about four months, and it averages monthly trends by taking three-month moving averages. But those characteristics, which make it a bad way of assessing developments in a particular month, are exactly why it is so useful as a gauge of

* See chapter 11.

longer-term trends: over a time period when the market has risen and fallen, these flaws cancel each other out.

Since autumn 2005, the time of the first credible report of the existence of a properly measured degree of overvaluation in the market,* I have stuck to the view that 2005 price levels – although modestly overvalued at the time – were defensible and sustainable. Had action been taken to stem the incontinence of bank lending in that year – and to gradually increase supply and densification in our urban areas – rising demand would have translated less into higher prices and more into higher skylines. Had that vision been implemented, a bumpy but safe landing could have been attained in the form of modest single-digit declines during 2006 and 2007.

Between February 2007 and June 2009 – a period the latter end of which was so crisis-ridden that trends in the property 'market' are hardly a guide to a stable equilibrium – prices fell by just over 20 per cent and are now back to levels slightly lower than those prevailing in 2005. In a falling market, the inability of many potential buyers to fork out 7 per cent of the asking price of a house in the form of stamp duty is preventing the market from functioning properly. At the same time statements of academic economists have struck irrational fears into buyers. For these reasons the volume of new mortgage lending at the start of 2009 is over 60 per cent down on a year before (Irish Banking Federation/PWC, May 2009). Any underestimate of price falls in 2009 caused by the time factor in the Permanent TSB/ESRI index is more than offset by the downward distortion in price levels caused by these temporary factors of stamp duty and negative comment. The crucial problem this negative sentiment is having is in depriving the housing market of something absolutely critical to settling prices at stable equilibrium values: multiple bidding. From the frenzied overbidding of 2005 and 2006, the

* Emmet Oliver, *Irish Times*, 5 November 2005.

market is now in the opposite extreme. Prices settled for houses are struck between often desperate sellers and buyers who for personal reasons have to buy immediately.

But NAMA* rests on the assumption that property price assessments should be based not on current crisis conditions but on 'the value that the property can reasonably be expected to attain in a stable financial system when current crisis conditions are ameliorated'. But some people don't want crisis conditions to ameliorate: it threatens to take away their badge of vindication. Nor, whether out of callous disregard for young people who need to buy property, or sheer Neanderthal ignorance of how damaging this tax is, do others want stamp duty to be abolished. The truth is we cannot as a country afford to indulge such need for validation and begrudgery. The rest of the country – the majority that wants it to succeed – must move on and leave them behind. We must do that by establishing a realistic view of where our property market is headed, one that is based not on reflexive, self-fulfilling and suicidal manias but on a reasoned and logical assessment of which property price levels are consistent with the relevant demographic, real income, competitiveness and interest rate realities that face us. We must then logically communicate the resulting view to the public, and remove any distorting taxes to allow the market finally to settle where it belongs.

Of course abolishing stamp duty on its own is not a panacea for the market. No credible person claims that it is. But that argument is a straw man advanced by some proponents of stamp duty to discredit the case for its removal. Like removing a tie and belt from someone who has just suffered a heart attack, abolishing stamp duty is not a sufficient condition for recovery. But it is clearly a necessary one. So is a final resolution of Ireland's banking crisis – a topic dealt with in chapter 11. So is a respite from

* Section 58, subsection 1 of 'Proposal for National Asset Management Agency Bill', Department of Finance, 2009.

the relentless barrage of emotionally negative comment on the market, based on superficial comparisons with the US.

Gently Does It

There is an apparent contradiction between two of the arguments made above. The first is that 2005 property prices constitute a reasonable point of return once the recession is over; the other, made directly above, that even 2002 prices were too high for the low-paid. The apparent conflict can easily be resolved, however. On average, 2005 prices are consistent both with a return to equilibrium and, if not a return to the competitiveness levels of the 1990s, at least a point where competitiveness is not unduly held back. The lack of variety and quality in property remains the crucial issue. As Peter Bacon puts it,* 'We in Ireland have to accept that in lieu of home ownership we must consider other options.' Even if 2005 prices on average are viable, Ireland still has a relatively low stock of rentable apartments suitable for family living at the lower-price end of the market. There is also a lack of variety between the traditional three-bed semi-detached and the apartment. If done now and immediately, implementing the Kenny report and achieving higher density in our cities would indeed make 2005 prices non-viable. Which is precisely why what is needed now is a comprehensive plan for rolling out such reforms over a decade or more – a time period short enough to make a difference but gradual enough to ensure market stability. By managing all policy aspects of our housing market – all its different components, not just in its entirety – between now and 2020, that can be achieved. The housing market will hopefully never again be a source of growth for the economy. But it can at least be an anchor of stability and, as discussed in chapter 9, a support for productivity.

* http://www.esatclear.ie/~buildingwithbacon/

It's time to implement the recommendations of a report that has been sitting on the government's desk for a generation. Reports that are not yet acted on are a curse of Irish government.

III

The Inchidoney Years: Ireland's Wrong Turn, 2004–2009

We know what to do. We just don't know how to get elected afterwards.

LUXEMBOURG PRIME MINISTER JEAN-CLAUDE JUNCKER

5

Denial and the Nile

Then let them gather all the food of these good years
that are coming, and store up the grain for food in the
cities under Pharaoh's authority, and let them guard it.
Let the food become as a reserve for the land for the
seven years of famine.

GENESIS 41:35 (NEW AMERICAN BIBLE)

When I have it, I spend it, and when I don't have it, I
don't spend it.

FINANCE MINISTER CHARLIE MCCREEVY

The Folly of Denial

Twice within a generation budgetary crisis has brought Ireland
to its knees. This time there was no excuse for avoiding it. All
the players in Ireland's political and business system had
lived through that last crisis, between 1977 and 1987. All
knew the perils of overspending and bad tax policies. In particular, they knew what could happen when, as in the 1970s, the

nation's future was mortgaged for short-term electoral gain.

They also knew – or should have known – that under EU rules governments weren't just supposed to keep their budget deficit below 3 per cent of GDP. That was certainly an important rule: it made sure no one Euro Zone country beggared the others by borrowing in ways that would raise costs for other member states. But the spirit of this rule, which said that governments had to maintain so-called 'structural balances', was even more important. More nuanced, it means that if a budget deficit does occur, it should be because a downturn in the economy reduces tax revenue or raises welfare spending. Not because the government is spending money on electoral projects. Likewise, governments only deserve surpluses caused by their own prudence. Crowing over a surplus caused by a surge in tax revenue in turn caused by an artificial boom cuts no ice with economists in either the ECB or EU Commission. Sure, the fact that a country is running a surplus during an upturn in the economic cycle is a sign that at least the government isn't squandering the fruits of an upturn. But when surpluses are the result of a non-cyclical credit boom it's a different ball game. An upturn in the cycle is a natural rhythm of the economy and is reasonably predictable in magnitude, if not timing. Credit booms are different, dangerous affairs. They create treacherous, never-to-be-repeated, self-reversing surges in tax revenues and falls in welfare payments (as the unemployed go to work in construction). They are dangerous beasts that smile at you when credit is flowing only to turn and savage you when boom turns to bust. Between 2005 and 2007, as the economy increased by almost one fifth in size – most of it artificial – revenues from stamp duty, Ireland's equivalent of a property tax, nearly doubled. The disproportionate relationship between economic growth – already too high – and the insane rate of this growth was a clear sign to any literate economist that government finances were built on sand.

On 6 July 2006 I wrote an article in the *Irish Times* entitled 'He

Had a Good Run But Now the Tiger is in Trouble'. In it, I stated that the government's financial position was way too dependent on construction. To my surprise, on 13 July, just a week later, the then Finance Minister Brian Cowen published a response that began 'We are managing the economy prudently and we are not depending on a surge in property-related revenue.'

It is probably fair to say that this difference of opinion has been resolved in one clear direction. During the years 2004 to 2007, however, the government, under pressure from social partners and shocked by the 2004 local elections, began a spending spree of unheard-of proportions. In just three years current spending rose by one third. Coming as it did from a one-off boom rather than from the natural operation of the economic cycle, the tax revenue boom was headed for bust. But current spending increases were being committed in ways that would be almost impossible to reverse. In fact, not even the cycle would have justified major rises in spending: after three years it was overdue a downturn, a downturn that would have been healthy. But inaction by the financial regulator interfered with Mother Nature's plan for the economy.

The even sadder fact – a fact examined in the next chapter – is that the opposition failed to shout 'Stop!' during the 2007 election. By going along with government forecasts on tax revenue growth in 2007 it was implicitly saying that what had happened between 2005 and 2007 was sustainable. And by assuming, as it did, that tax growth would match GDP growth it was in a state of total denial about the fool's gold impact the boom was having on tax revenues.

The busting of that boom now confronts us, with a gap between spending and tax revenues of over €20 billion. The first question is whether and how this gap can be closed. The second is this: can we redesign our tax system to make sure this insanity never happens again?

On the first question the signs are mixed. The government has shown an impressive resolve to deal with the crisis. Between July 2008 and April 2009 a budgetary correction of 5 per cent of GDP was achieved by the new Finance Minister Brian Lenihan. It is in the same league as Ray MacSharry's reduction of spending by 10 per cent of GDP between 1987 and 1989. But where MacSharry had cut spending, Lenihan increased taxes. Based on discredited advice that increasing tax rates necessarily raises revenues, Lenihan's decision may have been influenced by the imminence of a second vote on the Lisbon treaty and a fear of alienating public sector workers by the alternative strategy of cutting spending. Dominated by groups that wish to preserve high state spending, social partners were only too happy to see taxes rise. So were many academics dependent on the public purse for their lifestyles. But, as explained below, the tax rate increases of 2008 and 2009 backfired completely, economically and electorally. Just as they did in the mid-1980s, they produced less revenue and have dented consumer spending and confidence in the economy.

The answer to the second question is more hopeful. In 2006 Labour Party finance spokesperson Joan Burton proposed the creation of a Commission on Taxation. The overhaul of Ireland's taxation system was something that should have been done during the boom times and not under the intense pressure of a budgetary correction, but under Ireland's political system it took emergency conditions to get politicians to address long-term issues in any serious way.

Established on 14 February 2008 – by which time it was clear that even if a full-blown economic crisis wasn't around the corner, a crisis in budgetary finances was – the Commission finally reported on 7 September 2009.

In February 2006 – over three and a half years earlier – I had called on the government to abolish or at least reform stamp duty.* The tax was incompetent and iniquitous, not just in its

---

* Author, 'Unfair Stamp Duty Must Be Challenged', *Irish Times*, 24 February 2006.

existence but also its operation: by obliging buyers of residential homes to pay 7 per cent of the price of a typical house, the tax forced property buyers to borrow tens of thousands of euros when taking out their already over-inflated mortgages. Just to fund wasteful state spending. As house prices were rocketing upward, the capital gain on a house – even one the owner had bought recently – could fund the stamp duty. But once the property market stalled and reversed, stamp duty forced buyers to sacrifice their life savings or children's education, or saddle themselves with other debts, just to feed the state's need for revenue. And although a higher rate of income tax is only paid on income earned above the threshold for that higher rate, once a house price rose to push the payer of stamp duty into a new higher stamp duty rate, that rate was paid on the entire price of the house. Stamp duty was also a tax on Dublin, where most average house prices were above the threshold for paying the tax; in the rural constituencies of most government ministers and TDs stamp duty was a non-issue because house prices were low. Yet while the government was quick to ease the burden of stamp duty for farm land transaction, three years passed without any substantial reform of the tax.*

At the behest of incompetent advice, the tax was retained. While not the only cause of the downturn in property prices, the decline in transaction volumes was greatly exacerbated once prices started to fall. While competent economists accepted the need for prices to fall in order for markets to clear, this could not happen when buyers were forced to pay between 7 and 9 per cent of the price of a property in tax simply for the honour of buying it. Most of the 60 per cent decline in mortgage volumes is directly attributable to the existence of this road block. Thanks to

---

* The ungraduated nature of the thresholds and rates was removed in December 2007, but the size of the average stamp duty burden was not substantially altered.

declining volumes, prices may well have fallen faster than they needed to – a point argued in chapter 4.

In July 2006, in that *Irish Times* article I mentioned earlier,* I argued that the apparent forward motion of the Irish economy was like that of a headless chicken. The proverbial competitiveness 'head' of which had been cut off but the body was gyrating in an extreme way as a final adrenalin hit of credit surged through the system. The fact that stamp duty revenues had grown by 53 per cent in the first half of 2006 was not a cause for joy but alarm. 'If what has gone up comes down, that position [the government's budgetary position] could deteriorate rapidly,' I warned, adding that four years after the last boom/bust fiscal correction of 2002 exchequer revenue strength was 'even more illusory than before'. In a final comment I said that 'any subsequent deterioration [in finances] will be more severe than in 2002. So will the measures needed to balance the government's books. And so will the political consequences of not having taken pre-emptive remedial action now.'

Three years after this warning – three years in which the government did nothing but heed calls from incompetent academic economists to retain the tax – the Commission on Taxation has finally urged its abolition. It is a welcome shift in the power of decision-making, away from ideological and self-interested economists and towards professionals with real-world experience that produced the Commission report.

The Commission's other recommendations – introducing a property tax, water charges and carbon taxes – are also worth examining, but only once waste and excess have first been eliminated from public spending. For taxes like this, reform can be pre-announced and made contingent on other developments without any negative impact on economic stability. Transaction taxes are a different ball game. When they come, they must be like a

---

* 'He Had a Good Run But Now the Tiger is in Trouble', 6 July 2006.

thief in the night, swift and unannounced. Otherwise the speculation caused by the abolition of a large tax like stamp duty will simply cause buyers to defer purchase, depressing even further an already depressed market.

This point was proved in September 2006 by former Justice Minister and PD leader Michael McDowell. In the six months since my February article the clamour for reform had grown. By May 2006 even the left-wing Labour Party was calling for significant reform of stamp duty, and that September McDowell, a minister in government and leader of the junior coalition party, also called for reform. The public expected action, and for it to come in the budget three months later – or failing that, if McDowell pulled out of government he and the PDs would still be a major force to be reckoned with. In fact the whole face of Irish politics would be different, with McDowell enjoying the position Eamonn Gilmore enjoys now. But the real significance of the failure was economic rather than political: from sustainable growth of 2 per cent in the third quarter of 2006, the number of new mortgages taken out fell by 11 per cent in the fourth quarter. There were other factors in the falls in prices that occurred from January 2007, but the fact that those falls occurred a full year before the global recession and after the beginning of the decline in transaction volumes in the three months after McDowell's intervention shows how significant such a failed pre-announcement can be. If by the end of 2009 stamp duty is not abolished, needless misery will have been forced on thousands of young house buyers for the sake of government revenues amounting to just €85 million a year.

Wisdom of the Nile

For thousands of years, the Nile mystified Egyptians. Without fail it would rise, fertilize the soil, then subside. Aswan, Memphis and Dendera, among the oldest civilized settlements known to mankind, show how early civilized man respected the natural rhythms of the river that gave them life. The ancient Egyptians went to great lengths to predict its rise and fall. They sowed and reaped accordingly. Prosperity, employment and taxes depended on it. Four thousand years later, similar but more complex rhythms are at work in the world economy.

In the Book of Genesis, the prophet Joseph tells Pharaoh about a cycle that will last seven years[*] bringing great harvests, and then seven years of famine. In the first piece of economic advice ever recorded, Joseph urges the Pharaoh to save grain. Thousands of years later the idea of a seven-year cycle remains alive and well and has a monetary policy as well as a budgetary policy aspect. Two American economists confirmed the existence of seven-year cycles in 1946. One of them, Arthur F. Burns, became chairman of the Federal Reserve in 1970. Half a century later European Central Bank monetary policy, unwittingly or not, still seemed faithful to the idea. From a peak of 4.75 per cent in May 2001, ECB rates next peaked at 4.25 per cent in July 2008, just over seven years later. Perhaps it was coincidence. But perhaps not.

Even if it appeared to be following ancient wisdom, the ECB made one mistake. Perhaps indirectly influenced against its will by the US Federal Reserve, the ECB allowed interest rates to fall further than they should have. The Bundesbank, its predecessor as Europe's 'anchor' central bank, was respected for its tough-ness and had kept rates high enough in good times to stimulate savings. High enough also to prevent corporate balance sheets from overborrowing during good times so that when a downturn came and the central bank did lower rates they would be free to borrow. In the fifty years between its creation and the birth of the euro in 1998, the Bundesbank's 'repo rate' was on average 4.4 per cent. Whether by design or accident, since 1 January 1999 the ECB's main refinancing facility has averaged 3.2 per cent. The change

* I acknowledge that other economists and writers have spotted this parallel!

8. ECB's main refinancing facility 1999–2009

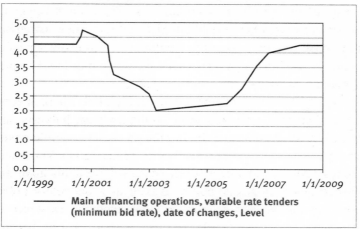

Main refinancing operations, variable rate tenders (minimum bid rate), date of changes, Level

seems slight. But Irish policymakers were to make a mistake that would cause that difference to wreak havoc on Ireland's economy.

The ECB at least never allowed its main refinancing to fall below 2 per cent, except during the abnormal crisis conditions of 2009. This was important. The ECB's mission is to keep inflation at levels close to 2 per cent. A floor of 2 per cent in base rates means that negative interest rates in Euro Land should, except for brief or abnormal periods, never occur. To ensure this, Euro Zone member states are supposed to work with the ECB, keeping inflation in check in their own countries. Some argued that the ECB regime was wrong for Ireland. The argument is ten years too late. Like stating that the rest of Europe drives on the wrong side of the road, it ignores the extensive preparations made by Ireland – and the extensive structural funding we got – in order to prepare for the rigours we knew were coming. Rigours we knew were good for us in the long run. Rigours, we have found out, our political leadership was incapable of preparing for.

Between 1993 and 1997 the Irish economy was successfully brought into synchronization with other Euro Zone entrants.

Inflation in 1997 was brought down to 1.5 per cent. Other steps that needed to be taken, however, were missing. To ensure that the low interest boom resulted in high output growth rather than high price growth, we needed to increase competition in the economy. We also needed to change our urban planning and financial system. Chapters 10 and 11 discuss these issues further. For now, let's focus on the key macroeconomic mistake that was made by the Irish government in the late 1990s and early 2000s: the failure to contain inflation, a process that would turn Ireland into one of the most expensive places in Europe in which to do business. And it had another effect far more insidious than that.

Although it has shared the same exchange rate and core interest rates with the Euro Zone since 1999, Ireland's real exchange rate and real rate of interest have diverged sharply from the Euro Zone. This is exactly what the Maastricht criteria – the Euro rule book we signed up to – was designed to avoid. It was to turn what was already a serious problem in Europe – as discussed in chapter 3, ECB nominal interest rates were already too low for anyone's good – into a chronic one at home.

The serious problem began in May 2001 when the ECB unexpectedly lowered its rates by twenty-five basis points, despite strong hints that it wouldn't.* On 9/11, the US Fed and the ECB conducted a further emergency half a per cent reduction in interest rates. At the time the uncertainty over the economic impact of 9/11 justified this. But as it became clear that the economic world wouldn't cave in, these cuts should have been reversed. As well as falling to 2 per cent in 2003 and 2004, rates subsequently peaked in 2008 half a per cent lower than previously. At each phase of the new monetary Nile's flooding, our modern-day

---

* This reduction was justified by the fact that monetary statistics for the Euro Area had been revised in a manner suggesting that growth in the money supply, which in the early years the ECB regarded as requiring control, was less than expected. It was therefore regarded as a 'one-off' reduction not relevant to the economic cycle.

Egyptians were becoming more and more lazy about respecting its wisdom, leading the economies of the world into a trap where the rod had been spared and the child had been spoiled.

At least in Euro Land real interest rates were never lower than zero for very long. Even at zero real interest rates, money is effectively free to borrow. But when inflation rises above the rate of interest rates, borrowing becomes too attractive to be healthy. With interest rates at 2 per cent and inflation at 5 per cent, a property buyer loses 3,000 for every year he saves to buy 100,000 worth of real estate. Where large purchases, particularly investment purchases, of property are involved then, as George Soros puts it, 'the rational lender will keep on lending until there is no one else to lend to'. But such a pursuit of self-interest by individuals, however rational, puts the entire economy on a yellow brick road to nowhere. It is exactly the sort of market failure – individual success but collective disaster – central banks and regulators exist to prevent from happening.

In Ireland inflation was so much higher than in the Euro Zone (see table 1 in Appendix I) that real base interest rates turned seriously negative. The awesome opportunity for profit-making drove the madness that gripped the Irish banking sector from 2004 on. Was it greed? Perhaps. But are investors in high-technology companies or manufacturing companies less greedy than those who invest in property? Arguably not. The real difference is that their incentives are not as distorted by central banks.

And were property investors really the only ones to blame? Local authorities and state planning policy had spectacularly failed to zone enough land in urban areas for the 300,000 new citizens that had joined the state between 1996 and 2002. The result was the state's failure to accommodate whole hosts of people, from nurses and teachers to Gardai and low-paid workers in the private sector. From just €206,117[*] in 2001, the price of a

* Department of Finance Budgetary and Economic Statistics, table 72.

second-hand house in Dublin was to rise 42 per cent by 2004, to €294,667 – over ten times a teacher's basic salary.

This result of high inflation was in ironic contrast to its cause. The result – the inability of public servants to afford a house – was to lead to exactly the wrong solution: raising incomes instead of lowering house prices. One of the causes, however, was that due to its lack of overall reform, inflation in the public sector has always run far faster than in the private sector (see table 1). In the clothing and footwear sector – a sector whose manufacturing, wholesale and retail parts are highly competitive – prices plunged between 1996 and 2003. But prices in the health sector ran much faster than the rate of inflation. Moreover, something curious was happening to healthcare inflation. Documented by the state sector, the cost of healthcare was driven least by competitive forces and most by monopoly power and political decision-making in government. As the general election of 2002 got closer, healthcare inflation sped up, but as it passed it slowed down (but remained high).

This was no coincidence, but part of a phenomenon that exists in most countries, but one which in Ireland was to get completely out of control. In the 1970s an economist called William Nordhaus noticed a tendency of governments to increase spending in the year before a general election (Nordhaus, 1975). By increasing spending and cutting taxes before an election in time for them to trickle down, governments found they could create a feel-good factor or, in really bad times, at least limit the electoral damage of unemployment and income decline. In the turbulent 1970s it was the curse of public finances. In the 1980s the beast was eventually tamed, and by the mid-1990s countries queueing up for Euro Zone membership were keeping their budgets in line. Once the EMU test was passed, however, spending habits went back to their bad old ways across Europe (Marco Buti, 2003). But no country was even to come close to the extent of what happened in Ireland.

From just 3 per cent growth in 1995, the rainbow coalition of Fine Gael, Labour and Democratic Left upped the rate of spending growth to 10.2 per cent in 1996. For a full year after taking office it looked as if the new Fianna Fáil government would restore order to the government deficit. Spending in 1998 rose by a modest 3.7 per cent. But in 2001 and 2002 the government increased gross current spending by a massive 26 per cent, before slowing it down to a still high but more modest 7.8 per cent in 2004. This was one cause of the rampant inflation that produced negative real interest rates. Another, discussed in chapter 7, was the failure of government to deal with the huge power of public sector companies to ratchet up the costs of doing business. In a boom, customers might grumble but could afford to pay up. But as inflation in the semi-state sector ran far ahead of inflation in the more competitive private sector, a competitiveness crisis of major proportions built up.

9. Real interest rates in the Euro Zone and Ireland

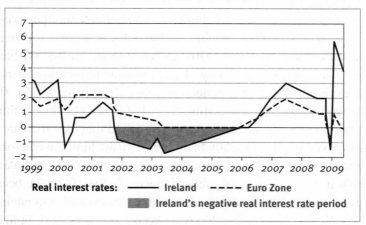

Real interest rates: —— Ireland — — — Euro Zone

Ireland's negative real interest rate period

2004: One Last Chance

No longer the lean beast of a few years before (see table 2 in

Appendix I), the economy had grown love handles by 2004, but was still reasonably functional. From 17.5 per cent in 1997, export growth had slowed to 7.5 per cent. Not great, but respectable. Growth in investment, 9.6 per cent, was inflated by negative real interest rates, but even half of this rate would have been acceptable. One in ten of the workforce was employed in construction – high compared to the ratio of one in fourteen for the EU but not outrageously so given Ireland's much younger and growing population. The economy's growth rate of 4.5 per cent was around 2 per cent higher than it should have been, and with retail spending growth playing a stronger role than it should have. But with exports growing, the economy was at least flying on all engines. The budgetary balance was in surplus, the illusory component of it was certainly present but not yet dominant. Sure, there was a property boom. But that boom had not yet spun out of control.

In the autumn of 2004 all of this changed utterly, and there was no beauty in what was about to be born. Over the next three years the economy experienced a rapid and frightening deterioration from healthy, if flabby, growth to bloated obesity.

Public spending was to grow by one third by the end of 2007. From €200 billion, the level of private sector indebtedness was to grow to €400 billion by the end of 2008, pushing the share of income needed to service that debt from 12 per cent of income to almost one quarter of income (McCarthy). From a point of modest but containable excess, the level of construction employment completely lost touch with reality. In every way possible, the economy was exposing itself to a global recession. In June 2006 the Economic and Social Research Institute warned as much (ESRI, summer 2006). Other efforts to warn the government in that year have been described above.[*]

* Brian Cowen, 'Headless Chicken Analogy Will Not Fly', *Irish Times*, 13 July 2006.

By the end of 2006 the government was relying on the property sector for almost one quarter of its revenue intake. And the sector's contribution to tax revenue growth was even greater. Perhaps two thirds of the increase in taxes in 2006 came from stamp duty, capital gains taxes and, more indirectly, income tax and VAT revenues linked to property, construction or related banking activities. The logical thing to do would have been to halt spending growth and start redesigning the tax base as soon as possible, as Labour's finance spokesperson Joan Burton had recommended. But from a normal level of 36 per cent of GDP in 2004, gross government spending rose to over 42 per cent of GDP in just three years. On an entirely illusory basis tax revenues grew by a third over the same period, disguising the deficit that was just waiting in the long grass for its moment to pounce. In 2008 it appeared with a vengeance, and by 2009 it was heading for a staggering €20 billion.

Anyone who really understood public finances and the dynamics of the property market knew that the huge increase in property taxes was of a one-off nature. Instead of spending them on current spending they should have been put into a long-term fund such as the National Pensions Reserve Fund, or just put aside for a rainy day. Instead, when revenues plunged by 13 per cent in 2008, and by nearly one fifth in 2009,* there was nothing in the kitty to compensate for it. The government came under pressure to increase spending on a number of fronts. Health spending rocketed during the period, as did spending on public service employment and pay and social welfare increases. The latter two were an understandable but misguided reaction to the appalling increase in the cost of living: instead of keeping prices, especially house prices (and the credit growth that drove them) and state-driven prices, down, the government was allowing them to rise

---

* Exchequer figures available at the time of writing suggested falls of just under 18 per cent in the first seven months of 2009.

and destroy our competitiveness, burdening future taxpayers by increasing the incomes of welfare recipients and state employees. Future taxpayers will for decades to come pay for the inefficiencies in our property market and public sector built up in the first decade of this century. What we needed was exactly the reverse: to keep incomes where they were and ease the cost-of-living burden by aggressively driving down prices. As a result of the approach taken, the report of An Bord Snip – a government body established to find cuts of €5 billion – now points out that an income earner with a spouse and three children can claim €41,690 in benefits each year. Given Ireland's chronic cost of living, it may not seem much; but compared to wage levels in other EU countries that are much lower, it presents Ireland with a chronic wage competitiveness crisis.

Where did this mistaken approach come from? In the local elections of June 2004 Fianna Fáil obtained 32 per cent of the vote. Although seven points higher than its equivalent 2009 result, the outcome shocked the party to the core. It was a cry from an electorate overburdened by high prices and angry at the benchmarking of public sector pay. But in September 2004 this fall in Fianna Fáil's vote was misrepresented as a cry for more spending and taxation. That month – the same month in which Bertie Ahern announced he was a 'socialist' – the party met for a think-in in the picturesque Cork town of Inchidoney to discuss its future. The Inchidoney project – increasing public spending on the back of property taxes – was instituted. Although he had made mistakes, Finance Minister Charlie McCreevy was not to blame for Fianna Fáil's drubbing, except in one respect: his pushing through of tax individualization was a huge injustice to stay-at-home mothers and had a severe impact on Fianna Fáil's traditional vote. Reversing that policy and strengthening measures to drive competition and lower prices, particularly house prices, by more competition and better planning, these were the initiatives that should have come out of that Inchidoney meeting.

Instead, an agenda of higher state spending and an antipathy if not hostility to competition were the result. McCreevy was exiled to the post of EU Commissioner in Brussels while Seamus Brennan, an influential and courageous Transport Minister, was punished by demotion to a non-economic ministry for having stood up to inept and inefficient practice in what is laughably called Ireland's transport system. The only minister with an economic brief opposed to this new socialist approach, Mary Harney, was too busy trying to control health spending from spiralling out of control.

The state was set for one of the biggest ever increases in public expenditure in any European country during peacetime. Taxes rise and fall with the economic cycle, but once increased, government spending is much harder to bring back down again. Even by April 2009, long after the need for urgent action, it was clear government spending was continuing to rise in both nominal and real terms. From around 25 per cent in 2008, government debt will rocket to almost 80 per cent by 2012. This final level is not, as chapter 1 argues, alarming in itself. But the speed of increase certainly is.

A Budget Backfires

With the public sector on average paid around one fifth more than the private sector – a situation unheard of in any competitive economy – and examples of wasteful spending hitting the headlines on a daily basis, responding to the full-blown budgetary crisis of 2008 and 2009 with tax increases instead of spending reductions was unjustified.

The first crucial step the government needed to take in 2009 was to reduce the high costs imposed on individuals and businesses through a constellation of state sector fees and charges. As a prelude to reducing pay across the economy, the state needed to lead the way. Public service reform should have been pursued during the boom years when the economy was best able to absorb a reduction in state expenditure. The next step was to begin to tackle Ireland's high accommodation costs. This in turn was crucial to what needed to happen next: reversing the 2002 benchmarking of public sector pay, an initiative driven largely by house price escalation. ESRI research shows that restoring parity between public and private sector pay levels requires an average adjustment of 12.5 per cent in public sector pay – even after the introduction of the pension levy. But to inflict this on lower-paid public servants before tackling the very high cost of living would be hugely unjust.

All of these steps needed to be undertaken years ago, before contemplating any tax rises. Tax rises without reform inflict on taxpayers the economically and morally unacceptable burden of paying for wasteful spending.

The government was about to heed advice of an entirely different nature. Despite the evidence from the 1980s to the contrary, in early 2009 respected economist Dr Alan Ahearne, former adviser to Alan Greenspan at the US Federal Reserve, used an *Irish Times* article to express a view that he and other public sector economists had been airing, namely that Ireland's tax rates were too low. He argued that 'substantial increases in taxes will be required to restore fiscal balance'.[*] Although superficially and theoretically attractive, the idea of raising tax rates to generate more revenue failed to understand the fact that the relationship between tax rates and tax revenues is a complex one. For all his failure to manage the fiscal cycle properly and lack of economic training, former Finance Minister Charlie McCreevy had at least grasped that raising tax revenues could be done by cutting tax rates. But he had been banished to Brussels after the Inchidoney consensus, and the other voices for tax restraint, Seamus Brennan and Mary Harney, had either been

---

* Alan Ahearne, *Irish Times*, 29 January 2009.

demoted or were too busy. Besides, opinion in the Fianna Fáil party on economic issues was dominated by public sector and academic thinking.

But as UCD economist Colm McCarthy showed in a presentation in Dublin that January (McCarthy, 2009), by 2008 total exchequer spending had increased to over 40 per cent of GNP, a level unseen since the early 1990s, levels that pre-dated Ireland's golden age and were not only symbolic of its past failures but well above levels to be seen in Ireland's hungry and emerging competitors. And they were shortly heading for 50 per cent of GNP. When another budget was called for in April 2009, it was time to recognize this and cut back on waste. But entirely the opposite direction was taken. Income levies were doubled in an effort to raise revenue. Unlike many of his peers, McCarthy was an academic with real world work experience.

On the basis of the latest exchequer figures available at the time of writing, raising tax rates has failed entirely. From just over 4 per cent in February and March, the annual rate of decline in income taxes had by September accelerated to 27.7 per cent. And this despite the fact that the rise in unemployment was moderating substantially. In the first quarter of the year the Live Register rose by 77,000. In the three months of June, July and August the rise was 28,000. But the September rise was just 600. While income taxes should still have been falling, the rate should have been moderating, but the reverse was happening. As well as failing to boost income tax revenues, tax increases pushed Fianna Fáil to its lowest vote in eight decades in the June 2009 European and local elections.

What else could the government have done? It could have taken inspiration from figures published by the Revenue Commissioners[*] showing that one third of income tax was paid by the top 2.5 per cent of income earners. At the other end of the

* Pat Leahy, *Sunday Business Post*, 8 February 2009.

scale almost two fifths of income earners paid little or no income tax whatsoever. In a year in which inflation and wage growth were likely to be negative – in the private sector at least – the clear and obvious policy measure would have been to reverse the indexation of tax bands and credits in previous years. Upward indexation was justified when incomes were rising. Now the reverse was happening and the state was gasping for money. On my own calculation, this would have netted the exchequer around half a billion euros, without creating either of the two disincentive effects of raising marginal tax rates. It would also have spread the pain far more evenly over the electorate. The reduction in popular support for the government would, although significant, have been less long-lasting as a result.

Just as seriously, tax increases are undoing the good work being done by the ECB. Since September 2008 ECB rate cuts had reduced the burden on the average mortgage borrower by well over a third. For a family with one earner on €50,000 a year and a twenty-five-year mortgage of €250,000, annual payments fell by around €4,000. Budget tax increases clawed back €2,500 of that. The net impact might still be positive, but the ominous reality is that interest rate cuts will eventually reverse, and as they do the destructive damage of tax increases will become apparent. Thankfully, the Commission on Taxation has implicitly accepted that the case for increasing tax rates is non-existent. But the government must go further. It must work to undo the increases in income taxes and fund this with a programme of radical public sector reform.

The immediate challenge, as I've already stated, is to reverse the benchmarking of public sector pay. Even former Irish Congress of Trade Unions General Secretary Peter Cassells accepts that public servants should on average earn less than their private sector counterparts. This should at least apply to public servants paid more than €40,000 a year; to reduce public service pay at lower levels before tackling Ireland's high cost of living would create injustice. The government's defence for doing nothing so far is the introduction of a pensions levy on public sector workers. But given the size of the liabilities of Ireland's extremely generous system of public sector pension provision – around €100 billion (O'Brien) – this merely scratched the surface of meeting these liabilities, never mind tackling public spending. In terms of restoring reality to public/private pay differentials, it is a mere accounting exercise. Only a new benchmarking exercise can resolve this issue in a fair manner. An Bord Snip has recommended that such an exercise be conducted. It does, however, appear that the public pension system is due for an overhaul.* Unfortunately, a new problem has been created. To deal with any current budget deficit, falls in spending should relate to current spending. By using the funding of long-term pensions to plug an overrun created by current spending the government has made it more difficult to deal with the €100 billion pension crisis as those affected by further proposed reform will object that they are already paying a levy to justify their better pensions. Again, cackhanded advice during 2009 has limited the government's future options.

There are other difficulties with the government's approach. In an effort to raise €95 million, a tax of €10 was slapped on flights. But on 13 July 2009 the *Irish Independent* showed how the state was wasting €98 million by paying eighteen times more for prescription drugs than was paid in the United Kingdom. Had this waste been dealt with, the air tax wouldn't have been necessary. There are many examples worth much more than these amounts and it is perhaps unfair to single out the pharmaceutical sector: it has contributed to employment growth and high-technology research. But the general principle of raising taxes before tackling waste is the prime reason for the state's current crisis.

* Ian Kehoe, 'Public Sector Pension System Set for an Overhaul', *Sunday Business Post*, 6 September 2009.

Not only do higher tax rates not guarantee increased revenues, their effect on competitiveness can be devastating. The tourist industry, in which we have some chance of generating jobs, is being crucified by a host of state-driven costs and taxes. By contrast, unproductive and inefficient sectors are not being taxed. Between January 2003 and June 2009, rail travel costs – a state monopoly sector – rose by almost 40 per cent, nearly three times the rate of inflation. The cost of air travel actually fell by 6.7 per cent. This is thanks to competition between Ryanair and the state-run monopoly Aer Lingus – a competition entirely absent in the rail sector. By putting a tax on air travel, the government is penalizing the sectors of the economy that are trying to cut our chronically high cost of living.

Planes v. Trains: transport and the great divide in Ireland's economy

	Jan 03	Jun 09	**Change**
All items	88.6	102.1	**+15.2%**
Rail travel	83.3	116.5	**+39.9%**
Air travel	111.2	103.7	**-6.7%**

Source: Central Statistics Office

Although not the sole reason for the collapse by one fifth in the number of tourists visiting Ireland (Central Statistics Office, 2009), it was clear that the air travel tax wasn't helping a situation in which a quarter of a million fewer visitors were coming to Ireland in May 2009 compared to a year before. The underlying cause was of course recession, but given that, the state should have been helping, not making matters worse. Ireland's high costs and the strength of the euro put an obligation on our tax system to work the other way. But economic advice to government is dominated by the mentality of those whose every instinct is to defend the public sector at the cost of taxpayers.

Stamp duty is another area where state policy has failed. In

1996 the tax, as intended, applied to just a small fraction of the country's housing stock. As house prices rose the government found that just by leaving payment thresholds untouched, ever more house buyers fell into the stamp duty net. Higher prices also allowed the state to cream off a capital gain that ought to have accrued to those who had taken the risk of buying the property. But the state had its benchmarking bills to pay; families' needs came second to the diktats of social partnership. From a few hundred million euros a year, stamp duty revenues swelled to over €3 billion by 2006. The rate structure was changed and the tax slightly reformed in December 2007, of course, but the size of the average burden remained the same; and in any case, by then prices had fallen to 2005 levels, reducing the number of buyers who had bought their current houses early enough in the decade to have any capital gain to cover the cost of stamp duty.

The contrast with the UK was instructive. Stamp duty in the UK was a relatively small burden compared to Ireland. For most buyers a rate of 1 per cent applied. Even that rate gave rise to concern, and in April 2008 the UK's Chancellor of the Exchequer suspended the operation of the tax below a threshold of £125,000 for at least a year (this threshold was later increased). By July, both the Halifax's and Nationwide's indices of UK house prices were showing a moderate but sustained recovery.

The maintenance of stamp duty for so long must rank as one of the worst policy disasters in fiscal history, and one on which the electorate of Dublin – the part of the country most affected by stamp duty – have delivered a devastating verdict by relegating Fianna Fáil to the status of a fringe party in the capital.

In May, the Minister for Finance signalled that future budgetary corrections would emphasize spending cuts over tax increases. An Bord Snip has been told to look everywhere but the public sector pay level. It was – bizarrely, at a time when unemployment was rocketing – allowed to advocate cutting public sector employment, however.

Political Conclusions

It's a well-worn truism that those who fail to learn the lessons of the past are doomed to repeat them. The only thing Irish governments seem to have learned properly is that they find it hard to learn, even from the oldest and most trusted sources of wisdom. The ancient Egyptians respected nature and tried to learn from it, building their lives around the life-giving cycles of the Nile. But by assisting the creation of negative interest rates, by raising government spending at rampant rates close to elections, and by depending on this for illusory growth in bubble-based tax revenues, the government showed that they didn't understand a basic wisdom that was over four thousand years old. Even lessons learned in our lifetime – that correcting a budget that's out of control is best done by cutting spending rather than raising taxation, as in the 1980s – has been disregarded.

The sage advice of T. K. Whitaker, who as Secretary General of the Department of Finance in 1957 charted Ireland's way out of stagnation, was also ignored. In June 2009 at a commemorative ceremony in honour of Sean Lemass, the Taoiseach associated with Ireland's escape from isolation, the ninety-three-year-old Whitaker told his audience that Ireland had a social obligation to explore every alternative to unemployment. His advice is sound. At around one third of a million and at less than one fifth of those in work, Ireland's public sector workforce is not overly large by the standards of any peer country. There were certainly grounds for employing some workers more effectively, but not for cutting overall numbers. It is pay levels in the public sector that are way out of kilter with both private sector pay and public pay in other comparable countries. The logical thing, therefore, would be to preserve numbers and cut pay levels. Cutting pay rather than increasing taxation is also good from a confidence point of view: tax increases affect mostly those in the private sector whose fear of job loss will cause tax hikes to damage confidence and spending far more. Restoring parity between public and private sector pay will still leave public servants as well paid as their private sector peers and will have a far softer impact on confidence and spending, given that public sector jobs are secure. But this more humane approach seems to be off the agenda. Labour and the trade unions oppose it. Fine Gael also opposes any cuts in public sector pay below a threshold of €100,000. Fianna Fáil appears – belatedly – to be accepting the need for some cuts in public pay levels at the time of writing. But trade unions like SIPTU are threatening to bring Ireland to a standstill if this happens. Despite this, it seems Fianna Fáil has nothing to lose by acting decisively.

When in June 2009 the people of Ireland got a chance to express their opinion on Fianna Fáil's newfound fondness for the policies of tax and spend, for the first time in Irish political history since 1927 Fine Gael outvoted Fianna Fáil in European and local elections (Fianna Fáil's share slumped to 25 per cent). This outcome was not a necessary one: despite the onset of recession Fianna Fáil had maintained a clear lead over Fine Gael until the tax increases of October 2008. But October's budget made a fatal mistake: it increased taxation but contained no clear measures to cut spending. The impact of this became clear on 14 November when over eighty years of Irish political history came to an end.

For the first time ever, the TSN/MRBI *Irish Times* opinion poll published that day showed that Fine Gael was the most popular party in the state, with a seven-point lead over Fianna Fáil.[*] Four days later, the reason became clear: a decisive portion of the electorate felt tax increases in the budget had been too severe. Most tellingly, the majority of voters supported pay cuts for public sector workers.[†] In other words, Fianna Fáil's disastrous

---

[*] Kilian Doyle and Charlie Taylor, www.irish-times.ie, 14 November 2008.
[†] Stephen Collins, 'A Majority of Voters Back Pay Cuts for Public Servants', *Irish Times*, 18 November 2008.

performance in the June 2009 elections was indeed a consequence of having listened to the advice of those who urged it to
increase taxes before first eliminating the huge amount of waste
in public spending, waste of a kind that did nothing to provide
real public services.

Despite this, and despite the party's apparent success, at the
time of writing Fine Gael offers no substantively clear alternative
in terms of a fiscal strategy. It does appear attractive as a protest
vote to those frustrated by inaction on public sector reform. But
even George Lee, a celebrated and respected economist whose
victory in the June 2009 Dublin South by-election for Fine Gael
stunned politics, retreated from arguing for a reversal of benchmarking. This was despite former Fine Gael Taoiseach Garrett
Fitzgerald, former Fine Gael leader and Finance Minister Alan
Dukes, and former Irish Congress of Trade Unions General
Secretary Peter Cassells all endorsing the need to restore parity.
If Fine Gael's seemingly strong support in current polls turn out
to be self-reversing, this may be the reason why.

In the first public speech he gave after accepting Fine Gael's
nomination for the election,* Lee defended Fine Gael's position
by saying that public sector workers had 'made commitments' on
the basis of their current pay levels. Indeed they had. And so had
many tens of thousands of laid-off private sector workers – commitments to repaying mortgages on houses with negative equity,
to their children's education, to paying outlandish taxes on property. Many tens of thousands more private sector workers had
seen their pay levels cut. But Fine Gael were only prepared to
countenance cuts in public sector pay for those earning €100,000
or more. This threshold was ironic: in that month it was the same
as the number of private sector workers who had lost their jobs in
the last twelve months. By contrast, public sector employment,
and incomes, were growing. CSO data also made it clear that

* The speech was given at a public meeting in Dublin's Goat Inn on Wednesday,
20 May 2009.

public sector wages, despite already being more generous than private sector wages before the recession even started, were increasing in real terms by 8 per cent a year.

But if one of Ireland's most renowned economists couldn't confront and address this reality, it was not his fault. There is a deeper underlying cause that prevents good politicians like Lee from standing up for the truth. When he accepted the nomination as Fine Gael candidate for Dublin South, Lee said he wanted to combat Fianna Fáil's 'failed approach' on the economy. In reality, it's Ireland's entire political system that has failed. We have an electoral system that is no longer fit for purpose. That is the subject of the next chapter.

6

Electile Dysfunction

An opposition which fails to challenge effectively a government pursuing economically disastrous policies and which goes along with those policies – as happened in 2007 – is not doing its job . . . What happened there was that they [Fine Gael] came to the conclusion in 2007 that if they criticized government policies they would lose credibility.

FORMER FINE GAEL TAOISEACH GARRETT FITZGERALD ON HIS PARTY'S PERFORMANCE IN THE 2007 ELECTION.

Fool me once, shame on you. Fool me twice, shame on me.

GEORGE W. BUSH

2007: The General Election That Wasn't

With one fifth of male workers in construction and property, one quarter of economic growth coming from those sectors and a quarter of growth in taxes from the same source, anyone reading

132

the state of the economy in 2006 knew something nasty was going to happen. It had happened before: in 2001 the government had overspent before an election only to cut back a year later (after the election of course). We were, in other words, fore-warned and forearmed.

And there had been many warnings since that election. In August 2005 the OECD stated that our property market was over-valued by 15 per cent. Our central bank did not disagree. A year later I told the annual conference of ISME that a downturn was due in 2008. And there had been earlier warnings than those, credible ones, as against the perennial stopped-watch warnings about Armageddon heard since the 1990s. The ESRI's 2006 summer Quarterly Economic Commentary noted that the domes-tic economy was over-exposed to construction, and to a possible crisis in the US economy and an increase in oil prices.

Some weeks later I sat within three metres of the then Finance Minister, Brian Cowen, at a press briefing on the economy given in the Galway Bay Hotel. 'Given the ESRI warnings some weeks ago, does the government have a contingency plan for recession, or for a drastic rise in the price of oil?' I asked him.

'No,' came the reply.[*]

In my *Irish Times* article of 6 July[†] I had written the following:

The Government was elected in 2002 on a tide of economic opti-mism, generated in no small part by the view that strong Exchequer revenues, published in the run-up to the next election, were proof of a strong economy. After the election those Exchequer revenues deteriorated rapidly. The resultant hole in the Government's finances was only plugged by unpopular cutbacks in capital spending and inflationary increases in indirect taxation,

[*] Author, 'Delegates at FF Conference Concerned Over Inflation and State of Infrastructure. Ministers Defend Coalition's Economic Policies', *Irish Times*, 18 July 2006.
[†] See chapter 5.

measures for which the Government reaped a bitter harvest in the 2004 local elections.

Four years later, Exchequer revenue strength is even more illusory than before and, if the OECD is indeed right, any subsequent deterioration will be more severe than in 2002. So will the measures needed to balance the Government's books. And so will the political consequences of not having taken pre-emptive remedial action now.

The last three years are history. But why was the government so complacent? Perhaps it was because in a world where political incentives determine policy they had every reason to be. The Progressive Democrats (PDs), self-proclaimed guardians of fiscal and monetary sanity, had gone along with the Inchidoney project lock, stock and barrel. By 2007, if any sanity was going to be injected it was the opposition that was going to do it. And the general election of that year was a perfect chance to do it.

The signs of slowdown were unavoidable. In the spring of that year successive organizations from Davy stockbrokers to the Central Bank and the ESRI were rapidly revising their forecasts for growth down to below 4 per cent per annum. And it was clear that further downward revisions would take place. As those forecasts made no provision for a global downturn, even they were optimistic. Yet both the government and opposition were to fight an election campaign on the ludicrous assumption that growth would average 4.5 per cent a year between 2008 and 2012. At the time of writing the economy looks set to *decline* by an annual average rate of 4.5 per cent between 2008 and 2010; whatever growth 2011 and 2012 manage to produce is unlikely to offset it. The government's position was, if not acceptable, at least understandable in terms of party politics. But why was the opposition endorsing its view of growth, and of tax revenue growth? Former Taoiseach and Fine Gael leader Garrett Fitzgerald has this to say about what went wrong: 'Most of the opposition parties were reluctant to challenge Fianna Fáil. They allowed a belief to grow that FF were effective in economic policies when in fact they were damaging the economy . . . What happened there was that they came to the conclusion in 2007 that if they criticized government policies they would lose credibility. They should of course have been tackling this competitiveness issue from 2004. If they had done that they could have fought the election a different way.'

Some parties were even more optimistic than the opposition. The party that claimed to have most credibility on economic issues, the Progressive Democrats, ended up in fact demonstrating that it had the least. Outlandishly it said that the economy would grow by 5.5 per cent a year! Only the Green Party, which assumed 4 per cent growth, was attempting to inject some realism into the debate. Fighting a joint election campaign, Fine Gael and Labour* produced economic forecasts that in all practical respects were identical to those of the government. But there was a much more fundamental problem: the pairings of parties facing each other in the general election were dysfunctional. Fianna Fáil's self-proclaimed socialism cancelled out the Progressive Democrats' free-market liberalism, allowing neither party to proclaim what they believed in. On the other side, Fine Gael's more moderate economic liberalism was paired with Labour's social democracy. This coupling might have worked. In times of prosperity. Indeed it had worked in the good years of the 1990s. But had the two parties been in government together after 2007 it is doubtful whether they still would be once the recession got into its stride.

---

* I note that there was a marginal difference between the opposition in terms of assumptions for average real growth in the economy, which it said would be 4.2 per cent a year. However it assumed higher inflation of 2.8 per cent per annum, giving it the same forecast for nominal GDP growth, and as a result the same forecast for tax revenue growth of 7.7 per cent per annum. Thus whatever minor differences there were between the opposition and government forecasts were not material for budgetary planning purposes.

In short, Ireland is suffering from electile dysfunction. The mechanism designed to blow the whistle and wake the nation up, the general election, failed to work in 2007. And the mechanism which ought to be confronting us with a real choice about which way to go is still not working. With Fine Gael and Labour contemplating government together, both are prevented from setting out their full stalls before us.

Three Reasons Why Politics Has Stopped Working

It wasn't always like this. Before 2004 a healthy alternation between left and right did exist. It was much more moderate than in other EU countries, but, after a fashion, it worked. Between 1982 and 2002 it had seen Ireland alternate neatly between a centre-left government (1982–1987), a centre-right government (1987–1992), a centre-left one (1993–1997), then a centre-right one again (1997–2002). The subsequent government involved a self-reversing u-turn in policy with the 2005–2007 period undoing any good work done between 2002 and 2004. Perhaps in 2002 it was once more time for a centre-left government. The Inchidoney project of higher spending was not wrong in principle – it was a valid ideological choice – it was wrong because it was based on a misreading of the reasons why voters had dumped on Fianna Fáil in the 2004 local elections. In 2002 they had decisively rejected higher spending and taxation. In 2004 they decisively rejected the government's benchmarking exercise and its lack of reform of public services. The fact that they used Sinn Fein, a party of the left, to express this anger reflected the fact that the party they might have used was either in government (the PDs) or hopelessly confused about where they stood (Fine Gael).

Voters were not calling for more socialism but for less of the culture of compromise that arose from trying to reconcile the PD philosophy with Bertie Ahern-style socialism. They were angry at the influence of vested interests that this culture fostered. A strong left-of-centre government that offered a principled, thought-out and cohesive socialism might have garnered their respect in the same way that the centre-left government of 1993–1997 did. Even if not re-elected, this period of government – effectively Labour-led – showed what the left could do when left-wing policies were formulated in a considered, disciplined and well-managed way. Ruairi Quinn was a highly competent Finance Minister. Although he certainly broke his spending growth targets at the time, he can be complimented for delivering the first balanced budget in two decades. And although Labour's aversion to income tax cuts prevented it from realizing full employment, it at least steered the unemployment rate down from 17 per cent to 10 per cent. For a four-year spell in government, this was impressive. As an approach to government, it beat Inchidoney socialism hands down.

In so far as voters did have a choice in 2007, they invalidated the interpretation put on the 2004 election results by Bertie Ahern by clearly rejecting higher taxes. From announcing in 2006 that 'the era of tax cuts' was over, in 2006 Bertie Ahern was forced into a u-turn by voter opinion. The public had turned decisively in favour of tax cuts, particularly stamp duty, and in the 2007 election Fianna Fáil about-faced and offered the public what they wanted. The economic forecasts on which they based this programme were, of course, illusory, but fortunately for Fianna Fáil the opposition validated those forecasts by adopting them for their own manifestos. Instead of being what it should really have been about – the inflated nature of the economy – the 2007 election became a Dutch auction. Faced with this less important debate, the electorate nonetheless showed clearly that there was no appetite for higher taxes and spending. Had there been, Fine Gael and Labour's menu of fewer tax cuts and more spending increases would have been preferred.

Also, two thirds of the electorate voted for parties whose economic leanings – as far as they had any – tended towards the centre-right. But these parties, who might together have provided stable and cohesive government, refused to do business with each other.

Labour's preference for coalescing with Fine Gael also denies those on the left – a growing share of Ireland's voters – the chance to elect a left-led government. And its refusal to coalesce with Fianna Fáil, the more pragmatic of the two civil war parties on economic issues, denies the same voters a choice of a more moderate centre-left alternative. Ancient and irrelevant divides and personal dislikes are holding back the effective operation of Ireland's politics. And this at a time when we badly need it to function properly. Labour's refusal in September 2008 to endorse the government's guarantee scheme for the banks is a sign of change, a sign that it is striking out in a more independent and left-wing direction.

The economy itself has impacted on politics. If the PDs could temporarily get away with going along with the rampant spending increases of the Inchidoney project, it was because of an illusory bulge in tax revenues. Thanks to that, the rise of one third in state spending didn't require an immediate raising of income taxes. They will of course eventually have to be paid for by our children and grandchildren who will inherit our debts, the size of which would become apparent later. But in 2007 no one in the political system was thinking that far ahead. Or if they were, they weren't prepared to base a credible manifesto on the consequences of that thinking.

Had the PDs taken a principled decision to leave government in 2004 and taken the Inchidoney world view to task from the opposition benches, an election could have been fought in 2004 on where the country was headed. Or Fianna Fáil could have made up the numbers with Independents or the Greens or Sinn Fein. Either would have been honest and consistent developments. The PDs would then have been able to fight the 2007 election based on credibility. Fine Gael in turn would have had to base its manifesto on its values rather than electoral expediency, and that in turn would have given Labour no option but to concentrate on assuming leadership of the left. Whether in 2004 or 2007, the vital issues facing the economy would have been debated and decided. Had it been in 2004, remedial action could have prevented much of the damage done to our economy by the recession. If in 2007, at least our banking crisis would be far less severe than it now is. But our political system – our entire political system, not just one party – failed us completely. And there is still no cohesive alternative to the current government.

Tragically for the country, there was a huge potential to harness growth in the economy in 2004. Having reformed its fiscal policies and entered EMU, Ireland reaped a macroeconomic dividend between 1997 and 2004; but there was and remains a huge further microeconomic dividend to reap from reforming public services and increasing competition in the economy. Instead, the government in 2008 and 2009 was raising taxes and inefficient state spending. With Ireland's population growing at a rate of 100,000 a year, a radical agenda of reform in all areas of government policy could have unleashed huge growth. It might not have prevented the recession – a necessary correction of excess – but it would have put the economy in a stronger position to pull through the recession, and rebound thereafter. Thankfully, Ireland is now recovering lost competitiveness, as of 2008, but the process could and should have begun in 2004.

The chances of implementing this reform are now becoming more difficult. As Fine Gael's refusal to acknowledge what even two of its most esteemed former leaders now appreciate, in relation to benchmarking, the absence of the PDs is having a detrimental effect. At least when they existed Fine Gael had to worry equally about the risk of losing votes to them, as they did about losing votes to the left. With the PDs gone, Fine Gael needs to worry only about losing votes to left-wing opposition parties. The entire political system is, under Ireland's electoral system, now intrinsically biased to producing left-wing outcomes. If this is the result of a balanced debate between left and right, then it is healthy, so long as it reflects the will of the people (as in 1992). But if it reflects the absence of any alternatives in a system where the only values-driven parties are on the left, it is unhealthy. Either a new party needs to emerge on the right or, as discussed in chapter 13, we need to re-examine the relationship between Fianna Fáil and Fine Gael.

Or we could take a hard look at our electoral system.

Ireland's Electoral System

In one sense, Fine Gael can be forgiven for avoiding reality in relation to public sector pay. For if one thing epitomizes the dysfunction at the heart of Irish economic policymaking it is his new constituency of Dublin South. Traditionally deep blue, it is a constituency that was once a jewel in the crown of Fine Gael when, back in the 1980s, John Kelly, Nuala Fennell and Alan Shatter held three out of five seats. Currently, Shatter and Olivia Mitchell hold two out of five seats, and with George Lee's arrival a return to the glory days for Fine Gael seems possible.

Fine Gael's problem is that the highly sensitive nature of Ireland's single transferable vote system means that a few hundred such transfers can often decide the outcome of the final seat in a five-seat constituency. For one of the two large parties winning three out of five seats, the first seat in Fine Gael's case and the first and second in Fianna Fáil's were usually won simply by retaining a respectable core vote (but see below). The third seat, which decides whether the party gets into government or not, is usually the last seat to be won in the constituency. Therefore wooing transfers is crucial in Irish politics. Whereas the German Christian Democratic Party or the Labour Party in the UK can, respectively under the list system and first past the post, both win an election by concentrating on their core voters, Fianna Fáil and Fine Gael are forced to seek transfers from voters whose ideological outlook could be significantly opposed to those who elected the first and second seat.

When the PDs existed, there were limits to the extent to which Fine Gael could alienate its core traditional vote. By going too far to the left in search of left-wing transfer votes, it would lose core voters to the PDs. But with the PDs now gone, Fine Gael can afford to woo those left-wing transfers in the knowledge that its core voters have nowhere else to go. In opposing cuts to public sector pay, George Lee showed that he was mastering his new profession with skill. The only trouble is that in order to get into power, Fine Gael is pursuing a fudge of a vital policy issue, a fudge that will effectively prevent it from solving the country's problems should it get into power.

This cross-breeds with the fact that Fianna Fáil and Fine Gael refuse to coalesce. It is no coincidence that the brief truce in this hostility (which dates from Ireland's civil war in the early 1920s) was the ultimate source of Ireland's boom. In fact, as chapter 13 explores, this is an absolutely critical insight into what needs to happen if the full potential of the economy is to be unleashed. To his eternal credit, Alan Dukes' noble decision as leader of Fine Gael in 1987 to support Fianna Fáil's implementation of stringent cuts in public spending was the genesis of the boom. But since then, Ireland's two main parties have resumed hostilities. With the PDs balancing the influence of parties on the left, this did not prevent the economy from growing. The emaciation of the PDs after 2004 in government and Fine Gael's continued preference for a coalition with Labour has stifled real political debate and choices.

Increasingly Variable Voters

Another aspect of this problem is Ireland's increasingly change-able electorate. Chart 10 shows how support for Ireland's parties is fragmenting, with two fifths of the vote now going to parties other than the traditional two 'pragmatic' parties, but with no clear focus or direction. The Irish electorate are searching for a new political system, but in the words of the U2 song, they still haven't found what they're looking for. The consequences for stable government in the future, whether of left or right orientation, are grim. Unless, that is, we change how we do politics.

It has already been mentioned that in a five-seat election – the kind a large party must do well in to get into government – that large party's core voters will elect its first seat in Fine Gael's case and, up to now, its first and second seat in Fianna Fáil's. This esti-mate of how many seats each party can win on the strength of its core vote is based on the approximation that in most constituen-cies Fine Gael can rely on around one quarter of the vote and Fianna Fáil can rely on slightly more than one third of the vote. This traditional difference between the parties has been crucial in explaining why Fine Gael has not won an election since 1982.* Through the vagaries of Ireland's PR system (which favours larger parties in terms of allowing subsequent transfer votes to boost its proportion of Dáil seats to a level above its first prefer-ence vote share), this allowed Fine Gael to rely on its core voters electing just under a third of Dáil seats. To win more, it would have to reach out significantly to floating voters. With the PDs in the background this was a zero sum game, as leaning too far to

---

* The party entered government in 1994 two years after the preceding election in which its vote fell significantly. This was due to a by-election in Dublin South Central which gave the Democratic Left Party a seat, allowing the Labour Party to form a coalition with it and Fine Gael. Although it improved its vote share and Dáil seat strength, Fine Gael failed to gain re-election in the subsequent election.

the left would lose Fine Gael votes to the PDs. Fianna Fáil, on the other hand, has (up to 2009) been able to rely on its core vote to give it a base of at least one third of seats in the Dáil. By levering its stronger core vote and its pragmatic political instincts, it has been more able to attract the transfer votes necessary to enter coalition with a small party rather than with a party like Labour. For this reason stable government, strongly rooted in the manifesto of one large party, has been possible.

However, the dramatic results of the 2009 European and local elections shows that a sea-change is taking place in Irish politics. The most commented-on result of that election is that for the first time since the 1920s Fine Gael overtook Fianna Fáil as the largest party in terms of the popular vote. Moreover, the *combined* vote of Fianna Fáil and Fine Gael continues to steadily decrease. It has now returned to levels unseen since the foundation of the state (see chart 10).

This means that unless they agree to coalesce with each other, both parties must now compromise more with their election manifestos if they are to hope to get into coalition government. Fianna Fáil won 25 per cent of the vote in the local elections and Fine Gael won 32 per cent. Despite Fine Gael's good performance, the dire state of the economy means that both parties are likely – unless one of them makes significant gains in public support – to be in a similar position, each henceforth relying on around one quarter of the vote. This will not be enough to govern without the support of several smaller parties. Unless Fine Gael truly replaces Fianna Fáil by gaining the 40 per cent plus levels of support that have characterized Fianna Fáil's electoral performance prior to 2009, agreement to the tough measures needed to curb Ireland's chronic fiscal imbalance will be much more difficult after an election than under the current government.

This problem would not be so serious if there was a third alternative. The corollary of the joint support for Fianna Fáil and Fine

Gael being at its lowest level since the 1920s is the fact that the combined vote for other parties is, at 40 per cent, at its highest. But where the 'pragmatic' vote is split between two parties, the 'centre-left' vote, broadly defined, is highly fragmented. The largest party, receiving between one tenth and just under one fifth of the popular vote, is Labour; then follows Sinn Fein with around one tenth of the vote, and after that a constellation of smaller parties each receiving low-single-digit-percentage support. Even were Sinn Fein and Labour to merge, they would face the same problem Fine Gael has faced up to now: making up the difference needed to get a majority of seats in the Dáil would involve much compromise with their core voter values.

10. Fine Gael and Fianna Fáil joint vote since 1927

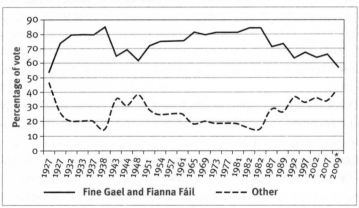

As table 4 (see Appendix I) shows, the key problem is a steady decline in the number of core voters. In Fianna Fáil's case this decline was massively exacerbated by the party's performance in the June 2009 election, though it was evident from 2004. The data in the table shows that back in 2004 at least two thirds of those aged over forty-five thought it mattered a great deal or somewhat which party got into power after an election, but half or fewer of those under thirty-five agreed. As time goes by, Irish politics will move more and more towards a system where traditional party loyalties are dwindling and large parties are increasingly unable to rely on core voters for a substantial base of seats; instead, they will have to haggle and bargain with voters, and with competitor parties. Unless they want to stay in opposition, they have no choice. In other words, unless we can find a breed of politicians who like to govern on core principles only to lose elections as a result, our electoral system dooms us to repeat the mistakes of the past every decade or so.

Why Inchidoney Happened

Now, at last, we are in a position to understand why the Inchidoney disaster happened. From being able to form governments anchored on a strong base of core support and given direction by a modest but significant ideological coalition partner, Irish politics degenerated into the Dutch auction that has characterized it ever since the infamous days of the 1970s and 1980s.

What makes the current situation worse than the 1980s, politically speaking, is declining voter loyalty. With party support now more fragmented, stable and coherent governments will in future be more difficult to put together. This has been made brutally clear by the results of the 2009 elections. If replicated in a general election, the only stable two-party government would be Fianna Fáil and Fine Gael. Of course some rebound for the bigger parties is likely in a general election. But if long-term trends continue, this will soon enough be true in a general election, perhaps not the next one but possibly the one after that.

Fianna Fáil policy in government has become strongly focused on winning targeted groups, like buyers desperate to climb on to an escalating property ladder on one side, and public sector unions seeking higher pay for their members on the other; like voters seeking tax cuts on one side, and welfare recipients seeking more generous entitlements. As they are all based on an unsustainable splurge in tax revenues, the long-term political impossibility of this coalition has now become apparent.

After the votes were counted for the 2007 general election, it looked as if it was working. Now reality has set in, the party is forced to choose between alienating one or other of its constituency base. Fianna Fáil risks falling between two stools if it does not act decisively.

Five years after it began, the Inchidoney project has been exposed as a political disaster for the party that developed it. As chapter 13 will argue, if Ireland is to pull through economically, the way our political system works must change.

7

For Whom the Dell Tolls

It's important that we don't end up believing our own guff.

SPEAKER AT FIANNA FÁIL CONFERENCE ON THE ECONOMY,
GALWAY, 17 JULY 2006

Between 2000 and 2007 Ireland forgot a golden rule of economics, one which of all the economies in the world's league of top performers Ireland needed to stick to most: if you can't be productive, be low-cost. Singapore had a low cost base and indigenous high-tech industries. Denmark, Sweden and Finland didn't have a low cost base but their high-tech industries were so good that even the highest wage levels and prices in the world didn't prevent them remaining in the premier league of competitiveness, year after year. For most of the 1990s Ireland had a low cost base. If by the late 1990s this was no longer true, it was at least true to say that Ireland was not chronically uncompetitive. But we still had no appreciable high-tech industries of our own. The ones we had were imported. For hugely profitable companies like Dell, Intel and Microsoft rising costs caused by the non-traded sector were, to a point, affordable, but for indigenous industries struggling to grow to the size where they could compete abroad, what happened in the Irish economy from around 2000 on was nothing less than a stab in the back. Relentlessly, and from behind a protective curtain of state monopoly power (or near monopoly power), the state-driven part of the economy ratcheted up the costs in a way that laid the foundation for a jobs haemorrhage once the recession came and the credit boom turned to bust.

Of course, none of those job losses happened in semi-state companies, or government departments, or among the permanent staff of universities, local authorities or the many quangos created during the Inchidoney years. Like a tapeworm in the economy's stomach, these sectors were draining energy and resources from the productive side of the economy without suffering from the recession themselves.

Action should have been taken years ago. Small businesses around Ireland, businesses that in 2006 according to Department of Enterprise, Trade and Employment figures accounted for 800,000 employees, were facing a rising iron floor of costs. As long as profits were high, they could survive. But in parallel with what was happening with state spending, costs were rising under cover of an illusory boom. When the bust came and revenues dried up, the implications of our higher cost base were brutally exposed in lengthening dole queues.

In September 2008 the government made an effort to do something. Minister for Natural Resources, Energy and Communications Eamonn Ryan announced a 10 per cent cut in electricity prices. Welcome though it was, however, it merely took Ireland from the most expensive to the second most expensive country for electricity prices. A far more radical programme of cuts in state-controlled prices and charges is needed right across the spectrum of state activity. As yet, nothing of the kind is forthcoming.

In December 2008 the impact of our high costs was brought home to government in the most shockingly embarrassing way.

One of the Industrial Development Association's flagship companies, Dell, announced the lay-off of 1,900 workers at its Limerick manufacturing plant. Fortune 100 companies, among which Dell itself ranked number thirty-four, did business with Dell and Dell's 'just-in-time' technique of delivering laptops was the stuff of MBA business cases. And along with Intel, Microsoft and others, its presence in Ireland was a badge of pride. Against job losses in the whole economy, Dell's tally paled into comparison. In seasonally adjusted terms, eight times more people had already joined the dole queue that month, and in January 2009 that multiple rose to eighteen.* But as the biggest single job loss in recent industrial history the Dell toll was tolling a death knell for Ireland's international competitiveness. And for an industrial strategy that rested on the pillar of foreign direct investment, it was a body blow.

In July 2006, a month after ESRI's warning that up to ninety thousand US-supported jobs in Ireland could be at risk if the US entered recession, Fianna Fáil held an economic conference in Galway city. One speaker at this conference drew an analogy between what hurricane Katrina had done to New Orleans and what a world recession could do to Ireland. 'It's important that we don't end up believing our own guff,'† she said. Two and a half years later, Dell's announcement proved that her warning had been overlooked. By 2006, even the American Chamber of Commerce – not noted for a willingness to comment on our economy – was issuing a warning. The top executives of American companies, it stated, were having difficulty finding affordable accommodation here. The minimum wage was the highest in the world, it added. Business costs like rates, electricity and waste charges were also decried by a whole host of business

* Live Register, January 2009, Central Statistics Office, February 2009.
† Author, 'Delegates at FF Conference Concerned Over Inflation and State of Infrastructure. Ministers Defend Coalition's Economic Policies', *Irish Times*, 18 July 2006.

representatives. But nothing was being done to overhaul the structure of government that gave rise to these costs.

Cost Competitiveness, 2000–2008: A Story of Decline

The fall from grace took place over a decade between 1997 and 2007. In 1997 Ireland's average weekly wage was €370 a week, significantly below the EU average. Its corporation tax rate was among the lowest in the world. In July of that year the cover of international magazine *The Economist* featured a luminous map of Ireland with the caption 'Europe's shining light'.

Competitiveness is a complex concept. Trade unions have often hit out at those who argue that keeping wages low is a guarantee of competitiveness. They are right. For economies with flexible, dynamic and high-technology private sectors, low wages are not a necessary ingredient in competitiveness. But that does not describe Ireland. Between 1997 and 2007 the likes of Dell, Intel and Microsoft were able to afford to pay Irish wage rates without any problem. Indigenous firms were in a different position, but those smaller firms were less represented at the social partnership table. On the other hand the unions and semi-state companies responsible for ratcheting up costs were represented strongly. Suffering from an outdated fear of public sector strikes – based on the wrong assumption that in such a circumstance voters would sympathize with the public sector – the government was terrified of taking action. And as former Taoiseach Garrett Fitzgerald pointed out to me in an interview for this book, the need for action was evident from 2000. 'Our relative costs vis-à-vis other countries in Europe . . . we were highly competitive, up to 1997, and after that we drifted,' he said. 'From 2000 to 2005 our prices rose at twice the rate of the EU and wages rose by more than twice as fast as a result of which we became uncompetitive.'

Chart 11 bears out the point, showing how our downward slide began in the year 2000.* Some in government blamed the strength of the euro for undermining Ireland's competitiveness. Just like those who argued that the ECB's interest rate was too low for Ireland's needs, they were like Irish tourists in France complaining about everyone else driving on the wrong side of the road. Not an intrinsic driver of competitiveness, exchange rates merely disguise or confirm the underlying competitiveness of an economy. That underlying competitiveness is revealed and ultimately driven by the cost of non-tradeable goods and services, goods and services that the trading side of the economy relies on but cannot source elsewhere. If Irish local authority rates on business are higher than those charged to Finnish business, that shows that the non-traded side of our economy (in this case local authorities) is less efficient than in Finland. Finland shares the same ups and downs in terms of the impact euro appreciation or depreciation has on the foreign currency cost of its goods, but you won't hear Finnish government officials complaining about the euro. The Finns don't do guff. They know, as we knew when we joined the euro, that it is up to them to counteract any rise in the euro, or any fall in ECB interest rates, by maintaining a tight control on inflation and public spending. This they learned during a hard recession in 1991. After taking a battering, the Finns relentlessly clawed their economy back over the ensuing decade. And they have, unlike us, never forgotten their lesson. By 2008 they were, in competitiveness terms, in the same excellent position as they were in 2000, ranking close to the top of the World Economic Forum Global Competitiveness Index. By contrast, Ireland's cost competitiveness deteriorated by one third between 2000 and 2008.

* Budgetary and Economic Statistics 2008, table 52, 'Harmonized Competitiveness Indicators', Department of Finance, September 2008. A rise in the graph indicates a rise in the relative cost of Irish exports to the rest of the world, hence a loss in competitiveness.

11. Ireland's falling competitiveness compared to Finland and Euro Land

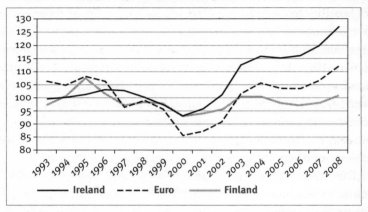

Source: Department of Finance, Budgetary and Economic Statistics, 2008

With high marginal tax rates, the chart illustrates a point made by Irish trade unions, albeit one those trade unions themselves don't fully understand: you can have high wages and taxes and still be competitive. The point not understood by trade unionists is that high wages and taxes are not in themselves a cause of competitiveness. To listen to some of the idiotic comparisons made by leading trade unionists and academics, you would think it was. Like Father Sean Healy, many on the left have argued that Ireland's tax take is too low. Pointing to high-tax countries in Scandinavia, they argue we should have the same levels of tax as a share of GDP – somewhere close to 50 per cent. But the reason that Finland has consistently been in the top four places in most indicators of global competitiveness is because its indigenous industry is productive and can rely on an effective public sector. Finland's trains and buses run on time, its civil service is excellent and free from the mind-numbing incompetence of restrictive practices in recruitment and promotion that have paralysed ours, and its education and health systems are consistently excellent. Finland has earned its right to have a high-wage and high-tax economy. Ireland is very far away from that place.

The public sector can't be blamed alone. Much of the private sector has been immune from any real competition. It's a situation that until the late 1990s was without serious implications for the economy. But when rampant growth in private sector credit and public spending washed over the economy, higher prices were the result. On its own, higher demand does not force up prices: if markets are competitive and business regulation light, high profits should stimulate more firms to enter the market and compete on price. As noted earlier, the existence of competition in the air travel market allowed Ryanair to push down prices dramatically during the 1990s and 2000s, in spite of rapidly rising demand. Had Ryanair not entered the market, air travel costs would have performed like train travel costs, where a hugely inefficient state monopoly still exists, and prices would have risen as a state monopoly continued to rip us off.

Unfortunately, much of Ireland's economy is immune from serious competition. Strong collaboration between dominant players in vital sectors of the economy contributes to Ireland having among the highest costs of living in Europe. And it is a vicious circle. Try blaming vintners for high beer prices and they will, quite rightly, point out how they are being squeezed by local authority rates and waste charges. Point the finger at the pharmacists and they will tell you that they pay the highest minimum wages in the EU. And as for the food industry, high electricity prices – 40 per cent higher than in the UK – are a major source of the higher costs of producing food in Ireland. The minimum wage itself is seen by some as the source of all evil, but in an economy with such a high cost of living, especially for basic necessities, reducing it is the wrong place to start the drive for competitiveness. High wages merely reflect the high cost of living; it is the cost of living that must first be reduced. Certainly Irish wages must come down relative to the rest of Europe.

But this will only be effective and just if it is preceded by a comprehensive and wide-ranging plan to bring down costs and prices across the economy. And there is little doubt where that attack needs to begin. Ireland's non-traded sector is behaving like the evil twin of the traded sector (see Appendix I, table 5). Between January 2005 and May 2009, the cost of computer products fell by 60 per cent as a result of dynamic change and innovation. In the health services, by contrast, prices rose by nearly 20 per cent. The cost of hairdressing rose by over 20 per cent. Here several trends are going on. The boom increased prices that customers were willing to pay. But as a relatively competitive sector – setting up a hairdresser business does not require a licence in the same way that setting up a pub does – this does not explain the full extent of the increase. The remaining extent is not the fault of hairdressers: high-street rents, many with upward-only rental revision clauses, not to mention high insurance costs and high labour costs, are a major part of the story. At the very least these are controlled indirectly by government.

The direct role of the state in driving our cost level is also strong. If Irish businesses could source public services abroad, as envisaged in the so-called Services Directive, it wouldn't matter. But the state's monopoly on a whole range of services imposes a huge cost burden on Irish citizens.

Central Statistics Office figures show that public sector earnings in 2007 were 47.6 per cent higher than in the private sector (CSO, 2009). Union leaders justify this by pointing to higher education levels in the sector. On the face of it, they have a point: CSO data also shows that 52.8 per cent of all public sector employees have degrees compared to 31.9 per cent of private sector workers. But the real question is this: are these higher-level qualifications justified by higher quality services provided to citizens? The civil service is famous for ignoring the qualifications of staff when deciding where to put them to work.

Many with oversight of our state finances and banking system in the past boasted of how they sustained the boom despite having degrees in classical literature. The verdict on this approach to recruiting management has been comprehensively served.

In some professions – teaching and nursing – there is a clear link between qualifications required and pay. But writ large, and particularly in the civil service, the real issue is not the level of qualifications – the intelligence and general ability of most of our civil servants being beyond question – but the chronic mismatch between what they do and what they know. Unlike the private sector, recruitment practice in the public service is in its infancy. In other words, we are paying over the odds for qualifications that are, with the exception of teachers and nurses, most unnecessary or, worse, destructive. And even where higher-level qualifications are needed, such as for university lecturing posts, salary levels are far higher than in the UK.

The fact is that differentials between public and private sector pay are not driven by productivity or performance but by the stronger bargaining power of those inside the social partnership tent. As argued in chapter 6, utility companies are the proverbial praetorian guard of the economy. Up until now they have had the power to bring the economy to a halt, and with it the career of any politician who tried to control them. But the dynamics of Irish politics are changing rapidly. Angry and increasingly self-conscious, voters in the private sector have been pushed too far by tax increases and public sector intransigence. The next chapter will argue that the representatives of public sector workers must now radically change their ways, or face the possibility of permanently alienating the vast majority of Irish opinion. From my own time in the public sector, I believe that if they did so they would merely be reflecting the views of a large but silent majority of public sector workers who secretly want radical reform but are afraid of saying so, given both the politicized nature of public sector employment and the higher propensity for bullying in that sector.*

2004: Another Last Chance

Action to reverse Ireland's competitiveness slide could have been taken as early as 2000 when it was desirable. By 2004, action was no longer desirable. It was necessary. The signs of decline were everywhere. Ireland's price level had by the start of that year risen almost twelve percentage points faster than the Euro Area average since 1998 (see Appendix I, table 1). Things were not so bad that recovery was impossible: as chart 11 shows, competitiveness fell 15 per cent between 2000 and 2004, but between 1996 and 2000 it had risen by 10 per cent. With a world recession still four years away there was time to prepare for the worst. 2004 was not, in other words, a point of no return. Neither is 2010. But thanks to the wrong turn taken in 2004 the road back to competitiveness will be longer and more painful than it needs to be.

Instead of increasing competitiveness and reforming the public sector, 2004 saw the government begin the Inchidoney project taking the economy in the opposite direction than the one in which it needed to go. A three-year bonanza of spending and credit growth began, and little or nothing was done to shake up the non-traded sector. On the contrary, state sector pay and employment levels increased rapidly over the following four years. Leaving aside its direct effects – the higher tax burden on businesses and workers that would become inevitable once the property taxes evaporated – this expansion was to have devastating indirect effects on the economy. As Garrett Fitzgerald put it, the building boom was one of the 'huge errors' contributing to our current crisis.

Dr Fitzgerald was not alone in issuing warnings like this. In

* See the ESRI report into bullying in the workplace, *Irish Times*, 30 March 2007.

July 2005 central bank governor John Hurley stated that there was 'no longer any doubt'[*] that private sector lending was beginning to get out of hand. Still, he added, a serious crisis could be averted if house price inflation was brought back under control. He had every reason to speak out, for it was in August that year that the OECD in a confidential report warned our central bank Ireland's housing market was 15 per cent overvalued.[†] As if to up the ante, credit growth not only failed to slow down in response, it actually sped up, causing house price inflation to return to double-digit growth. In the 2002 and 2003 period, such growth could be justified by population growth. After all, even up to 2004, the competitiveness of the economy had not deteriorated too much. By 2005, every economic indicator, whether it was house prices, credit growth, building employment or competitiveness, was travelling rapidly in the wrong direction. House prices were particularly scary. From 6.2 per cent[‡] in August 2005, house price inflation rose to 8.2 per cent by November and eventually 15 per cent by September 2006.

As that happened, warnings from the Central Bank and National Competitiveness Council (NCC) – in successive reports – became louder and stronger in language. But according to Garrett Fitzgerald, too many people had a short-term disincentive to confronting reality. 'The Central Bank tried to talk about competitiveness but were inhibited,' he told me. 'Economists in the private sector said nothing about it, businesses were delighted with their higher profitability and trade unions were delighted with their bonuses.' With the exception of ESRI, the Central Bank, the NCC and some economists in the media, no one was crying out for this to stop, certainly no one with any clout.

[*] Author, 'Central Bank Warns of Danger Posed by Credit', *Irish Times*, 13 July 2005.
[†] Emmet Oliver, 'OECD Believes Irish Property Market Overvalued by 15%', *Irish Times*, 5 November 2005.
[‡] TSB/ESRI House Price Index, www.esri.ie

Given its mandate, the National Competitiveness Council has been the most consistent voice of all. Despite a mix of outlooks on its council, from industrialists to trade unionists, its warnings and calls for action have been unambiguous. In 2003 it warned that Ireland was the Euro Zone's most expensive country for consumer goods and services (NCC, December 2003). A year later it warned that the state's 'deteriorating competitiveness' was undermining its exporters on world markets (NCC, September 2004), and that our rates of wage growth were outstripping our competitors'. But it noted that the economy was still performing well. By 2005 that had changed. As some were touting as 'healthy' or 'strong' Ireland's economic growth rate of over 5 per cent, the NCC had no illusions. Ireland's economic performance was 'relatively weak', despite strong growth, as was our performance in the non-price aspects of economic competitiveness: research and development, competition policy and, most crucially perhaps for a country claiming to have a high-technology economy, the use of information and communications technology in business.

One government minister, Michael Martin, tried to take action. The abolition of the Groceries Order in the spring of 2006 was a small blow for the consumer with limited prospects of delivering lower prices. However, the evidence now is that prices of processed food and alcohol, which the order effectively put a floor under, have grown more weakly since the abolition, and more weakly than other food prices. But the main impact of the order was political. As a template for what needs to happen right across all sections of the economy, the abolition of the Groceries Order was a major milestone.

Thanks to rampant inflation in other parts of the economy on which the food sector depended for input costs, Ireland's food costs in 2007 were still 40 per cent higher than the EU average and the second highest in Europe.* This didn't prove that abol-

---

* Eurostat 2008, price comparisons of EU member states for food, alcohol and tobacco.

ishing the Groceries Order had failed. What it proved was that without widescale reform across the whole of the economy, one reform alone could not deliver results. The food industry greatly resents the abolition of the order. Like trade unionists who resent attempts to lower the minimum wage, it is right to feel some resentment, but also like those trade unionists, it doesn't properly understand why it is right to feel resentful. The reason is not in the reform itself. The reason is that, like taxi drivers and minimum wage workers, the food industry has been singled out to bear the brunt of reforms, without other key players doing likewise. The result is that it still pays local authority charges, electricity costs and insurance costs – and minimum wages – to the sectors of the economy that provide its input costs. But unlike those highly controlled or monopolistic sectors, it must alone face the squeeze of international competition.

According to the latest NCC report at the time of writing (NCC, 2008), Ireland's industrial electricity prices are still the second highest in the EU. They increased by 70 per cent between January 2000 and January 2007, and the reasons are clear: the uncontrolled boom between 2004 and 2007 and the failure to liberalize the market in time for that boom as well as the build-up of the inefficient and costly generating capacity. The fault cannot be laid solely at the door of the ESB,* however. By spreading Ireland's population growth around the country like butter over bread, bad spatial planning and urbanization have made it more expensive to provide electricity than it should be, as has the poor design of Ireland's energy-inefficient housing stock – something the Green Party in government is now trying to correct. Political pressure to create jobs in remote areas has led to the building of peat-based electricity generation plants that are not just cost-inefficient but bad for the environment. Which all goes to prove that pointing the finger at one group to accuse them of 'ripping off' everyone

* Ireland's quasi-monopolistic electricity distributor.

else – beloved of some in the media – misses the point. Ireland is based on a vicious circle of everyone ripping everyone off.

But the circle has a beginning and an ending. Like a food chain, the government is at the top. Unlike the private sector, it need not compete and faces no pressure to be cost-efficient. With the power to legislate and coerce everyone else, it can charge and tax what it likes to whomever it likes. At the bottom of the food chain are tax-paying citizens, consumers, those laid off – thanks to mismanagement of the boom and the high costs imposed by the non-traded sector – and our exporters.

2009–2016: The Route Back to Competitiveness

The climb back up the competitiveness league will be steep and painful, but it is possible. We cannot devalue our currency. As well as the letter 'r' and the benefit of a higher and growing population, the euro is one of several crucial factors that separates Iceland from Ireland: without it, the cost of servicing Ireland's huge borrowing – €20 billion during 2009 – would escalate, pushing the fiscal system to the point of collapse, resulting in the country being taken over by the IMF. 'Economists' who argue that leaving the euro is an option either don't understand fully the ramifications of what they are saying, or they do and are just having some fun.

Even if public finances were stable, the competitiveness effect of devaluation is questionable. Rather than devaluing our nominal exchange rate by leaving the euro, what Ireland really needs to do is devalue what economists call the real exchange rate – the rate at which foreigners can buy our goods and services.* That is done by reducing state fees and charges and rates, business costs, prices and wages, and in exactly that sequence.

* This depends not only on the nominal exchange rate but also on the prices of those goods and services faced by a foreigner wishing to buy them from us relative to the price they could be obtained for in a competing economy.

There is evidence that this is happening. In April 2009, UCD economist Colm McCarthy reviewed a number of surveys undertaken by business organizations as well as a survey undertaken by the Central Bank. Taking them as representative[*] would indicate that since the recession began, nominal wage cuts of around 5 per cent have occurred in the private sector as a whole (made up of cuts of around 10 per cent in half of industry respondents). Further good news comes in the form of a 2009 survey by the National Consumer Agency showing a fall in food prices, with the gap between the cheapest and dearest supermarkets widening thanks to competition from 1.8 per cent to 4 per cent for a typical basket of goods – a very significant fall in grocery terms (NCA, 2009).

In 2008 the NCA warned that our food prices were too high (NCA, 2008). Then in June 2009 Tesco took the unprecedented decision to roll out cheaper food products sourced from UK rather than Irish wholesalers (as had been done up to then). Ciaran Fitzgerald, a food industry lobbyist, complained about the decision. A key problem for Irish food producers, he argued, was that they faced higher electricity prices than their UK counterparts. It was a fair point, and one which revealed the way the Irish economy still works: in order to mitigate the effects of one injustice – the burden that high electricity prices put on food producers – other sectors of the economy are supposed to facilitate those food producers passing on those higher costs to consumers by way of practices that minimize competition. Fitzgerald's views are perfectly understandable, but from the point of view of Ireland Inc. they are no longer viable. But the challenge of government is to end the injustice its pricing policies impose on the food industry before blaming it for rip-off Ireland.

The vicious circle of high costs, caused by a lack of reform and competition, is what is really damaging producers. Another is the

---

[*] Not everyone accepts that this is so. When presenting ESRI's summer 2009 Quarterly Economic Commentary in July 2009, ESRI economist Alan Barrett asserted that there was no evidence of substantial declines in private sector pay.

legacy of bad planning. In 2008 NCA chief executive Ann Fitzgerald called for planning guidelines to change so as to lift restrictions on new retailers opening up. The call ignores the fact that Ireland already suffers from excessive retail capacity. But in substance, it is right. The problem isn't an overall lack of retail outlets but the fact that in too many centres of population there are too few retail outlets within convenient walking or commuting distance. Moreover, the sprawled nature of our population puts many consumers at the mercy of car-driven shopping trips, for which outlets like Tesco – powerful enough to provide car spaces – have a natural advantage over smaller retailers.

As with so many other problems, our high food costs are part of a deeper problem of governance.

At last, there is some good news in terms of Ireland's overall competitiveness rankings as measured by the World Economic Forum: for the first time in several years Ireland's ranking in the Forum's Global Competitiveness Index stopped falling in 2008. Its ranking of twenty-two remains, however, considerably lower than it once was.

Two Tribes

However constrained, however motivated by self-interest and however limited, the private sector is at least playing its part in bringing Ireland back from the brink. The public sector is playing no such role. The hostile reaction to the only request made of it so far – that public servants start making a proportionate contribution to their pensions – has demonstrated how far removed its leaders are from the centre of Irish opinion. Either that or it shows how deluded they were in thinking that the benchmarking exercise was ever sustainable.

The growing divide between the two sides of the economy could result in serious consequences for Ireland's political cohesion. The contrast between the downward wage pressures in the private sector and rising pay in the public sector is significant. 'On average they were significantly overpaid ... and there is some evidence that the public/private sector pay differential has been aggravated but we won't know until later in the year [2009],' says Garrett Fitzgerald.

With inflation likely to end 2009 at 5 per cent, anything other than a pay cut of this magnitude would worsen cost competitiveness. Larger cuts are needed to improve it. But as the inflation figures given above demonstrate, the overall decline in inflation masks two very different trends. Private sector prices are falling in line with the pressures of lower demand and rising competition while protected sectors continue to raise prices well above the rate of inflation. As the private sector generates competitiveness, the non traded sector is busy eroding those gains.

How can workers in the private sector be asked to take more wage cuts, or suffer property tax rises, when the non-traded sector is immune from pay cuts? And how can any worker, particularly a low-paid one, be asked to take pay cuts, or a reduction in the minimum wage, when the state sector is doing so much to maintain Ireland's status as one of the most expensive places in the world to live? The salaries of nurses and teachers may be high by international standards, but when they try to live on their salaries Irish teachers and nurses are no better off than their German or French counterparts. They too need to accept changes in the way the education and health sectors work, so that cost efficiencies can be passed on to users in the form of better services and lower charges. But their pay levels should not be cut until costs and prices have fallen first. This is why, as I will argue in chapter 13, a comprehensive economic plan is needed to coordinate the different policy measures in a way that does not cause injustice and undermine political stability.

Competitiveness must be restored, and all but the very lowest income groups must bear some of the burden. But the burden must first be imposed on the most protected and safe sectors of the economy. There are two reasons for this. The first is that, as ESRI research has shown conclusively, the public sector is the higher-earning sector of the economy and it can bear the brunt the most. The second is that having security of tenure, public servants are more able to absorb pay cuts without losing confidence. In the private sector the loss of income from pay cuts (usually on lower salaries) is greatly exacerbated by fear of job loss, hence pay cuts here hurt confidence and spending much more.

These points have been valid for most of the last decade, a period in which, even before benchmarking, public sector pay was higher than private sector pay. But up to now politicians could avoid it: those in the private sector were doing well enough, and felt safe enough, to put up with it. But as the Lisbon Referendum result of June 2008 and the election results of June 2009 make clear, two phenomena have combined in a way that has the potential to drastically alter Ireland's political economy, and to do so in ways that are extremely dangerous.

8

Two Tribes (About to) Go to War

Ye went off to America, but we stayed! We stayed!

BULL MCCABE IN *THE FIELD*

It is ironic that the city of Lisbon is associated with two crucial debates in Ireland. The beautiful Portuguese capital gave its name to both the Lisbon Agenda of 2001 and to the Lisbon Referendum of 2008. The former plans to create jobs in Europe by making its labour markets more flexible. The latter is an attempt (finally successful) to get Ireland to vote for what is in effect a new EU constitution. As well as a poor campaign in favour of the referendum, the negative outcome of the first Lisbon referendum was influenced by immigration from other EU states, something the Lisbon Agenda encouraged. One could say that in that referendum of June 2008, two Lisbons cancelled each other out.

The reasons aren't hard to understand. Over a year later Ireland has passed the second referendum on the Lisbon treaty. But at what cost? In an analysis of voting intentions, Stephen

165

Collins of the *Irish Times* reported – some weeks before the second vote on 2 October 2009 – that, despite a majority intending to vote Yes, strong class divisions were surfacing in attitudes to Europe. When undecided voters or those not intending to vote were excluded, 39 per cent still opposed the treaty; but among so-called AB voters opposition was just 19 per cent. By contrast, 52 per cent of voters in the lower-income DE voting category were opposed to Lisbon. Although carried, the Lisbon referendum – particularly because of the resentment caused by the perceived refusal to accept the first referendum – could cause a political divide that will never heal.

It was of no comfort to the lower-income side of this divide that immigration, which they resented, was of benefit to the economy as a whole. Had the economy treated everyone fairly, they might have accepted this. But in the Ireland of 2009, taxi drivers are being drowned in competition from an army of laid-off workers seeking refuge in their industry, while well-paid sectors of society – the sectors that made up the AB voting category – are immune from any competition at all. These protected workers included not just civil servants but many professionals and semi-state workers who benefited from government regulation. Worse still, the most vocal exponents of a Yes the second time out were members of the most protected bastions of the state sector, such as senior academics and former civil servants.

For example in September 2009 Professor Klaus Zimmerman, an esteemed German economist, delivered a paper entitled 'EU Labour Markets after Post-enlargement Migration' in which he argued that some concerns about immigrants were nonsense. Migrant workers were not 'welfare tourists', as many had thought. A co-author of the report, ESRI's Professor Alan Barrett, was also right to point out that the three countries most open to

---

* '46% Back Lisbon After Drop in Support and Rise in "Don't Knows"', 4 September 2009.

immigration – Ireland, Sweden and the UK – had benefited most from EU enlargement, far more than countries with closed economies. Some weeks later, the heads of Ireland's seven universities called for a Yes vote in the second Lisbon referendum.

Unfortunately, with security of tenure, noble academics are less than exposed to the downside of immigration. And it wasn't a matter of welfare tourism. Rather it is the pressure created by the hard-working immigrant ethic that they are praising. AB voters of this kind are not losing their jobs like many DE voters are. Of course Lisbon II has nothing to do with immigration. But in a political system that failed to represent growing divisions in a stable and fair manner, it has become a valve for expressing the anger of those who felt they were being lectured at by an elite. An elite which had all the advantages of free movement of labour but none of the disadvantages. In an Ireland where voter dissatisfaction with all parties is at an all-time low, this has explosive potential.

That the 2008 referendum was going to be a close-run thing should have surprised no one. As chart 12 shows, support for a 'pro-European'* position has declined since the 1980s. As the initial advantages of EU membership and integration became harder to appreciate, this was only natural. But the fact that two out of three referenda before 2008 had been defeated should have given politicians grounds for reflection. The Inchidoney experiment had shown how badly politicians misunderstood the electorate. The illusory boom of the ensuing period disguised it, convincing them that the public approved of what they had done. As chapter 6 argued, they had little choice. In 2008 there was a clear choice, and having been denied a clear debate on the economy in 2007 – and in particular on issues like immigration – the only way the public had to channel their frustration was to use the Lisbon

---

* I place this expression in inverted commas to respect the fact that many opponents of those referenda would regard themselves as pro-European.

referendum for a different purpose entirely: to express their exasperation with the extent to which Ireland's tyranny of political consensus was choking debate on crucial issues, social as well as economic.

12. Votes on European Referenda

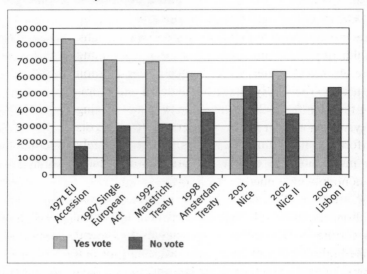

Source: Various

As an exercise in closer cooperation, the European project is for Ireland an undoubted good. But it is seen by many as part of a neo-liberal economic order. It is anything but. Europe's traditions of economic management are neither socialist nor neo-liberal, but Christian democratic (see chapter 13). If any collection of nations has a destiny to point a straight path between the two extremes of rampant individualism on the one hand and totalitarianism on the other, it is the EU. But Ireland's unquestioning political climate in relation to key issues precluded serious debate. Immigration is only one of those key issues and there are many more.

Ireland's ascent to the ranks of rich nations – an ascent immune from the current recession – would have been unthinkable without openness to the inward migration of capital and technology. How then could we, as a nation that had benefited from Europe so much, complain about inward migration of people? Some have speculated that it might be because globalization didn't bring benefits to all Irish people and that the large numbers of those supporting the 'No' side reflected this. The reality is more subtle.

In Ireland during 2001, labour markets were working flexibly, perhaps too flexibly. In that year unemployment fell to 3.6 per cent of the workforce. Three years later Ireland embraced the concept of labour market freedom in an even more determined manner by being one of only three of the 'old' EU states to take in workers from the new states in Eastern Europe without a permit.

Social partnership was highly effective at redistributing the fruits of Ireland's globalized economy, arguably too much so. But that decision in 2004 to expose Ireland's labour market to an additional layer of international competition by allowing in migrant workers from accession states was not so much a step too far as a step taken only by one foot of the economy and not the other. That the number of migrant workers still exceeds the number of unemployed at the time of writing is a fact that could be abused by xenophobic comment. That would be unjustifiable. It could be argued that immigrants are preventing Irish workers from getting jobs. But that is not the real story.

The real story is the gaping divide between the traded and non-traded sides of the economy. In the previous chapter we looked at how this drives costs in Ireland. It is also having a dividing effect on our labour markets.

For well-paid public servants like academics, senior medical staff and civil servants, and also for highly paid professions, immigration is a universally positive thing. It makes access to au pairs easier, leads to quicker service in restaurants, and provides cheaper workmen to renovate or decorate the house. The solicitors, academics and teachers who dominate our political classes – and the big business leaders who dominated the Yes campaign – receive all these benefits but do not themselves face a threat to their own jobs. The folly of the Lisbon campaign is that it was led by those who, although their motives for calling for a Yes vote were not selfish in any way, nonetheless were not suffering from a phenomenon that many associated, wrongly, with Lisbon and the EU. Whether due to job security or the highly specific and 'Irish-oriented' nature of the work (solicitors rarely cross frontiers, except at very high levels of work, for example), those on the Yes side had no conception of the pressures immigration were putting on other kinds of workers. This was not the fault of the immigrants. Nor is it an argument against immigration. What it is is an argument for a consistent approach to competition across the economy.

As in relation to property, the story of Bull McCabe, like all great stories, has a wider relevance. A man who himself had never been abroad, the Bull confronts the cosmopolitan American who is about to buy and bury in concrete what he has coveted for decades. But this is more than a fight over a single transaction. Decades of bitterness over how Bull's ancestors were abandoned to their fate by those who left – those who now have the audacity to come back and use their money to take away the only thing they had – sharpens his hatred of the American. Before killing him in revenge, Bull screams, 'Ye fecked off to America, but we stayed! We stayed!'

In many ways the exchange echoes the Lisbon Referendum. The cosmopolitan elites were quite rightly telling us that Lisbon was good for us. But they forgot the disparity that existed between themselves and those to whom they were talking. Yes, if competition and integration were widely distributed, then they and other things Lisbon symbolized would not just be good, they would easily be seen to be good. But like the American in the story, those arguing for Lisbon were in effect having it both ways, enjoying the benefits of globalization while forcing others to suffer its risks.

As the dole queues started to lengthen in 2008, the electorate's resentment at the reversal of their expectations – expectations validated by all political parties in their election manifestos of 2007 – mounted. There had been a foretaste of what was coming when the Irish Congress of Trade Unions managed to assemble tens of thousands of workers in a demonstration against Irish Ferries' attempt to hire Latvian workers at less than the minimum wage. That specific dispute may have been resolved, but the issues that lay beneath it continued to build like magma under a volcano.

Migrant workers from accession states had lower costs of living in their home countries, to which they would presumably return when Ireland's boom had given them what it could. Trade union leaders alleged that immigration was leading a race to the bottom by forcing down wages in already low-wage sectors. Up until 2008, the facts did not support this. But there was a problem waiting to be born. That problem was not the workers themselves, but the fact that the jobs they were coming to service were about to disappear, and quickly. Given the high and rising share of construction employment, policymakers should have grasped how additional employment from 2005 was going to be temporary. Accordingly, workers coming to service those industries from abroad should have had their employment status more clearly matched with the durability of their jobs.

Thanks to Ireland's minimum wage and the impact of the boom in pushing construction wages way above it, the state's open-door policy was going to set some sectors up for a harder fall than others in employment.

Although not the prime reason – a poor Yes campaign and a vibrant No campaign were the main reasons identified by commentators[*] – on the defeat of Lisbon I immigration was cited as

---

[*] Jamie Smyth, 'No Campaign Convincing – Yes Voters', *Irish Times*, 21 June 2008.

one of the direct causes of its defeat. Fear of the 'Polish plumber' had also played a strong role in the defeat of the first attempt at EU reform, the EU constitution, in France a few years earlier. In Ireland, unemployment in early 2008 was still relatively low by EU standards and immigration was more of a nascent factor. But the speed at which it was rising in affected sectors was high enough to impact politically.

With the dole queues now lengthening dramatically, the fact that 923,000 PPS numbers have been issued to non-national workers since 2002 might not be something politicians are talking about. But workers are. Of course that number involves significant double counting; by spring 2009 there were 287,000 non-nationals working in the economy. Compared with an unemployment total that was less than this, it would be tempting for some to conclude that immigration is causing unemployment. The reality is different. Without the demand created by large-scale immigration, many Irish people would not currently be in employment. Employment figures also show that despite making up one eighth of the workforce, non-nationals make up a third of the 150,000 workers who lost their jobs between February 2008 and February 2009. Far from pushing Irish workers on to the dole, non-nationals are getting hit harder by rising unemployment. Nonetheless their strong presence in some sectors combined with their absence from others is having a serious impact on the labour market, and potentially on politics.

The Time Bomb Ticks

The deadly serious issue with immigration is not the thing itself but the other issues it could interact with. With Ireland's government comprising one half teachers and the other half lawyers[*]

---

[*] One minister at the time of writing, the Minister for Communication, Energy and Natural Resources, Eamonn Ryan, is a former businessman.

there is little ability in government to grasp public fears in this area. That inability is clearly replicated in the sectors that dominate social partnership. As the table shows, only 6.6 per cent of workers in the education sector are non-national. Even if this share were higher, it would have little impact on those Irish workers in this sector, which is largely immune from recession and where employment defied the recession by actually rising between early 2008 and 2009. In the sector of public administration and defence the share of non-national workers is even more slender, at just over 3 per cent. This is the other of the two sectors, both state-run, in which employment levels are rising and in which no one faces the threat of redundancy.

The contrast with other sectors couldn't be clearer. Over one third of workers in the hotels and restaurant sector are migrants, while one in seven construction workers are migrants. Irish workers in those sectors, where wages are far lower than in the public sector, might fairly ask why competition with migrants was pushed on them when the public sector was effectively protected from it. And, however illogical, the referendum on the Lisbon Treaty is the proxy for the debate on the Lisbon Agenda that should have occurred but didn't.

The share of non-national workers in key sectors

Construction	Hotels and Restaurants	Public Administration and Defence	Education	All workers
14.9%	34.8%	3.1%	6.6%	14.6%

Source: Quarterly National Household Survey, Q1 2009

Between the first quarter of 2008 and the first quarter of 2009 some 72,100 people lost their jobs in construction, 30,600 lost their jobs in the wholesale and retail sectors, and 16,600 lost their jobs in finance. This was the flip side of unsustainable expansion in those sectors in previous years. But the public sector was also unsustainably expanded, if not in terms of numbers (which as a share of the labour force are not excessive) then very definitely in terms of pay levels. As the private sector corrects itself both by shedding jobs and freezing or cutting pay, the fact that the public sector is doing neither is a serious sign of two sides of an economy drifting further and further away from each other.

Cooperation or Conflict?

In 1997 there were approximately 1,380,000 people at work in Ireland. Had Fianna Fáil made the election commitment that, were it to hold power for the next fifteen years, employment would rise to 1,850,000 by 2010, no one would have believed it. A rise of half a million in the workforce was more than had been achieved in the preceding four decades. In proportionate terms the workforce will by the end of the recession be one third higher than it was just over a decade before. But such analysis is not good enough for the third of a million persons who may by that time will find themselves out of work.

Even the most pessimistic forecasts agree that we will end the recession with employment levels that are significantly higher than ever before, with the exception of the 2005 to 2007 period of course. The fact that even pessimistic forecasters (ESRI) put Irish employment levels back where they were in 2004 is in one way encouraging. But as this year is the year in which we opened our labour markets in a highly generous manner, it forces our policymakers to think about how to bring Ireland back to full employment.

Firstly, for Ireland's policy of welcoming migrants to be fair and credible, all sectors – including the public sector – must be equally exposed to its risks as well as advantages. Thanks to a closed-shop approach of internal recruitment and promotion, that is not the case in the public sector. A continuation of this risks creating a situation where immigrants are unfairly scapegoated for economic injustices that are in fact created by Ireland's unfair and divided economy.

Secondly, as David Grubb of the OECD has pointed out (Grubb, 2009), Ireland is almost unique in Europe in that the numbers claiming unemployment benefit are 61 per cent above the numbers actually unemployed. In May 2009, for instance, the Live Register climbed above 400,000 persons for the first time but the true unemployment level, as measured by the Quarterly National Household Survey, was under a quarter of a million. This fact, plus the relatively higher level of benefit in Ireland compared to that in most accession states, may act as a disincentive for non-nationals who have lost their job to return home.

This point needs to be qualified carefully. Of course those who wish to stay should be made welcome. Neither can we blame those who responded rationally to economic incentives put in front of them availing themselves of Irish welfare benefits which are superior to what they would get at home. But with a budget deficit heading for €20 billion in 2009, Ireland can no longer afford to provide welfare benefits to a number of claimants that is 61 per cent above the true unemployment level. These two issues are considered in chapter 10.

Neither can the economy continue with a system of pay determination which allows those in public sector jobs who face no risk of redundancy to earn more on average than in the private sector. As advocated in chapter 12, a new benchmarking exercise must be conducted with a view to examining the relevance of the costly qualifications of public sector staff – claimed to justify salary differentials – to the provision of real public service value.

This question goes beyond the importance of restoring normal pay differentials between competitive and non-competitive employment. The restoration of parity between public and private sector pay is, politically, a prerequisite to many other radical changes that need to occur in Ireland's economy. On 21 July in a speech at the McGill summer school in Glenties, Finance Minister Brian Lenihan said that if Ireland's minimum wage – at least the second highest in Europe, possibly the highest – proves to be a barrier to employment in certain sectors then it would need to be re-examined. The statement came a week after the report of An Bord Snip in which cuts in social welfare were advocated. There may be a case for freezing or even cutting the minimum wage – arguably less so for cutting welfare payments – but not before addressing the equally damaging competitiveness legacy of the 2002 benchmarking exercise?

And reversing benchmarking is not the only prerequisite for broader reforms. It must, as argued above, be preceded by an across-the-board reduction in the state's contribution to our high cost of living. In 2009 the Irish Hotel Federation, representative of an industry in which immigration levels are high, spoke out against what it described as 'crippling' local authority rates. Mostly highly inefficient and over-numerous, Ireland's system of local government is one of the ultimate sources – all of them state-driven – for the huge cost burden placed on our private sector. Not only is it insidious, the system of taxation they operate is incompetent in the extreme. 'Local authorities extract taxes relative to the size of the premises without any recourse to the level of turnover or overheads of the business,' IHF president Matthew Ryan told the *Irish Times*.[*] According to the IHF's chief executive John Power, a hundred-bedroom hotel, for example, is charged between €150,000 and €200,000 a year in local rates. It begs the question: what services do local authorities provide that are worth such exorbitant amounts? And why do we need more local authorities (there are 129 such structures of varying status and authority) than Paris Hilton has shoes? The really dangerous

[*] Laura Slattery, 'Hoteliers Want Cut in "Crippling" Rates', *Irish Times*, 13 August 2009.

aspect is that here is a sector immune from reform whose employees cannot lose their jobs imposing crippling costs on a traded sector where a key contributor to job losses are the high costs imposed by the state. In this case, Bull McCabe has every right to be furious.

However genuine their support for it, protected sectors of the economy have not accepted the downside of globalization. Instead they have inflicted it on others. Certainly, voter misunderstanding of the Lisbon Referendum, thanks to a poor campaign, was a significant factor in its defeat first time around. But the double standards of those sectors in relation to competition was an additional factor, one without which the referendum might have been carried, albeit marginally.

Commenting on industrial Britain's severe social divisions in the nineteenth century, Benjamin Disraeli remarked that Britain was made up of 'Two Nations'. Ireland today is made up of 'Two Nations', and those two nations are either going to have to come together – which means the protected nation finally accepting its share of the economic burden that restoring competitiveness requires – or fight it out. At present, there is no sign of willingness on the part of the public sector or private non-traded sector to reduce pay or prices. With a huge disparity between working-class No voters and more prosperous voters voting overwhelmingly Yes – and by a margin of two-to-one – Lisbon was carried on its second attempt. But the first defeat was a symptom of voter anger and frustration against a broken system of party politics. A system that made the Lisbon Referendum the only tool voters could use to express their anger on issues with nothing to do with the Lisbon Treaty. If voters voted Yes it was only out of apprehension – if not downright fear – of the consequences of voting No. As one newspaper headline put it on the day after the count: 'We've put our anger aside, but not for long.'

IV

The Road to Recovery

The thing we're most afraid of is finding out how much we're capable of.

SØREN KIERKEGAARD

9

The Smart Economy

We need to identify . . . those skill sets that allow
some businesses to grow to the 100-million-euro
turnover level.

PAT COX

Building a smart economy requires smart people. The ministers
who make decisions, the civil servants and advisers who assist
them, the bankers who lend money, the media pundits who drive
debate and, most of all, the business people who take risks and
create jobs. All of these people have to be smart. A failure in one
link in the smart chain can bring down the whole system.

Goodness knows, there is no shortage of smart people in
Ireland. In 2009, John Collison from Monaleen, Limerick was
one of them. One of eleven students in the country to get eight
A1s in state examinations, he was more than just bright. In
transition year he founded a software company with his brother
Patrick, helping eBay to manage large-volume transactions. It
was the kind of enterprise that Ireland Inc. – a self-professed
high-tech economy – should be all about: not just high-tech, but

exporting international services. This should be a cutting-edge activity in an economy trying to create the thousands of jobs needed for a growing population. That the company was bought in 2008 by Canadian firm Live Current Media for €3.2 million[*] was proof of its success. Selling a business for over three million euros at the age of eighteen – here's someone smart enough to do what Pat Cox tells us we need to do.[†] Unfortunately, the system in which John Collison was operating was nowhere near as smart as he was. In fact, it was incredibly stupid.

In the years before Collison set up his business, our banking sector had just poured tens of billions of euros into the property sector. Despite the latter sector being clearly overvalued and having no export potential whatsoever, the banks continued to do so as Collison went looking for finance for his business. He was refused a loan in Ireland. It is a tribute to him and his brother that they didn't give up. Private investors from the US – a breed increasingly vilified in the media – took an interest. Once again we relied on foreign direct investment to do what we were perfectly able to do ourselves. Now Collison has sold his business and is planning to study in Harvard. The system – the state, the banking system and the university sector – has failed a person who could have brought jobs and prosperity here. Failed hierarchies, retarded, bureaucratic mindsets and a thinking dominated by begrudgery are the biggest blocks of all to achieving a smart economy.

Despite half of Ireland's cabinet ministers being teachers and the other half lawyers, the government is now making an honest effort to deliver a smart economy. Through no fault of their own, many, like their Fine Gael opposite numbers, are hereditary politicians, inheriting their Dáil seats from their fathers. Some of them are highly capable. But until those governing us begin to

---

[*] Kathryn Hayes, 'Eight A1s Puts Software Millionaire on Track for Harvard', *Irish Times*, 13 August 2009.

[†] See quote at head of chapter.

reflect the new reality of a competitive economy, mistakes like the failure to finance the Collison business will continue.

Small 'c' conservatism is deeply entrenched in our system of government and social partnership. To many in social partnership, entrepreneurs are enemies, tax dodgers, potentially corrupt. Even those who don't vilify them don't understand them and how they work. Taxes, red tape and bureaucracy are killing their dreams and dashing the hopes of those they might otherwise have employed. Neither do social partners understand how their failure to do the things they should be doing is holding the country back. The fact that Ireland took over ten years to expand Dublin airport because of inter-partnership wrangling is testament to the bankruptcy and irrelevance of a smart economy imposed from above. The smart economy must come from below. The only contribution social partners can make to this process is to remove the blockages of a high-cost, high-tax economy and fulfil the few tasks for which taxpayers provide ample funding: the maintenance of law and order, the provision of broadband, good spatial planning, proper public transport and control of public spending.

The phrase 'Celtic Tiger' was invented by economist Kevin Gardner to associate Ireland's strong growth in the 1990s with the so-called Tiger economies of Asia. But Ireland can't emulate those economies. Nor should it. Their low labour costs and autocratic political and social cultures are alien to us. The Celtic Tiger concept needs a fundamental review after the last few years. We need a new model.

Ireland is best off looking for inspiration in countries that are as similar to us as possible, culturally, geographically and historically. That way we have the best chance of replicating what they've done right without compromising our identity. Thankfully, there are small peripheral countries in Europe with similarly independent-minded citizens and political cultures. Even more thankfully, they happen to be the richest and most successful economies in the whole world.

Smart from the Start

Hopping on to our shores with blond hair, beer, currency and an ability to build cities – things we'd never really seen before – the Danes arrived in Ireland over a thousand years ago. Their arrival still benefits us in some ways today, such as coinage, international trade and, yes, the ability to build cities.* But a millennium later it seems that of all the invaders ancient Denmark had to offer, we got the dumbest of them. Perhaps it was a scam: the Danes sent their most violent and troublesome kinsmen abroad to pillage and loot while the smartest of them stayed at home.

In 1945 Ireland was having trouble producing anything other than beer and butter that anyone else in the world wanted to buy. Two decades before then, Ireland and Denmark were both agrarian economies. For another fifty years Ireland was to stay that way. But taking their farming roots as a base, as early as the 1920s the Danes started to cluster industries around what they had been doing best for hundreds of years. From their bacon industry sprang one of the world's leading makers of insulin, when HC Hagedorn founded Nordisk Insulinlaboratorium. Unlike Ireland's picturesque but inefficient patchwork-quilt farms, Denmark's intensive grain farms lent themselves to greater productivity. More profitable than their Irish counterparts, larger Danish farms enabled enough Danish farmers to invest in agricultural machinery in a way that created a demand for native manufacturing of agricultural machinery. If Danish companies are now exporting machinery to the US, China, UK, Norway, Finland and, of course, Ireland, that's because the Danish economy has been smart from the start.

In 1945 a Dane by the name of Peder Hansen founded a company called Vestjysk Stålteknik A/S, or Vestas for short. Initially

---

* Dublin, Limerick, Cork, Waterford and Wexford were all founded as Viking settlements.

manufacturing household appliances, Vestas then started to produce agricultural equipment and hydraulic cranes before being inspired by the oil crisis of the 1970s to begin production of wind turbine electricity generators. When the rest of the world was throwing its hands up in despair at the rocketing price of oil, the Danes were exploiting an alternative to it on their very own doorstep. Now called Vestas Wind Systems, this company is the largest of its kind in the world, with a 28 per cent world market share. In February 2009, when Ireland was digesting the news that the Live Register had risen by 36,000 in the preceding month, Vestas announced the production of two new turbine types, the 3-megawatt V112 and 1.8-megawatt V100.

In a policy document published before the previous Christmas break, the Irish government announced its intention to create a smart economy[*] – a worthy if overdue initiative. The Danes already had one. Like Ericsson and Volvo in Sweden and Nokia in Finland, the Danes have not allowed their small size or relatively peripheral position, dominated by big neighbours, to let them off the hook. Ireland does have overseas industries, but hardly cutting-edge ones. A thousand years after the Viking invasion, the Vikings who stayed at home have something to sell that is new and needed. With the exception of the best music in the world and low-cost air travel, what is Ireland selling abroad that the world really needs?

The answer is plenty. The only problem is that the knowhow to produce it is imported. One amazing statistic is that on a per-head basis Ireland's imports of royalties – a measure of the extent to which we import knowhow before re-exporting it – is not only the largest in the world, but exceeds that of the next ten largest importers put together. In so far as we led the world with this approach, it's something that former International Development

---

[*] 'Building Ireland's Smart Economy: A Framework for Sustainable Economic Renewal', Department of An Taoiseach, 2008.

Authority chief executive Padraig White is proud of: 'The IDA laid the basis for pioneering a foreign investment drive when Ireland was mainly an agricultural country . . . we identified the pharmaceutical industry, the emerging electronics industry, and then set on ways of marketing Ireland and also offering an environment with no red tape, a one-stop shop, and repackaging and presenting what was essentially zero tax on exports.'

When we were a low-cost economy, innovating foreign direct investment policy was the way to go for industrial policy. It is part of making Ireland what economist Con Power has described as a 'Global Office' for leading world businesses. Over three decades this 'global office' approach has attracted 580 US enterprises that employ 100,000 people directly and support the employment of 200,000 more.

In 1982 White and his associates pulled off a coup that other foreign direct investment-hungry states would envy for years to come. IBM had a traditional policy of putting its headquarters for particular services only in countries large enough to sustain significant markets in them. Convincing them that the location of its software development centre in Ireland was – despite its small size – entirely consistent with accessing world markets was a huge achievement. The template was repeated in 1985 when Microsoft, then in its infancy, established its European base in Sandyford in Dublin. And again four years later when Intel chose Leixlip. Even in the darkest days of the current recession, the IDA's strategy paid off. It still is: as the dole queues were rocketing in January 2009, Hewlett Packard – another trophy catch – announced the creation of an additional five hundred jobs in Leixlip. And as Power points out, the concept can be and is being extended from manufacturing to a whole host of internationally traded services (Power, 2009).

But with a quarter of a million now unemployed, it is no criticism of the IDA to say we can't rely on this strategy any more.

As the appalling crash in Ireland's stock market has made abundantly clear, Ireland's economy is over-reliant on the three Bs, Building, Banking and Booze, all of which are highly responsive to the economic cycle. This is no foundation for the future. In the long run, innovation in attracting foreign direct investment is no substitute for innovation in goods and services that the world wants to buy.

Moreover, the contrast between the dazzling sophistication of high-tech multinationals and what rubs off on the Irish-owned economy is ironic, as the most recent example of high-tech foreign investment shows. Flagship companies like Schering Plough, Pfizer and Merck Sharp and Dohme are a badge of honour for Ireland's economy, making it a world centre for leading pharmaceutical research and production. But in August 2009 Ireland was coming to terms with a surprising aspect of that success: in December 2008 a report to the Health Minister by Dr Michael Barry showed Ireland to have some of the most expensive prescription drugs in the EU. When nine months later the minister moved to reduce the costs, pharmacists responded by refusing to give out prescriptions under the Community Drugs Scheme (a government scheme whereby the state funds drugs for those on medical benefits). It took a court injunction to ensure their cooperation and months of wrangling to enforce a result that in other EU countries would have been taken for granted.

Ireland's low quality and percentage of broadband penetration is another case in point. You would think a country that could boast the headquarters of Dell, Intel, Microsoft and Hewlett Packard would have one of the best broadband records in Europe. Despite the efforts of Communications Minister Eamonn Ryan, we continue to have one of the worst in the developed world. According to Martin Cronin, the chief executive of Forfas – a body that researches the productivity of Ireland's economy on an ongoing basis – we have much catching up to do, even though the country has the infrastructure needed to provide broadband not just for residential but cutting-edge industrial use as well, the kind of high-tech sectors that could generate indigenous spin-off industries. 'We have the so-called fat pipes needed to compete on a global level in areas like cloud computing,' he said, 'but we aren't exploiting them.' Semi-state companies like ESB, Bord Gais and even Iarnrod Eireann have these 'fat pipes'. In other words, right under the nose of the state, a crucial asset that could make or break our position in emerging sectors is going to waste.

Nor is there much transfer of the modern management techniques and dynamism these multinationals have to offer. According to Padraig White, 'Foreign companies have been able to create these oases of world-class companies, management and staff which outperform their peers and which are highly flexible, highly adaptable and highly committed, and these examples stand in marked contrast with the lack of flexibility, lack of service and lack of efficiency in many other sectors of our economy, both in the private service and public sector.' The jobs are welcome. So is the reputational kudos. But too much else of what multinationals have to offer seems to shoot through our economy like grain through a goose.

Pat Cox, former European Parliament president and currently working with the Innovation Board,[*] praises the IDA, but says we have to stop relying on it. 'We won't win twenty-first-century battles with twentieth-century battle plans . . . mobile foreign capital is dramatically more competitive.' To grow our own high-tech industries, he adds, we need to look to countries of similar size to Ireland. 'We need to look at some Scandinavian countries, maybe Finland but not exclusively Finland, and I would say Israel, as two models of small open economies who have come to terms with the necessity to grow your own.' In a crucial insight, he highlights in a positive and encouraging way why many of our

* A think-tank funded by Microsoft.

188

indigenous organizations have failed: 'Successful innovation models are very flat organizations, they are non-hierarchical, they are transdisciplinarial and multidisciplinary.'

With these words Cox identifies a key reason why Ireland's economy lacks smartness. Despite doing much excellent work, the disconnectedness of many successful government organizations is undermining what they are trying to do. The trend of agencification – creating ever more quangos to deal with specific problems – is making this worse. The truth is that we can't create a smart economy until we smarten up our structures of government. Cox praises what state institutions have done to date, but says we need to move on. 'There is another issue of the state or its agents – whether it's the IDA or Enterprise Ireland or county enterprise board, incubation centres . . . I think maybe we need to re-look at these organizations that have served us really well. A lot of them can trace their origins back thirty, forty, fifty years and I think maybe we just need to rethink some of the models.'

The question begs asking: with a plethora of state bodies producing relatively modest results, how can the Irish learn from Denmark, a country that built a smart economy with relatively few state institutions?

Science and Technology

Denmark is committed to education and investment in science and research, and has been for generations. In order to turn core sectors in international services and life sciences, like web-based computing and clean technology, into indigenous success stories, we'll have to follow suit.

Later is better than never. Ireland's third-level sector, funded by the Science Foundation Ireland, is beginning to deliver excellent results. At least Padraig White thinks so. 'You see extraordinary collaborations between these companies in Ireland,' he says, 'the foundation for the jobs of tomorrow. Other sectors are emerging, clean tech, renewable and sustainable energy, and there's scope for more of those companies and collaboration with the university sector.'

Ireland spent €2.8 billion, or 1.7 per cent of GNP, on research and development* in 2008, most of it private sector spending. It's not up at Nordic levels of above 3 per cent, but Minister of State with responsibility for science, technology and innovation Conor Lenihan says it's a vast improvement on before. 'Overall in the last ten years we've tripled the amount of money we spend on research and development. Two thirds of that comes from the private sector, a third of that comes from public institutions, be it agencies like the Enterprise Ireland IDA, and of course the universities deliver a key part of that money.'

For money spent in 2008, we'll need to wait until 2018 to get a return on it, says Lenihan. But he points at some metrics from past investments that seem to be coming good. Perhaps because of the statist mindset and public sector or legal background that subconsciously still dominates the thinking of our politicians, it is difficult to get them to think in terms of actual results rather than money spent. But they are at least beginning to try. 'It's something that delivers basically over a seven- to ten-year cycle and I think what we can see particularly since 2005 is very, very strong evidence that the embedded spend we began ten years ago is now beginning to pay off . . . the number of patents and registered discoveries from Irish universities has doubled since 2005. We've also doubled the number of spin-out companies from university campus.' Research and development spending between 2000 and 2007 has, so Lenihan reckons, supported 430 high-technology start-ups employing 5,500 people. In 2008, 838 small- and medium-sized enterprises (SMEs) got assistance with R&D, and in 2009 an estimated 3,100 jobs are supported by government

* Strategy for Science, Technology and Innovation, Summary of Issues and Progress. Innovation Task Force, 17 July 2009.

spending in the area. Those numbers need to start increasing.

The key to developing indigenous productivity is to engender a culture of basic and applied scientific research, no one doubts that. And no one doubts that it's a long-term process. But if we're not getting results from past investments, how can we know that what we're currently spending is useful? Lenihan's department is working on the development of a set of metrics to measure the impact of our science spend. Not before time.

But an axe is about to fall hard on all government spending, and Lenihan is anxious to point out that when Finland was dealing with its fiscal crisis in 1991 it put a steel fence around science spending. 'They cut public spending by 25 per cent but increased spending on research and development by 20 per cent in response to their particular crisis.' One of the results of that decision, Nokia mobile phones, are now in almost every jacket pocket and handbag in Ireland. 'They picked a very clear winner, technology, where they felt they had an edge in relation to Nokia and they backed that company and they backed that research around that company and around the supply companies to that company.'

A few days before telling me this, Conor Lenihan's brother, Finance Minister Brian Lenihan, published a report recommending swingeing cuts across the public sector – the so-called An Bord Snip report. Included in the list of things to be cut was PhD research in third-level education. Conor Lenihan is strongly opposed to the cuts. So is Padraig White's successor, outgoing IDA chief executive Sean Dorgan. In an article for the *Irish Times*, Dorgan warned that even if they don't guarantee results in the form of indigenous high-tech companies, PhD graduates are a precondition for it.* There are certainly grounds to be cautious in cutting back on the number of science graduates.

* 'We Would Be Foolish to Derail the Smart Economy', *Irish Times*, 14 July 2009.

But the standing of PhDs has been undermined by the unwillingness of many PhDs to accept the importance of other contributions to the economy. The flair of John Collison, at just eighteen and with no primary degree let alone a Masters or PhD, proves that excellence does not always require a PhD. PhDs are of course still important, but the inability of universities to interact with practical and real-world activities in relation to the services they provide shows the dangers of an excessively theoretical culture.

Besides, the most pressing problem in Irish science education isn't a lack of PhDs. Rather, it is the worrying failure rates in second-level state examinations for mathematics and science subjects. Figures released in August 2009 showed a 16 per cent fall in the numbers taking maths at higher level. Only 8 per cent of students took higher-level physics and only 10 per cent took higher-level chemistry. Worse still, the numbers obtaining the highest grades in all their subjects fell from 216 in 2008 to 143 in 2009. As the chief executive of Chambers Ireland Ian Talbot reminds us, 'As a knowledge-based economy we rely heavily on graduates with a deep knowledge of mathematical sciences.'

Universities can recognize and shape genius and entrepreneurship but they cannot create them. Primary and secondary schools, on the other hand, can. If the state devoted half the resources to improving the teaching of maths and science subjects, and removed obstacles for the likes of Collison in terms of access to seed capital, it would be doing more for the future of the smart economy than a year of research spending. And as Pat Cox explains, it's something we need to start doing now. 'Whereas we are not in the healthiest zone, in the Pisa tests [of international educational performance] the Scandinavians are well up there and Finland and South Korea are vying for being the best in the world. This is a product of a deliberate policy over thirty years so it's not a quick journey, but if you're in a race to the top you have to start at the bottom in terms of your thinking, how you get up that ladder. We've catching up to do.'

As for the case for continuing to fund PhDs, in science as in other areas this depends entirely on the 'left-shoe–right-shoe argument: whether PhDs can work with other equally important people. It says something that someone who has both a PhD and commercial experience – Chris Horn, former chief executive of one of Ireland's few indigenous high-technology companies, Iona – is not calling for more PhDs to save our economy, but more engineers.

As far as allowing universities to take the lead in research is concerned, Sean Baker, chairman of the Irish Software Association, sounds a word of caution. Real-world commercial perspectives will, he says, make or break the value of spending on research to the economy and he criticizes the 'waterfall model' of funding where money is poured into the early stages of research in the brave hope of commercial output. 'I just don't think it works,' Baker says. 'It's inefficient. For me, to commercialize research, you have to have commercial input from the start.'[*]

Conor Lenihan is, to a degree (no pun intended), right about protecting science and research spending. But Finland shows how commercially driven spending on research is what produces technology winners. Sean Dorgan is probably right about keeping a minimum flow of PhD graduates in science coming down the line. But the role of PhDs in universities needs to radically change in ways that end their monolithic dominance and allow their contribution to be complemented by other types of contribution. If universities cannot themselves innovate, they are in no position to spend taxpayers' money on innovation.

In any event, the debate is academic. With over a quarter of a

[*] Ian Campbell, 'College Research Needs Business Input Early – ISA', *Irish Times*, 22 June 2009.

million unemployed the most important people in our economy right now are not PhDs. They are entrepreneurs.

Entrepreneurship

One of the most self-destructive reactions to the financial crisis in 2009, in Ireland and around the world, has been the re-emergence of a disease we thought was banished. In truth, it was lurking in the long grass waiting for its moment. Begrudgery towards entrepreneurs, or towards anyone who tried to make themselves or things around them better was always a famous trait of the Irish. Perhaps there was good reason for it in the past. Genuine and justified anger at a lack of equal opportunity in Ireland has caused a traditional antipathy to those who do well. The rules of the success game in Ireland have been too stacked in favour of those who inherited wealth, or who enjoyed superior educational opportunities or access to privileged social networks. Instead of levelling the playing field, we've sought to drag down those who benefited from them. However understandable, it was never a productive approach. It could be said of Irish entrepreneurs and begrudgery that never had so much been done for so many by so few only for the many to bite the hand that fed it. Once the boom years were over the memory of all the jobs and wealth created since the late 1980s, most of which is still intact, was forgotten in a welter of misdirected recrimination against high salaries and bonuses, most of which, but not all, were deservedly earned.

Entrepreneurs are the drivers of any economic recovery. According to a recent report there were in 2007 almost a quarter of a million of them (GEM, 2008) in Ireland. The recession will have taken its toll but their number is still likely to exceed 200,000. For whatever reason, compared with their peers, Irish people are more likely to get up and start a business. It is a vital national advantage in fighting a recession, but only if we avoid recreating the barriers to entrepreneurship that existed in the past. And only if the government gets out of their way.

Ireland ranks fourth in the OECD for early-stage entrepreneurs.* Partly this reflects the traditionally small size of Irish businesses. Many Irish small companies are mom and pop operations. Portugal and Greece, which rank higher than Ireland, are hardly models for entrepreneurial economies. Unlike those countries Finland, which also ranks above Ireland, has made the vital connection between enterprise and technology.

There are, says Pat Cox, three critical kinds of entrepreneur our policies need to identify: 'The ones who are capable of leaping from the ecology that they are in into the wider global market and to be a reasonably substantial player. Then there are those skill sets that allow some businesses to grow to the 100-million-euro turnover level. Then there is a more elite group of players that can grow a 100-million-euro business into a 100-billion-euro business.' He calls on the government to build up an inventory of our skill set. 'The Irish diaspora is all over the place and I would have a wide view that my inventory would include the sum of the parts because there are connections and values and openness to doing things.' We also need, he says, to create a 'stock exchange' for good business ideas. 'I am not talking here money but intellectual capital, human capital, and connecting it.' Such an exchange could allow the government to participate more successfully as a catalyst to start some new businesses, while the inventory could pull in auxiliary talent and funding. With regard to state support, Cox thinks the approach should be driven by quality rather than equality. 'I'm talking about commercial sense being hard with the numbers and following the hard logic of the numbers. The state shouldn't pick these people; guys like, say, Gerry Connelly with his Photoshop down in Tralee who was able

---

* This assessment is based on 2007 data. Data on company formations in 2009 suggest the rate of new company formations has decreased by 20 per cent in the second quarter of 2009 compared to a year before.

to build a business that the Gettys paid 110 or 120 million euros for – they should. But we need to say we'll take a slice of that thank you very much.'

To support entrepreneurship, our culture also has to become more tolerant of failure in the private sector. That is one of the areas where Ireland has improved. Traditionally wary of starting business in a high-tax economy, Irish entrepreneurs' fear of failure stands at 37 per cent, now not much higher than the average of 35 per cent for the OECD (GEM, 2008). One worrying statistic, though, is that Irish entrepreneurs tend to quit more easily than their peers in other countries. Could this be because of a lack of government support?

In August 2008 Tom Cooney and Etain Kidney of DIT conducted a study of enterprise and innovation policies in EU countries (Kidney, 2008). The conclusions were stark and included sentences like 'There is currently no comprehensive policy for entrepreneurship' and 'There is a low uptake of R&D and innovation schemes in SMEs'. The first finding can be laid at the door of government. The second reflects in part the fact that the sectors in which Irish business boomed in the years before the report – construction, luxury services and retail – were ones in which sustainable research and development spending was either irrelevant or too time-consuming.

Innovation

The Cooney and Kidney report also concluded that there is 'a lack of monitoring of policy' and that the links between innovation policy and entrepreneurship policy are more implied than real.

As Pat Cox explained to me, the situation couldn't be more different in Finland. There, a state body called Citra – the Finnish Innovation Board – has pioneered Finnish industrial development in a way that is fully integrated with other arms of government.

Established by statute, Citra reports to Parliament, and parliamentary leaders from all main parties sit on its board. By not being an instrument of the government it escapes what Cox describes as the 'silo' logic of departments of state. Like the IDA here, it is constantly scanning the global horizon for opportunities. But instead of getting just foreign firms to rise up to them, Citra is about getting Finnish businesses to meet them.

And in Finland, the state provides innovation parks that are able to evolve the services they offer companies as they go through their different phases of growth. Cox describes a system that is designed around the needs of the innovators, allowing them to share not just their canteens and other facilities, but also their perspectives.

Policies like this make the pieces of the Nordic productivity puzzle – the apparent contradiction between the high prices of Nordic countries and their high productivity – easier to understand. Day-to-day interaction is often where the genius of innovation comes from, as Cox confirmed with this anecdote from a visit to one of these parks. 'I met there over lunch one day – again, quite by accident, it wasn't an appointment – a young man from Norway who was working with some young guys from Finland and Denmark who had developed some piece of microbiology that eats its way through the inside of the empty vats you brew beer in when you are doing the cleaning. They have now connected their small business to Carlsberg and through the connection went global with their microbial agent. That happened out of that business park environment.'

The Irish government, to be fair, created an Innovation Task Force in July 2009. Its goal is described as 'positioning Ireland as an International Innovation Hub', its immediate focus, self-proclaimed, to 'increase rates of innovation and commercialization; intensify foreign direct investment in high-value areas; develop Ireland's indigenous enterprise sector; scale innovation-intensive companies; increase the intellectual property and talent pool in Ireland; and foster entrepreneurship, creativity and innovation across the economy and society as a whole'.

There are no shortage of policy documents setting out such high-sounding ideals. Key targets of the group would not look out of place in a Stalinist propaganda movie, suffering as they do from the persistent delusion of government – that attaining some target of spending as a share of GDP is a meaningful policy objective. The objective of increasing research and development spending to 2.5 per cent by 2013 is a case in point. Another concern about the approach is a reference to the rise in the rate at which Irish research is cited around the world. Academic citations are a typical measure of research output, but one that has no correlation with job creation or profitability. As for raising the share of the economy devoted to R&D, the objective is desirable. But only as the indirect outcome of private-sector-driven initiatives and not as a state-driven target to be achieved regardless of quality. The first priority of innovation policy must be to critically assess the results from R&D spending to date. The next priority is to improve the quality of that spend.

Having said that, the government appears to have taken a cue from Finland in starting to adopt a 'whole of government' approach, involving all relevant departments of state and semi-state bodies. There is also a real and increasing focus on spending R&D money on commercially driven outputs.

New laws on the treatment of intellectual property assets are allowing Irish-based companies to pay an effective corporation tax rate as low as 2.5 per cent. It will attract international companies, if not to develop their ideas here then at least to trade them. In 2003 tax credits for R&D expenditure were introduced in Ireland, and thanks to more recent changes these can now be set against payroll costs. This will help bring more highly skilled professionals into the economy. But only when state innovation policy is overhauled in the way Pat Cox talked about can changes like these leave anything of lasting value behind.

The Smart Economy

The smart economy can be envisaged by government but only private individuals can make it happen. The Spirit of Ireland, a remarkable idea not just in its potential to create jobs but also as a strategic response to a looming energy crisis, is a prime example of what Pat Cox described. But instead of waiting for the government to take the initiative, they just did it anyway.

A team of fifty are engaged in a project to turn Ireland's vast potential for wind power into a more stable and reliable source of energy. The idea is beautifully simple: use wind power to pump water into a dammed-up valley. An energy form that is erratic – wind – can be gathered and stored in a form of kinetic energy – water – that can be held in a valley area and put on a reliable tap. With less access to wind and wave power, and few valleys to exploit in this way, Denmark has already planned to be 100 per cent independent of fossil fuels by 2030. Chapter 2 argued that one of the reasons for the fall in share prices – effectively a fall in the value of the world economy – during 2008 was the realization that fossil fuels are limited. Here is a country with Ireland's population, on an even smaller land mass, that will have already moved on. Ireland needs to do much more than it is doing in this area. To really harness the potential of renewable energy, for instance, we need to build fewer, larger-scale wind farms. Instead of a confetti of small-generation efforts dotted around the country, a plan on the scale and grandeur of the Shannon hydro-electric scheme in the 1920s needs to be envisaged. A few big bold steps rather than many small ones are in order.

Although it contains many useful ideas, the government's paper *Technology Actions to Support the Smart Economy* still lacks the vision needed. It unfortunately falls back on a jaded rhetoric of national advantage that is long out of date. Ireland's low-tax status and 'Anglophone' status are, for example, still regarded as comparative advantages. They are nothing of the sort.

If anything they are fig-leaves that have up to now helped us to disguise our lack of real competitiveness, a competitiveness that comes not from speaking someone else's language or having low taxes but from cultivating unique national genius and abilities (as in Scandinavia and Israel). The reference to our English-speaking status is a particularly pathetic perennial that fails to embrace the real reasons why our indigenous industry has not yet met the standards of countries like Denmark, Finland and Israel. One story I heard illustrates the problem of this psychology very well. A leading business person told me how he had lobbied for his niece to get a job in an international organization on the basis that 'she spoke excellent English and had a B in honours French'. He was told by the organization concerned that there were plenty of candidates for the position with better English, and all of them were from non-English-speaking countries! Ireland needs to stop believing its own guff here. Our ability to speak the international language of business is no longer a competitive advantage in a world where tens of millions are learning English as well as retaining their own language. Our inability to speak our own language is, on the other hand, a serious threat to our economy, as argued below. Population growth, high rates of participation in third-level education and Euro Zone membership are also referred to in the *Smart Economy* document. Again, these are not sources of indigenous excellence and productivity, only weak and temporary stopgap substitutes.

On the positive side, the document begins to inventorize the sectors in which Ireland can thrive. Smart communications networks, cloud computing, content service centres for digital creative arts and legal and professional services – these are all part of the international goods services sector that has shown such huge potential for growth. In pointing to where the jobs are, the document is on the money.

Examples of how this could work abound. Smart metering is one, where national necessity and international opportunity could go hand in hand to make Ireland a world leader, like Denmark. Key drivers of a smart economy are policies and infrastructure based on knowledge and sustainability, thinking ahead and planning policy over a long time frame, and the government taking a holistic and long-term approach to strategic thinking. Smart metering for electricity is a classic example of an industry of the future that combines all three. Thanks to long commutes and poor insulation standards, Ireland has a far higher carbon footprint than it should have. And over the next fifty years global population is set to rise by 50 per cent, with fossil fuel production peaking in the next decade. How we manage a dwindling resource – fossil-fuel-driven electricity – could make or break our economy. In a world where most countries face the same challenge, Advanced Metering Infrastructure* is an industry we need to develop at home to help the households and industry of the future. So why not be a world leader in this industry? Why not develop the highest possible standards in this arena, successfully patent them and lead world production as a result?

A Cultural Crossroads

Ireland can continue on borrowed wings. But not for much longer. Ireland's cost competitiveness must be improved, but it can never be restored to the point where we can compete on low costs alone. We have to innovate, to do original things. But to do original things, you have to be original in the first place. The remaining non-cost advantages we have, a low corporation tax and income tax wedge, are being rapidly copied by countries with

---

* A technology that allows consumers to see in more detail, and based on real-time information, the cost of the electricity they are using as they use it. The information flow is two-way so that electricity generators and suppliers can see more accurately when demand is peaking. This allows them, in turn, to manage their purchase of fossil fuels by buying cheaply and storing in preparation for peak demand, rather than getting caught unawares and having to buy at peak demand.

better innovation and lower costs than us. The so-called 'unique' advantage of speaking English is also being copied. 'In Poland today there are a quarter of a million youngsters studying in the medium of English their primary coursework,' Pat Cox says, 'so in other words the knowhow on how to compete internationally is becoming a common currency.'

Even if that wasn't true, a future based on advantages like these constitutes being a low-tax airstrip stopover for US multinationals and a retail extension of UK multiples. The country is already becoming a cultural annex of Anglo-Americana.

Such a future does no justice to our distinctive heritage and potential as a people. The insights you get from being different to other countries are the ultimate source of the native genius that produces inherent comparative advantage. That is why culture and language, though seemingly unimportant, are in fact the long-term life source of a nation's trading advantage. Denmark's homegrown knowhow is unique to it and hard for others to replicate.

Here Ireland is at serious risk. On a daily basis, the increasing penetration of American and British television and media undermines our cultural distinctiveness. That distinctiveness was recently recognized as critical to developing homegrown competitive advantage (Finbar Bradley, 2008). It cannot be an accident that Denmark's success as an economy is related to the ability of Danish children from an early age to speak both English and Danish. Too many Irish policy documents on productivity and innovation policy have, in the sections devoted to education, stressed our status as an English-speaking country. But the fact that we are a country which is only able to speak English is a devastating indictment of our education system's failure, not its success. Finland's revival of its language in the 1850s and 1860s[*] was, as an effort of national will, a major contributor to its identity, independence and will to succeed today.

[*] As in Ireland, a serious famine wiped out much of the Finnish-speaking population and increased the share of Finland's population that spoke Swedish or Russian.

Ireland's absorption into this new bland and dumbed-down cultural orbit is also detrimental to the intelligence of our young people. The collapse in the take-up of maths and science subjects in Ireland, mentioned above, mirrors what is happening in the UK and US. By contrast France and Germany, and most of Scandinavia, are maintaining a solid performance in the Pisa tests. This is largely because the quality of television in those countries is of a higher standard. The mass moronization of Ireland's children by modern media is a process that desperately needs to be reversed. The contrast between the highly intelligent output of TG4 on the one hand and commercially driven output of non-Irish programming shows how our native culture offers far better food for the minds of our children than the prevailing diet of intellectual junk food coming from abroad.

Promoting the Irish language – actively and particularly by immersion education – is also crucial to avoiding this. Policymakers have failed to realize this. Sacrificing the Irish language for the sake of proficiency in English, they have demonstrated a stupidity of unbelievable proportions. I believe from first-hand experience that the antipathy towards the language is not just born of total ignorance, it also stems from resentment, partly understandable, at both the frustrations of learning the language in what is a highly flawed system for learning it, as well as the requirement for Irish in promotion in the civil service.

In the most successful countries of the world, Finland, Sweden and Denmark, knowledge of English is a contributing factor to success, but not the base. Knowledge of English merely opens the gateway to foreign investment and international markets; it does not provide the spark of native genius that creates goods and services those markets want to buy. In Sweden, for instance, the concept of 'Volkshemma' – collectively caring for the community – is a key plank in the excellent relations between its workers and managers.

While leaving far greater amounts of wasteful spending

entirely untouched, particularly spending on third-level salaries, the An Bord Snip report recommended the abolition of the Department of An Gaeltacht and a cut of one quarter in overall spending on the preservation of our language and heritage. The savings arising from this virtual castration of the country's ability to preserve what is best about its traditions will yield a pathetic €151 million, less than could be saved by freezing public service pay increments for one year. But the authors of the report, through no fault of their own, had been mandated by government not to touch the issue of public sector pay. Effectively, then, in order to protect the public sector from any kind of contribution to budgetary correction (other than a modest contribution to their hugely generous pensions), three thousand years of history is to be overturned. The 23 per cent reduction recommended in spending here was in sharp contrast to the much smaller reductions recommended in much larger spending items.

Irish language summer colleges, the only surviving institutions where our cultural uniqueness can be fostered, are also facing destructive penny pinching in the autumn of 2009 as the government considers cutting subventions to providers of Irish-speaking accommodation.[*] If vast sums of money could be obtained from these savings and if no other less objectionable cuts were available, these cuts would be justified. But the lack of any effective economic planning and strategy in any government department is proof positive that cuts of this nature are desperate attempts to avoid cutting back in areas where the real savings need to be made. Instead of cutting back on subventions that protect jobs and culture, the government should be cutting back on the massive number of quangos created since 1997, many of which do nothing other than duplication. In fact they do more than this. In a seminal study on the impact of state agencies, Orlaigh Quinn has found how they have contributed to failed governance in the

---

* John Fallon in the *Irish Times*, 3 September 2009.

state and incoherent and uncoordinated policy outcomes[*] of which the proposal to save paltry amounts of money by downgrading funding for the Irish language is a clear example.

Prostituting our culture simply to sustain a so-called competitive advantage that other countries are rapidly adopting is a form of cultural, and in the long run social and economic, castration. In a few years' time Poland will have the competitive advantage of a significant English-speaking population, and will have preserved its culture. Ireland will, if it doesn't watch out, soon lose both.

Secondly, children who fail to learn their mother tongue find it more difficult to learn subsequent languages. With growing evidence of secondary students opting out of Irish language obligations on the grounds of psychological inability to learn it, a significant minority wants to turn its back on Ireland's indigenous culture. Those students are undermining themselves: many employers will think twice about hiring someone who shirks unpleasant tasks that more dedicated students can take on and conquer. They are also undermining the cultural capital of the country. In turn they are slowly destroying the hidden magic of distinctiveness that feeds the real source of a nation's competitiveness: native genius.

---

[*] Orlaigh Quinn, 'Advisers or Advocates?', Institute of Public Administration, 2008.

10

City Smart, Country Cute

Cities are, first of all, seats of the highest economic
division of labour.

GEORGE SIMMEL

The denser the population, the more intensive the use
of land becomes . . . the more highly developed must
be the control of land utilization exercised by or on
behalf of the community.

EXTRACT FROM THE KENNY REPORT, 1974*

Nothing Rotten in the State of Denmark

Comparing the price levels and global competitiveness rankings
of Ireland and Denmark nearly a thousand years after the Battle
of Clontarf, one could be forgiven for thinking it was won by the
wrong side. Denmark's average price level exceeds the EU

---

*Committee on the Price of Building Land Report to the Minister for Local
Government.

average by some 41 per cent (Eurostat, 2009), but the country's overall competitiveness – both cost and non-cost dimensions – are consistently in the top five of international rankings.* Once, Ireland was in that space. In 2000 Ireland was the world's fifth most competitive nation. Thanks to the rapid increase in prices we have fallen steadily over the course of the first decade of the third millennium to position twenty-two in 2008. By comparison with many of our peers, the ranking is still good. If we didn't have to create 200,000 jobs between now and 2016, it might even be acceptable. But re-ascension to the top ten is not an option for Ireland. It is an imperative.

One of the things the Danes introduced to Ireland was the concept of urban living. Most of our cities – Cork, Waterford, Dublin, Limerick, Dundalk – are founded on Viking sites. A thousand years later, though, we still don't seem comfortable with the idea. The bad way in which urbanization has been handled in Ireland is an invisible but powerful drag on productivity. It is also a huge contributor to the potential cost to the state of bailing out our banks, as chapter 4 discussed. Population growth offers exciting possibilities to reverse this mistake and unleash long-term productivity gains.

As well as good industrial policy, Denmark's urban profile is one of the reasons it can combine high productivity with high costs of living. Urban Copenhagen has 1.2 million souls in a land area of 455 square kilometres. Urban Dublin has less than that, a million souls, spread over 921 square kilometres. The International Financial Services Centre (IFSC), which in spite of recession still employs around 27,000 people, shows that focused planning in one part of Dublin has resulted in the kind of high-value-added economic activity that is robust to recession. It is the only area that possesses the kind of density – not just population density but density of services and facilities – most

*According to the 2008 WEF rankings, Denmark was in third place.

Europeans would recognize as appropriate in a capital city.

Berlin is an interesting second check on Dublin in that while Dublin and Copenhagen have the same populations, Dublin and Berlin have comparable land masses. Where Dublin puts its million souls in 921 square kilometres, Berlin comfortably packs 3.8 million people into an even smaller area of 890 square kilometres, with huge benefits in terms of access to convenient transport, access to shops and facilities within walking distance and well-planned public amenities that are cheaper to provide for Berliners than for Ireland's sprawled population. But while having a higher skyline than Dublin, Berlin is devoid of skyscrapers. If Ireland is to reap the density dividend, as I argued in November 2007, its cities need to cluster and concentrate its population more.

A month later Dublin City Council agreed. In a draft report, it urged greatly densifying Dublin, building up and in rather than down and out (Dublin City Council, 2007). A council report on the implications of Dublin's skyline contrasts Dublin's density of 4,400 people per square kilometre with that of a similar bayside city, Barcelona, at 16,000. Thanks to that difference and despite having an even more beautiful bay (if not climate) than Barcelona, Dublin has extracted only a fraction of its potential for waterfront living. The Dublin Docklands Development Authority has done excellent work in starting to change this, but so far the surface has only been scratched. Once its redundant power stations and warehouses are dismantled and Dublin port's commercial activities are moved north, Poolbeg peninsula has huge potential to house tens of thousands of people in high-quality residential living space at the edge of one of Europe's most pleasant bays. The depths of a property crash may seem the wrong time to be thinking about this. But with land and construction prices at rock bottom, it is precisely the right time to be thinking ahead.

Dublin city centre's current north–south orientation from Parnell Square to St Stephen's Green needs to be complemented by a second, perpendicular axis running from Phoenix Park at one end to Poolbeg lighthouse at the other.[*] To make that axis work there must be a sufficient density of population in between. But census data for 2006 shows that while approximately 155,000 people were working in this central area between Dublin's two canals, only around one tenth of this number were living there. Extending the Luas to Connolly station gets us part of the way in providing facilities, but building further up along the quays and providing high-quality apartments suitable for families is essential to maximizing the financial and social return from these and other transport investments.

Of course densification is controversial. The decision by An Bord Pleanala to turn down planning permission for a thirty-two-storey building on a site in Ballsbridge reflects that fact. It could have been a showcase development. For several reasons the Ballsbridge location was inopportune, but the concept was not. Designed by Ulrik Raysse of Danish firm Henning Larsen, the proposed building had the approval of Dublin City Council planning officials. A thousand years after the first Danish visitors jumped off a longship just beside Dublin City Council headquarters[†] their ancestors were finally bringing us round to the idea of urban living. Or were they? The ultimate failure to achieve planning permission for this project shows how carefully densification will have to proceed. The right location, heights, timing and arguments need to be combined. Endorsing an early version of the plan, city manager John Tierney praised it as being like New York's Rockefeller Center. The remark probably did more harm than good, conjuring up an image of Dublin transformed into a forest of high-rise buildings. Neither was Ballsbridge an ideal site for high-rise. It wasn't even mentioned as a suitable location for high-rise development in the city council's policy document on high-rise (Dublin City Council, 2008).

[*] This point has been made by Kevin Myers in the past.
[†] This building is located on the riverside Viking archaeological site at Burgh Quay, the heart of old Viking Dublin.

To gain traction, high-rise building will have to be concentrated in areas that are virgin territory as far as residential development is concerned. To that end, the future plans of the Dublin Dockland Development Authority offer a cogent, credible long-range objective around which the city council's and the government's visions need to crystallize.

As I argued in *The Best is Yet to Come*, cities should look like cupcakes, with the city skylines rising in the centre but tapering off to the edges. Up to now, Dublin has adopted the reverse 'Donut' model of development, maintaining an extremely low-rise profile in the centre and along the bay but building up in outer suburbs. Young first-time buyers, who should be enjoying the coast and the centre of the city, are living in leafy West Dublin in the type of suburbs that in other cities are reserved for more mature residents with families. And as any visitor to Dublin's newer suburbs will see, they are living in high-density apartments that belong in city centres. There ought to be a trade-off between high density and facilities. The quid pro quo for living in an apartment rather than a house with a garden ought to be easier access to place of work, shopping, entertainment and night life. The quid pro quo for moving away from city centres that provide these things, conversely, ought to be more greenery and space. In Dublin, too, many of our young people are suffering the disadvantages of high-density living without enjoying the advantages of a central location.

As well as harming our quality of life, long commutes, congestion and high commuting costs are affecting our economy. According to the Dublin Transportation Office (Department of Transport, February 2008), the average peak-hour speed for traffic in Dublin city is 16.5 km/h. The contrast with Copenhagen's 28 km/h underlines the damage being done by Dublin's sprawled development and lack of public transport. Copenhagen is, incidentally, a city where thanks to good planning and higher density one third of the population commutes to work by bicycle.

When the Irish government tried to encourage its civil servants to do the same in the summer of 2009* a mere 170 out of a total of 28,000 took up the offer. Who could blame them? With its suburbs that spread for miles in every direction and congested traffic, the layout of Dublin is hostile to bicycles.

But the most damaging economic consequence of all is the high prices created in many Irish towns by the scramble to buy the low supply of accommodation in our town centres.

In short, we have no option but to change our ways and change the model of how we urbanize. The vast opportunities for gain are not just a Dublin affair: Cork, Galway, Waterford, Sligo, Athlone, Dundalk and Limerick all have massive potential to cluster and densify their populations into regional powerhouses that combine high-quality living with access to amenities, infrastructure and employment opportunities.

Why Cities are Good for Productivity

I interviewed chief executive of Forfas Martin Cronin about how, as the dole queue spirals upwards, we can create high-productivity jobs to replace the credit-fuelled mirage employment of the boom years. 'We can only succeed by proactively targeting the internationally traded sector,' he replied. There is little arguing with this position. Certainly, Ireland's share of internationally traded services fell back during 2008. But between 2000 and 2007 – an era when, as we've seen, our cost competitiveness collapsed – services exports trebled at a time when our high-tech sector grew by 'only' 60 per cent and our more traditional indigenous export sector barely at all. Between 1990 and 2007, some 80,000 jobs have been created in the sector.[†]

To survive and prosper, Ireland will have to trade services and

* Paul Cullen in the *Irish Times*, 6 August 2009.
† Source: Forfas 2008, taken from 'Summary of Issues and Progress Innovation Task Force', July 2009.

trade them big. Even into the first year of recession, financial services and insurance employment continue to hold up reasonably well. Computer and business service exports continue to rise.

13. Traded services exports compared with modern and traditional manufacturing exports

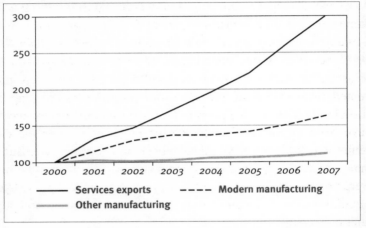

Source: Forfas Enterprise Statistics at a glance, 2008

The premise of any economic strategy, Cronin adds, is to target areas where we are strong internationally – where specific niches exist where the value we add is high enough to counteract our higher cost base. To make that strategy effective in combating Ireland's rising unemployment levels, it has to be done by building industries that are large in scale and high in quality.

Cronin also sits on the National Competitiveness Council and is co-author of the annual NCC report. In a ground-breaking edition entitled 'Our Cities: Drivers of National Competitiveness', the NCC repeated many of the arguments I'd made in *The Best is Yet to Come* (NCC, April 2009). Unlike November 2007, however, recession has finally woken us up to the fact that Ireland's dysfunctional approach to land planning and spatial and urban development, and all the problems that creates in providing state-of-the-art education, telecommunications and transport, has greatly contributed to our current crisis.

As chapter 4 argued, the failure to adopt the recommendations of the 1974 Kenny report, which urged controlling the price of land, has greatly contributed to the devastating mess the National Asset Management Agency must now clean up. But the financial damage to the state is just one part of this. Combining that with a failure to densify the city in a strategic way helps explain why developers like Sean Dunne had to pay €59 million for an acre of urban land and why, once they had done this, they were prevented from exploiting the site's full potential by building up sufficiently high. With a proper system of planning Dunne would have been incentivized to locate his project closer to the city centre where his plans would have been more appropriate. But in many respects, the poor decisions made by developers like him were not essentially the product of incompetence, but arose from a complex array of incentives created by poor planning. And poor land management.

Like electricity and gas, land is not an internationally traded commodity in the real sense of the word. Instead, its price constitutes one of those non-traded costs that the internationally traded sector must bear. And in Ireland, the burden is crucifying. As the NCC's 2008 report on cities exposes, the cost of office rental in Dublin in that year, even as the recession was biting, was still around €110 per square metre, nearly twice the cost in Copenhagen or Singapore. Is it just a coincidence that Copenhagen and Singapore are much more clustered than Dublin?

Building up facilitates a clustering of businesses within short commuting and walking distance. There are several studies to show that this approach enhances innovation over time (O'Leary, 2007). In the OECD, more than four fifths of all patents are produced in regions dominated by a strong and clustered urban centre (OECD, 2005). The reasons are obvious: internationally tradeable services of the kind we need to compete on the world stage require international standards in staff and infrastructure. To achieve those standards something only cities can create is required: deep pools of specialist workers with high-quality expert knowledge. As recent research from the IBM's Institute for Business Value (Susanne Dirks & Mary Keeling, 2008) points out, in most countries the percentage of workers with third-level education is significantly higher in urban areas. This doesn't mean city slickers are smarter than their country cute cousins. The same IBM report also points out that three fifths of leading international companies say that access to qualified staff is vital for their business. Whether those qualified staff are from urban or rural backgrounds – and often the best of them are from rural backgrounds – cities are where they choose to spend their working lives.

There are many other things higher-density cities provide much more easily than low-density ones. A greater choice and competition in products and services leads to lower costs and prices. Rolling out better public services – broadband, high-quality health services, public transport, third-level education and so on – is also more cost-efficient when ten thousand rather than four thousand people live in each square kilometre. Provided that green lungs are built in, the high quality of life that springs from all well-densified cities is also a major attractor to the internationally mobile entrepreneurs, innovators and professionals needed to pollinate a high-tech economy with ideas.

Slowly but surely we're getting the message. In December 2007 a Dublin Council draft policy identified the potential for high-rise buildings to be erected in the city's eastern inner city core area, as well as certain other districts. Situated between the city centre shopping axis between Parnell Square and St Stephen's Green to its west and the Poolbeg peninsula to its east, and also located next to the Dublin Port tunnel link to the airport, this location is the perfect place to build up. It will provide the sort of low-cost, high-quality residential and commercial space needed for competitive traded services to flourish. If this dream is realized then Dublin, one of the world's oldest cities, can start to aspire to be one of its most dynamic and productive.

But where will we get the people to fill its new and thriving centre? As it turns out, that's the easy part.

Here Comes Everybody

In *The Best is Yet to Come* I argued that we would have to harness future population growth to direct the growth of our cities in an upward direction. Much opportunity had been lost, I pointed out: in the four short years between 2002 and 2006 the Republic's population had risen from 3.9 million to 4.2 million – a rise, staggering for such a short period, of 8 per cent. But instead of population growing faster in urban areas, the reverse was happening. Due to completely wrong spatial and urban planning, population in some urban areas was actually falling. In terms of achieving the gains from productivity described above, Ireland was going into reverse. At the time of writing I was confident of our ability to reverse this in relative terms over the coming decades, but somewhat apprehensive about whether this would be true over the coming half decade, a period when I suspected population growth would either stall temporarily or go into reverse. But I still believed that by 2020 the Republic's population would rise to around five million people and that by targeting this growth into strategically chosen locations we could begin by then to realize critical mass in our cities.

Far from ruining that dream, events since then have made it more attainable. And more necessary. The recent growth in our population has been staggering, all the more so because by a full year into the recession – the start of 2009 – the 4.2 million recorded in the last census had become 4.5 million, as recorded in the latest short-term population estimates.* This time it isn't immigrants who are driving the process. Natural population increase in Ireland is the highest in Europe, and even if the rate of child birth slows once the recession impacts fully – which it will – it is liable to remain high enough to offset both deaths and most if not all of the net outward migration likely to have occurred by the time the recession ends in 2011.

In December 2008, long after it became clear that net outward migration would resume for a few years, the Central Statistics Office produced long-term population projections (CSO, 2008). Those show that if Ireland can regain its cost competitiveness, there is nothing stopping the state from growing to five million people by 2020. In fact this is a cautious estimate, based on two scenarios set out in the report. In one, conservative estimates of fertility and migration put the state's population at 4.8 million persons; in the other it could rise to 5.5 million. The state's population will, it seems safe to assume, spend the decade between 2010 and 2020 rising by half a million people. That is the same population as Dublin city proper now, so where are these people going to live? So far the projections have been based on the old National Spatial Strategy and, thanks to that fact, a continuation of sprawl is forecast: the highest population growth will be in the Mid-Eastern region, where population will rise by an annual average of 2.3 per cent. Neither growth in Dublin nor growth in other metropolitan areas will be significantly faster than in the country as a whole. For a few years – until 2014 perhaps – such trends might be useful in restoring demand for property in over-built areas. But in the medium to long term they are a journey on the road to nowhere.

As Copenhagen and Malmö have shown, the benefits of urbanization are increased when there is more than one population centre of critical mass in a region. To realize that increase,

* Central Statistics Office, September 2009.

governments need to enhance communications and transport networks between them. In the 1990s Denmark and Sweden collaborated to build a bridge over the narrow Øresund that separates the two countries. As a result, these two cities are turning eastern Denmark and southern Sweden into a thriving economic region.

The growing cooperation between the north and south of the island of Ireland presents the same opportunity for Belfast and Dublin to grow. But what about the rest of the country? The west and south of Ireland cannot be abandoned as the whole island's economy tilts to the north-east. Nor should it be. There are urban centres that over the coming two to three decades have the opportunity to grow to levels of population that are significant in economic terms: Cork, Limerick-Shannon, Galway, Sligo, Letterkenny-Derry, Waterford, Athlone and Dundalk. The first six are on the Atlantic corridor, a project the completion of which is of vital economic and social importance. Short-term cost-benefit analysis of this project has been used to discredit it, but this demonstrates precisely the flawed approach to infrastructure – a failure to understand the long-term dynamics that, interacting with well-planned and targeted population growth, infrastructure development can bring. On their own, Galway, Limerick and Cork have, respectively, some of the world's leading companies in the fields of medical technology, informational communication technology hardware and pharmaceutical products. The NCC has rightly pointed out, and events at Dell have proved it, that on their own, these urban specialisms leave those cities vulnerable to sudden changes in global demand. And it has rightly called on the government to prioritize the completion of the Atlantic corridor between them. The residents of Sligo have also pointed out that their town is bereft of high-quality medical facilities. At present population levels it would be hard to justify heavy investment in hospitals in Sligo town, but it must be a national priority to put the people of Sligo and Donegal within the shortest possible commuting distance of those available in Galway. Connecting Donegal and Derry, the island's two most economically challenged counties, to regions further south should also merit a high priority. The advantages of rapid transport between these cities are multiple. A blow like Dell – a company in a sector where Ireland is losing advantage – would be far easier to recover from if its laid-off workers were within an hour's commute of jobs in newer, more robust sectors. And if workers did not have to move house to move job, the local economy of Limerick – its housing and retail markets – would be less impacted. Businesses also benefit from a wider range of labour and suppliers, not to mention the higher worker productivity that flows from easier commutes.

Why City Smart is Country Cute

Building and linking cities is one thing. Making them smart cities means giving them the powers and structures.

In 2002 both the Decentralization plan and the Spatial Strategy document showed how self-destructive rural politicians could be in trying to help their own areas. By countering the natural forces of urbanization – incentivizing relocation away from larger towns and cities – they thought they were being typically 'cute', in the Irish political sense of the word, by doing their constituents a favour. They weren't. Much of our current property crisis and unemployment crisis – not to mention the water crisis in Galway, the growing problem of alienation among the rural elderly, and the tragedy of suicide among the rural young – can be traced to this. This country cuteness has backfired. Decentralization has resulted in small towns becoming over-reliant on public sector employment of a low-technology and low-value-added nature. It has also distorted local labour markets, making it more difficult for private sector employers in towns affected by decentralization to compete for skilled workers with the local public sector employer.

Spatial strategy itself needs to be drastically overhauled. It presumes that in order to keep the small towns of Ireland alive economically, employment has to be provided in the small towns themselves. Obviously the lessons had not been learned from similar mistakes made in relation to healthcare provision – the urge to provide a hospital in every small town in Ireland regardless of cost, efficiency or the quality of care. A smarter strategy is to identify seven regional urban centres outside Dublin – Cork, Galway, Limerick, Waterford, Sligo, Athlone and Dundalk – and make sure transport infrastructure in the hinterland makes for easy commuting to their nearest regional centre for the inhabitants of all towns and villages.

Along with this, Ireland's current local authority structures – 129 county councils, town boroughs and other bodies – should be replaced with eight local authorities that correspond to Dublin, the South-East (centre Waterford), the South-West (centre Cork), the Mid-West (centre Limerick), the Midlands (centre Athlone), the West (centre Galway), the North-West (centre Sligo) and the North-East (centre Dundalk). An Bord Snip Nua does recommend some consolidation in this area but, through no fault of that body, it neither goes far enough nor is it properly joined up with planned reform of local government. This is due to its understandable and urgent focus on finding ways to cut expenditure; establishing the ideal structure of local authorities was, quite reasonably, a secondary if not tertiary consideration of its mandate. But the fact that it didn't recommend consolidating the four separate authorities which, ludicrously, still carve up Ireland's most important and only internationally competitive urban centre is a wasted opportunity.

So, without matching reforms, is the proposal by government for elected mayors in Ireland's major towns. Radical consolidation of local authority structures is essential not just for public finance reasons but for good governance. A city like Limerick cannot recover from the blow dealt it by Dell's lay-off of 1,900 workers if, as is the case currently, three local authority structures are responsible for its development. Electing a mayor for a city such as Limerick or Dublin without first consolidating the structures he or she will oversee is a recipe for dysfunctional government.

Reform must go further than urban consolidation. The fact that cities drive regional economies means that local authorities, which are crucial for planning the infrastructure that aids growth, must also encompass hinterland areas as well. Even the population catchment areas of the suggested eight regional areas would be small by the standards of many local authorities in Europe. They would begin the work of getting those regional economies on their feet in terms of independence from Dublin, helping to end the dominance of the capital city so resented by rural politicians. Ironically, some rural politicians are too short-sighted to see this. They object to consolidation in larger regional towns on grounds of diminished democracy in the smaller towns around it. If anything, the reverse is true. The greater sense of identity and local loyalty in smaller towns would translate into more, not less, power for small-town Ireland and would do so in newer, bigger and more effective local authorities.

If those concerned about Dublin's excessive dominance of Ireland really want to see the creation of alternative sources of economic power, they must accept that a rival to the capital can only come with serious urban growth elsewhere. Just as Dublin's development is good for the rest of the country, rapid growth in cities like Cork and Galway will, as in the case of Copenhagen and Malmö, create a positive dynamic for the whole of Ireland.

But that, I repeat, means consolidating governance structures, the total reform of local government finances, and the election of mayors who would govern not just cities but the regions whose economies depend on them. Instead of a high turnover of local councillors giving part-time attention to local government on their way to Dáil Eireann, having a situation where elected local councillors were fewer in number but well paid and incentivized to focus on local government by the prospect of mayoral or executive office in a regional authority of significance will greatly raise the quality of local governance and democracy. And the amazing thing is that the main advantage of these reforms would not be the directly intended ones. Despite the huge financial and efficiency gains this would bring to local communities around Ireland, the main advantage would be this: finally, our national legislators would be free to focus on governing the nation as a whole rather than as a loose federation of 129 independent republics.

11

Goodbye Yellow Brick Road I: Banking and Finance

> One wouldn't have lasted very long by saying 'We're losing market share and our earnings per share is down because we don't want to be part of this'. Anglo-Irish Bank's performance put pressure on other banks to follow the trend.
>
> FORMER BANK OF IRELAND GOVERNOR LAWRENCE CROWLEY

> As long as our civilization is essentially one of property . . . it will be mocked by delusions.
>
> RALPH WALDO EMERSON

The Wonderful Wizards of Oz*

In the rush to make sure a financial crisis of the kind we have just had never occurs again, all sorts of one-shot solutions have been

---

* This allegory was drawn in an article I wrote in the *Sunday Independent* on 23 August 2009. I refer readers to this in case of any doubt as to its originality arising from its use by other commentators between that date and the publication of this book.

advanced. Set up new systems of financial regulation. Abolish bonuses for bankers and cap their salaries. Nationalize banks. Merge banks. Establish an asset management agency. Hire more expert staff in regulators and central banks.

As if the entirety of what has just happened was that simple. The peddlers of this creed – that bankers alone can account for our economic crisis – are leading us down another blind alley. If another crisis is to be avoided, all of the causes – all of the true causes – must be addressed.

But that's a hard slog. How much easier to come up with a simple slogan that vilifies an easy target. How much easier to slake the public thirst by demonizing an easy target, or anyone else whose massive creation of wealth and jobs was enjoyed without question by a receiving public while things were going well. But what about politicians – opposition politicians included – who conveniently chose to ignore economic warnings? Or investors who blindly ignored the old advice of not putting all your eggs in one basket? Or voters who voted for politicians who were plainly incompetent in terms of economic issues, but who had provided some local favour? Or a media that played along with the property boom by relying almost completely on it for revenue growth.

The idea that one single target can be blamed is too easy to be any use. Of course, there are many in this story who are completely innocent, most particularly those young people whose stage of life forced them into a choice between the instability and poor quality of rented accommodation on the one hand and shackling themselves to a lifetime of debt on the other. There are also those who are extremely guilty – some estate agents and mortgage lenders who indulged in sharp practice. But in between there is a hierarchy of responsibility, with various degrees of culpability. Many individuals and groups have travelled down the frenzied yellow brick road. But, however foolish they were for following the leader, there were prime movers.

We saw in chapters 2 and 3 how negative interest rates created the disastrous incentives for overinvestment in property. The fact that they preceded the splurge in property by a year or more may remove them from the scene of the crime at the time of its commission, but it doesn't prevent them being an accessory. Huge personal failures among bank management also played a key role. But to what extent was this due to moral turpitude rather than a system of incentives that were wholly dysfunctional? Weak regulation played an enormous role. But as the source of money creation, central banks are the first port of call for ensuring mistakes of this kind never happen again. And, strangely enough, there is no better place to look for a model of how to do things right than in a land whose economy has completely avoided recession in spite of strong trading links with the stricken Anglo-Saxon economies of the US and the UK: the Land of Oz itself.

Why Monetary Policy Rules OK in the Land of Oz

With GDP figures in for Australia, in the second quarter of this year, it looks like the lucky country is being true to its nickname. Actually, it isn't really luck that's kept Australia's economy in check. When the central banks in the northern hemisphere were bringing their rates down under, the central bank down under was doing the opposite.

As the US Federal Reserve and the European Central Bank lowered their policy rates to 1 and 2 per cent respectively, the Wizards in Australia's Reserve Bank never allowed its policy rate – the so-called cash rate – to fall below 4 per cent. It brought benefits to Australia's economy that would be evident once the global recession started. Banks had more incentive to keep money on deposit, boosting their capital reserves. Secondly, short-term interest rates never fell below 4 per cent until the crisis began; thanks to that, when it did begin the subsequent reductions in the cash rate towards 2 per cent had more of an effect. Australia's central bank never spared the rod and never spoiled the child. Thirdly, Australian interest rates were never less than the rate of inflation for any prolonged period of time. Fewer Australian companies were overborrowed as a result so that when recession came they could borrow when they needed to.

While US and Irish economists decried interest rates of 4 per cent as hostile to economic growth, the Australian central bank understood better: economies that are reliant on low-interest rates for growth are like people who need coffee to stay awake – fundamentally unhealthy. Low interest rates are a stimulant to use in an emergency, not a normality. If used when not needed, their usefulness in emergencies is fatally undermined.

14. Australian Reserve Bank daily cash rate

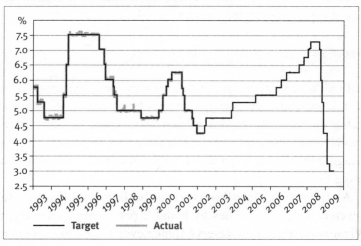

Source: RBA

The Celtic Kangaroo?*

As the US, UK and Japan were gripped by terrible recession in the first quarter of 2009, Australia's economy was actually growing.

* See previous footnote.

And it was balanced growth, both exports and consumer spending doing well. The jobless rate in Australia climbed in 2009, but to a rate of 5.4 per cent – still one of the lowest in the developed world.

If a nation of ex-convicts can have one of the most ethical and successful banking systems in the world, then so can Ireland. We should take inspiration from the discipline and toughness of Australia's economic management, and not just in banking: its fiscal prudence during the good times under conservative-leaning Prime Minister John Howard left Howard's successor Kevin Rudd with a huge war chest to fight the recession. If we want an animal to replace the Celtic Tiger, perhaps it should be the Celtic Kangaroo – a bounceback economy resting on two strong legs: tough regulation of money and banking on one side and prudent fiscal management on the other.

The idea isn't far-fetched at all. Ireland should certainly take inspiration from Denmark, Finland and Israel for its industrial strategy, but for its financial regulation it needs to look at countries that are culturally and politically similar. With one third of its citizens claiming Irish descent, Australia is an excellent model. But to learn from that or any other model we need another analysis of what went wrong in Ireland.

Back to Basics

Before even addressing the problems of regulation and banking conduct – vital, no doubt – global monetary policy must be given its fair share of blame. The wickedly false and destructive allure of loose monetary policy is a yellow brick road to nowhere. The time has come to bid it goodbye. For ever.

Both the US Fed and the ECB must adopt an iron rule of never again allowing the central policy rate to fall below the rate of inflation, except for very brief periods when caused by surprise rises in inflation. To do that, and given that targets for inflation rates in central banks tend to be in the region of between 2 and 3 per cent, a floor of at least 2 per cent must be put under key policy rates such as the main refinancing facility. Presently the ECB's main refinancing facility is at 1 per cent, and unlikely to fall. It is in the Euro Area economy's interests that when it does rise, this rise is slow and gradual. But the rise must not simply be a sequence of short-term rises based on the ECB's usual analysis of monetary and economic conditions.

As well as the short-term management of the economic cycle, the ECB and the Fed must repair the long-term structure of policy rates, steering them back to levels that restore reasonable averages for real interest rates. It may take a decade to do so, but it will be worth it in the long run. It will deter the kind of insanity that occurred in Ireland where real interest rates were negative for two years. Of course an element of Ireland's negative real rates was our fecklessness in controlling inflation. In the spring of 2009 German Chancellor Angela Merkel and Finance Minister Peer Steinbruck signalled that they would, if needed, bail out Ireland's economy. But do we really want as a sovereign nation to be in a position where we are reliant on another country for such assistance? National pride demands that we start shoving an iron rod of prudence down the back of our fiscal and monetary management and show the world we can stand on our own two feet. Besides, Germans might ask why their rates should rise to pay for our stupidity. And they would be right to do so.

An average real interest rate of 2 per cent is a healthy benchmark for the Euro Zone economy. Higher rates are needed for the US, given its desperate need to incentivize depositors to do something they have been disinclined to do for quite some time – save money.

The last issue in relation to central banking is the role of variable-rate mortgages. The German and French economies are suffering contractions of far lesser magnitude than Ireland and the UK simply because the impact of the rise in ECB rates (in Ireland) and Bank of England rates (in the UK) were greatly amplified by the greater prevalence in those countries of variable-rate mortgages. The swings in after-mortgage payment income this causes result in larger than necessary reductions in consumption when rates rise, and larger than healthy increases in consumption when rates fall. These large changes in purchasing power, always temporary, can also tempt governments into raising taxes. The profound impact of the reduction in the ECB's main refinancing facility from 4.25 per cent to 1 per cent between the autumn of 2008 and spring of 2009 in Ireland was a key consideration in the government's decision to raise income taxes in the budgets of October 2008 and April 2009. With mortgage repayments reduced by one third thanks to rate cuts, the government realized it could increase income taxes without reducing take-home pay. The logic was, of course, flawed. Not being stupid, taxpayers realized that interest rate cuts would reverse themselves while tax rises were likely to hang around for longer, if not for ever. Sharp falls in consumption and unemployment during early 2009 were in no small part a result of consumers cutting back their spending in preparation for the permanent reduction in income they knew the government was going to inflict on them.

Although not the only variable influencing house prices, in a country like Ireland a fixed-rate system of mortgages would lend stability to fluctuations in house prices.

Putting world interest rates back to a sensible level has to be a priority for the world's central banks. And that's just the start of what needs to happen.

See You Later Regulator

With the loosest monetary policy in Ireland's history, it was crucial to have a strong line of back-up defence in the form of tough regulation. But just as Ireland's interest rates were turning negative, it was in the process of creating the loosest and most ineffective system of regulation in Western Europe. Within three short years of the establishment of the Central Bank and Financial Services Regulatory Authority, our regulator was to stand back and watch as credit growth surged to annual rates of almost 30 per cent, turning a modestly overvalued housing market into a seriously overvalued one.

But anyone who thought the resignation of the regulator himself, Patrick Neary, in January 2009 would rectify matters was deluding themselves. As the nation was rocked by the revelations of the Ryan report, the scandal of wasteful spending in the state's employment agency FAS and the huge amount of waste and ineptitude in our public sector, the story of Irish financial regulation was telling us something very deep about ourselves and our culture. Whether because of the need to be furtive and evasive under centuries of British rule, or some other reason, Ireland suffers from a strong cultural disinclination to lay down rules and respect them in a rigorous manner. And when they are broken, as they invariably are, we feel honour bound to say nothing.

At least in 2009 that most ancient of institutions, the Church, was coming clean about its failures and trying to do something about it. The story of the awful goings-on in industrial schools was exposed in horrifying detail. Thanks to the vigilance of Senator Shane Ross and Nick Webb, the waste of money in FAS also came to light. But as an *Irish Times* editorial on 22 June pointed out, we still had – at the crucial time when a new system of regulation was being announced – no clear analysis of what went wrong in our banking system. What did go wrong?

The state had little short-term incentive to stop the property boom. As short-sighted as any trader in credit default swaps, for a government that couldn't see beyond the next election the short-term tax revenues from the boom – all unsustainable, of course – were irresistible. Former IDA chairman Padraig White points out how development levies mesmerized the local authorities – themselves an arm of government – into granting planning permission left, right and centre. 'Local authorities got about twelve thousand euros per apartment so there was a huge incentive for them to zone land for building. There's also a lack of transparency surrounding the figures collected as local authority finance doesn't come under the Comptroller and Auditor General.'

The story of Ireland's latest episode of misregulation has its roots in Ireland's status as a small country where key players in finance and politics know one another. One of the reasons the philosopher and social reformer John Stuart Mill advanced against Irish independence was that Ireland's small size would lead her people to be constantly exploited by powerful networks of friends at the top of Irish society. Mill was wrong about Irish independence, but he did have a point: in small countries where the culture of adhering to strong and transparent rules is weak, either a very strong ethical system or a strong regulator is needed. When informed that Irish Life & Permanent had deposited €4 billion with Anglo-Irish Bank in September 2008, regulatory authorities should have taken a stronger line than they did. The deposits, made just before the end of Anglo-Irish's financial year, offset withdrawals of €4 billion made just before the announcement of the state's guarantee of all deposits. It was investigated by the financial regulator in February 2009. But they had been notified to the regulator by IL&P as early as 1 October of the year before.

In a small country where not being an 'insider' can harm your career prospects, it is hard and usually wrong to blame individuals. Cultural and institutional weakness – collective failures – are what needs to be examined. We have been here before. In the 1980s and 1990s Ireland witnessed banking scandals in relation to the use of offshore accounts in Ansbacher Bank and National Irish Bank to help account holders evade tax. In 2002 a debate began on how to establish a regulatory system to avoid this happening again. The minority party in government, the Progressive

Democrats, proposed the creation of an entirely separate regulatory entity, fully separate from the central bank.

No one can make a hard and fast rule about what structure is right for which country. In larger countries, or ones where relations between work and business colleagues are less characterized by intimacy, the existence of a single structure for both a central bank and a regulatory authority for the financial system could work well. In a country where networks are powerful, there is a strong case for what the PDs were arguing for. There was also a strong argument that as an institution that requires deep thought and academic brilliance, the culture of a central bank needs to be very different from that of a regulator, whose task requires vigilance, dynamism and an orientation towards action. As many writers were acknowledging in 2009, the failure to regulate Ireland's financial system was as much a failure of culture as anything else, and it is hard to see how these two divergent cultural requirements can be accommodated in one organization.

Then again, perhaps they can. There is and was a case to be made against what the PDs were proposing, that is for the retention of a single entity. Unfortunately the case made against the PD approach was not derived from the healthiest of motives.

In a rearguard action, both the central bank and Department of Finance opposed what they saw as an attempted incursion on their powers. In 2003 the Central Bank and Financial Services Regulatory Authority of Ireland was created. Under a single umbrella, the central bank and regulator operated with two separate boards. It was a typical Irish compromise between the ancient regime and what the PDs wanted. And it has failed spectacularly. But what aspect of it has failed? Are the failures down to the proximity of the central bank and regulator under the same roof? Or down to the fact that they were not integrated enough? The latter argument could be advanced by pointing out how the central bank governor, John Hurley, could issue warnings about borrowing growth until he was blue in the face, but under the separate structure he could do nothing. Then again, given that his warnings were regularly getting into the newspapers (thanks in part to my efforts), what was to stop the financial regulator from acting on them, no matter how institutionally separate he or she was?

Perhaps the true answer is revealed in the fact that although the head of the regulator's consumer affairs Mary O'Dea was given a place on the board, such a place was – amazingly – denied its director of prudential affairs, Con Horan. Yet the board of this institution contained a representative of the country's main farming organization and its main trade union federation! The institution couldn't have sent a clearer signal to the banks that it didn't take regulation seriously.

Under the 2003 legislation the board and governor of the central bank were both appointed by the Minister for Finance and were therefore in effect appointees of government. The chief executive of the regulator was appointed by its board with ministerial approval and was therefore in the same situation. And while the regulator balanced a consultative panel for the industry with one for consumers, there is no doubt which was the more powerful. The industry had a seat at the social partnership table, the source of most decision-making in government. The consumer wasn't even present.

When announcing an overhaul of financial regulation on 19 June 2009, Finance Minister Brian Lenihan said there would be an 'expansion in regulatory capacity' with a substantial addition to staff. It was certainly welcome. So is the decision to break with tradition by allowing those outside the civil service to be considered for top jobs. But it is hard to avoid the conclusion that an opportunity has been missed for a more precise analysis of what went wrong, institutionally, culturally and managerially. In his defence, the minister's proposals mirror the De La Rosiere report of March 2009, which recommended a single institution encompassing a central bank and regulator, a principle on which it proposes creating a European Systematic Risk Council under the arm of the ECB to monitor and blow the whistle on future episodes of reckless lending.

In the US, the need for stronger regulation is greater. In June 2009 Barack Obama announced a reform of the US patchwork quilt of regulatory bodies. The Federal Reserve Authority will regulate major financial institutions, capital requirements for big banks will be more exacting, and the federal government will be able to rescue banks before they fail. Regulation of hedge funds and derivatives will be toughened, and those issuing securitized mortgage loans will have to keep part of each loan they issue, exposing them to the risks involved.

In a small country like Ireland, the changes need to be cultural as well as institutional. The Financial Services Consultative Industry Panel has pointed to 'critical characteristics' of a new financial system. Knowledge among regulatory staff of what they are regulating will be crucial. But this needs to come from the top. Using the board of the financial regulatory body as a mechanism of social partnership – i.e. to give representation to various vocational interests – has had its day. The panel rightly says that first-class regulation 'can only be achieved if the regulator takes on experienced senior managers from the private sector'. Its opposition to a rules-based system is questionable, but it is on the money in identifying the need to focus on the quality of the personnel in financial regulatory bodies as much as the institutional make up. The closed monasteries of officialdom, cultures that wear down the best and brightest of our public servants, must be replaced with dynamic, flat organizations that release their huge potential and allow their public sector ethos to be balanced by fresh thinking from outside. This approach should be followed in government departments as well.

Thankfully, an excellent start has been made here with the

appointment in September 2009 of Professor Patrick Honohan as new central bank chief. As well as complementing the skill sets in the central bank with outside expertise – Honohan is a respected World Bank economist and Trinity College professor – Honohan shows the diaspora principle in action: he has gone abroad, harnessed top-level international knowhow and is now in a position to bring it back home. On monetary policy if not taxation matters, Professor Alan Ahearne's appointment is another welcome example of the government bringing in a highly qualified expert to help steer the nation out of crisis.

Back to Bailey

Although they weren't a huge problem in Ireland, one aspect of sub-prime mortgages is common to a key problem Irish banking shares with banking in the UK and US. To an increasing geographical, informational and cultural degree, mortgage borrowers on the one hand and savers on the other have been growing further and further apart. As this occurred, it became more important to be able to trust those on the other side of a transaction; but at the same time, trust was arguably on the decline. Although former Fed chairman Alan Greenspan presided over one of the biggest 'macro policy' mistakes in monetary policy, there is nothing untrue about an important observation he made in 2004 about the changing morality in financial markets: 'In a market system based on trust, reputation has a significant economic value . . . I am therefore distressed at how far we have let concerns for reputation slip in recent years.'

About a decade after *The Wizard of Oz* was made out of Frank L. Baum's book, another Frank – Frank Capra – made another of Hollywood's best-loved films. In *It's a Wonderful Life* the hero of the film, unlikely though it might seem today, is a banker by the name of George Bailey. The film is set in 1930s America where fear of banking collapses is driving panicked depositors to withdraw funds. When a run on the banks happens in his little town of Bedford Falls, Bailey is confronted with a crisis. Although his own bank is secure, Bailey's customers don't have the same degree of information as he does and rush to withdraw their deposits. The problem is referred to in economics as 'moral hazard'. It is at its most dangerous when trust in society has broken down. Those who have borrowed those deposits will, Bailey is confident, be able to honour their debts once the economy turns around. If everyone keeps their nerve and their money in the bank, the situation can be saved. And in the most touching way, that is what happens in the film. But only because Bailey the banker is trusted. In the film, Bedford Falls is a close-knit community where everyone knows everyone else and bank managers can base such confidence on long-standing financial knowledge of the people around them. This is exactly the model of financial market intermediation that three decades of innovation and change have swept away. The personal relationship of trust between borrower and banker and banker and lender is broken. Mortgage sub-prime borrowers' requests for a loan application became aggregated with tens if not hundreds of thousands and funded en masse by an ever-globalized financial system which was so removed from the borrower that vital links of knowledge were broken. When the crisis hit there was no George Bailey who knew both lender and borrower to restore overall confidence in the system. Instead there were unscrupulous profiteers determined to sell the lowest-quality investment to risk-mad investors with neither the sense nor information to screen them. Or, like the surplus cash economies of Asia – thanks to a decade of superb export performance and a very high savings ratio – to investors who had nowhere else to invest their money.

As this book is being finished it can't be ruled out that Ireland's entire banking system will have to be nationalized and entirely restructured. If that occurs, the government must ensure that mutual societies – the George Baileys of our banking system – continue to play a strong role in our housing market. Apart from ensuring competition in the market, this is essential to bring back the trust and long-term relationships between borrowers and lenders that, despite some drawbacks, were what was good about Ireland's mortgage market for so many decades.

And if that reshaping is to be credible, it must take a strong account of the events of 2008 by ensuring that those leading the banks and building societies of tomorrow are not associated with the mistakes of the past. I asked former Bank of Ireland Governor Lawrence Crowley – a conservative and cautious banker of the old school – which of the mutuals he thinks should survive, and he answered, 'I would think it would be EBS. They seem to have got less involved than the others in what happened.' Some building societies have generated considerable controversy during the financial crisis. By publishing a comprehensive report on that crisis it would be easier to chart a way forward for Ireland's banking system.

Ireland's new financial services regime, when it emerges at the start of 2010, must be based on experience and knowledge of the Irish market. But it also needs to be based on competition in the banking sector and have no link with past failures. But as yet, our knowledge of what those failures were is incomplete.

NAMA: Fail or Bail?

Establishing a strong and competitive financial sector, with banks and mutual societies operating together, is the end-game goal. But there is a much more immediate one to be dealt with first. In February 2009 former Danish Prime Minister Poul Rasmussen visited Ireland and gave a speech on the global economic crisis. When I interviewed him I asked him, as someone who had helped create perhaps the world's most successful small economy, what the most urgent task facing Ireland was. With typical

Danish efficiency, his answer consisted of a sentence containing no more than eight words. Half a year later, we are still waiting for the government to take his advice: 'Clean up the banks, and do it quickly.'

Richard Curran, deputy editor of the *Sunday Business Post*, pointed out that Ireland differs from the US and UK in that we have yet 'to hold any kind of formal public inquiry into how we ended up in this mess'. Bad bank loans to be taken over by the National Asset Management Agency were valued in August 2009 at around €90 billion. It is the price tag for a complex array of mistakes, from the very heights of monetary policy to greed and incompetence in banking, but also chronic dysfunction in state planning and – last but not least – a failure of banking regulation.

No event illustrates the latter more than the failure of Anglo-Irish Bank. Demonizing its former chairman Sean Fitzpatrick cannot take away from the fact that this was a bank which was lauded for a decade for putting its faith in the Irish economy. It was at an unacceptable extreme of banking, but it got there by reacting to another unacceptable extreme: a banking system of the kind that failed to give the likes of John Collison a break. Before becoming warped by the Celtic Tiger and when extreme conservatism in banking was holding the entire country back in the 1980s, it did much good. With typical Irish fickleness, in 2009 the public and media turned on it. But three years before that few if anyone had a bad word to say about it.

We could attack the greed of Anglo-Irish Bank, but we could equally attack its sheer stupidity. Although monetary policy and bad regulation contributed to Anglo-Irish Bank's mistakes, it should have seen the signs of excess in Ireland's property market that from 2005 on were patently obvious. If a €2 million bonus in 2007 created anything, it was an obligation on the CEO bene-fiting from it to spot and arrest the dangers of further overinvestment in property. It did the reverse, and by 2008

Anglo-Irish Bank had a loan book of some €72 billion, some 94 per cent of which was in property. This was three years after the OECD had warned that property prices in the Republic were overvalued. Who in Anglo-Irish Bank was looking at the big picture? Who was assessing and reporting to the chief executive on its exposure to an overheated economy? And if they were, what incentives did they have to shout 'Stop'?

On 29 September 2008 the bank's recklessness ceased to be its problem and it became ours when the government decided to guarantee for a period of two years all deposits – retail, commercial and inter-bank – and all debts of six of the state's banks. Some argued that banks could simply have been let go to the wall and were not systemic to the economy. Perhaps they were right. But in an economy like Ireland's where one quarter of GDP was generated by the property sector, was there enough information to make this call immediately? Lehman Brothers was not systemically important to the world economy yet its collapse was a profound catalyst for the world recession. In a panic-stricken economy, the government's decision was the least worst option.

No, the trouble with the guarantee wasn't that it was introduced. The devil – more than one, in fact – lies in its detail. Why, for instance, was dated subordinated debt included in the guarantee? And although Anglo-Irish Bank's inclusion in the guarantee in September was a prudent precaution in case it was systemic, the immediate priority should have been to assess whether this was really the case, and if not, perhaps wind it down.

On 4 October Sean Fitzpatrick defended his bank's record. 'Have we been reckless? No, we haven't. We cover all our loans in a belt and braces way.' He was referring to the bank's collateralization of loans. But as most bankers were to find out, the collateral behind their loans was overvalued in ways that would not have passed any rigorous assessment of macroeconomic risk. For all the derision thrown at economists about their inability to agree, it is worth noting that Anglo-Irish Bank had no senior economist. Critics of Sean Fitzpatrick after-the-fact were close conceptual cousins of those who heaped praise on him when the going was good. Swimming with the tide is easy. Fitzpatrick was, as Anglo-Irish Bank chairman Donal O'Connor said, a visionary driving force, but a visionary whose force went out of control.

All of these factors have now combined to inflict a high price on Irish taxpayers. As the chicken said to the pig on the morning of the farmer's breakfast, 'I'm involved but you're committed.' The taxpayers' involvement in the rescue of Anglo-Irish moved increasingly towards commitment status on 21 December when the government took €1.5 billion in preference shares in the bank. On 20 January 2009 the degree of commitment became total when emergency legislation was brought through the Dáil to nationalize the institution.

The first incision into the taxpayers' flesh came in May. Unlike the purchase of preference shares – an investment with a conceivable chance of getting a return – the government sank €4 billion into the bank to keep its capital above requirements. In his analysis of this decision, Richard Curran pointed out that €31 million in unpaid directors' loans had been written off by the bank and that €1.2 million of a €4 million loan to an employee to buy a house in the US was written off as the house's value collapsed. So it seems that at least some of the loans intended to cover emergencies have been used in relation to activities the systemic importance of which is unproven. The fact that another €3 billion in further capital injection may be needed raises the financial and political stakes of this.* If needed, that injection will be made during a winter of discontent in either late 2009 or early

---

* On Friday, 29 May 2009, Anglo-Irish Bank reported a €4.1 billion rise in its bad debts in the six months to March 2009, but the bank's stress tests indicated that a further €3.5 billion in bad debts could arise.

2010, at a time when the public will be digesting savage cutbacks and possibly tax increases.

The rationale for saving Anglo-Irish is, according to its chairman, that a wind-down of the bank 'could be a very costly operation for the Irish taxpayer'. Thanks to the guarantee of bank debts, a wind-down of Anglo-Irish Bank would indeed force the taxpayer to stand in and repay the debts of those funding the bank. As a going concern, those debts are treated as the debts of a semi-state company and are not part of the national debt.

But why should the taxpayer have guaranteed the debts of Anglo-Irish Bank in the first place? Before becoming adviser to Brian Lenihan, Professor Alan Ahearne was highly sceptical about the need to save Anglo-Irish Bank. Professor Brian Lucey of Trinity College remains not just sceptical but totally opposed to bailing out the bank. He has rightly pointed out that its depositors come in different shapes and sizes. Commercial and retail depositors – about half of the €60 billion on deposit at the bank – are accessing a relatively high rate of interest. They are able to do so because their deposits are largely underwritten by the taxpayer. Arguably a tooth-comb analysis of all depositor types should be presented before the public in advance of any further funding going into this bank. For a further injection of taxpayers' money into Anglo-Irish to be justified, the link between international confidence in Irish banks and the individual depositors of Anglo-Irish Bank needs to be established in the public mind.

Including Anglo-Irish Bank in the state guarantee was arguably the right thing to do during the crisis-ridden period of September 2008. It was the safest action to take and in the absence of full information on Anglo-Irish's loan book and depositor base it would have been extremely risky simply to let the bank go under. But with international financial markets now settling back towards pre-crisis levels of trust and confidence, the generalized and blanket panic has been replaced by a more discerning and calm atmosphere. The government's approach to the banking crisis is now gradually coming down from the red alert state to adopt a still vigilant but more differentiated approach to depositor protection. One year after the original guarantee, in September 2009, the Finance Minister Brian Lenihan said that when the current guarantee scheme runs out in September 2010 he will replace it with a less 'universal' guarantee. The question is, what funding will by then have been committed to the banking system, funding made necessary by the existing scheme?

More to the point, Anglo-Irish Bank will be made effectively redundant in the course of 2010 as much of its loan book is dumped in the National Asset Management Agency – the government's new knacker's yard for bad loans.

BaNAMA Republic?

The risk to the taxpayer from NAMA has been greatly overstated. Still, even assessed at its most prudent level, that risk is still huge.

The final legislation outlining how NAMA will work was published in September 2009 but at the time of writing had not yet been passed by the Oireachtas. As envisaged, the agency will operate by purchasing, at a discount, bad loans from banks currently worth around €68 billion*. The agency will force banks to take a hit on their capital base, writing down by the discount factor the value of assets being sold. In return, the banks will get mostly cash which the government will raise by selling bonds. But in a move that was not envisaged in the first draft of the legislation published in July – and thanks to a suggestion made by Professor Patrick Honohan, before he became central bank governor and before indirect criticism of the original draft legislation by the European Central Bank† – the banks will now share the

---

* When rolled-up interest payments are accounted for the loan liabilities total €77 billion.
† On Monday 31 August the ECB warned that the original approach of paying 'long-term economic values' could pose risks for the taxpayer.

risk with the taxpayer. Part of the payment for loans will be made in the form of subordinated debt, allowing the state to withhold interest payments to the banks if NAMA fails to recover loans. Those who borrowed from the banks will still have to repay their loans, but to NAMA rather than the banks. Freed from these bad loans, and with reduced but more secure capital bases, the banks can – in theory – start lending again.

Many questions arise with this approach. How many borrowers can pay, will pay, their debts? With the government able to raise funds for this scheme at rates of 1.5 per cent and with interest rates on NAMA loans likely to be around 4 per cent, if more than half of the borrowers repay then, on the funding side at least, all will be well. The outlook for this at the time of writing is, on balance, mixed.

In the worst annual performance of the worst bank in Ireland, Anglo-Irish Bank confirmed that 54 per cent of its loan book was 'good quality' (Anglo-Irish Bank, 2009). In case this appears to provide comfort, it shouldn't necessarily: the 46 per cent that aren't are the ones destined for NAMA. The more it becomes a toilet bowl for the very worst of loans, the more NAMA risks not even being able to fund itself. If the taxpayer is to be asked to undertake a risk of this magnitude, NAMA must acquire a rea-sonably mixed portfolio of assets. At the time of writing that mix remains to be seen.

Even if it can fund its borrowing, NAMA may not break even for the taxpayer. It will base the price paid for the loans on cur-rent market prices 'adjusted for long-term economic value', thus creating a huge dilemma. If what Alan Ahearne believes of the residential property market is true[*] then property prices generally need to fall by 50 per cent from peak to trough across the econ-omy in the long term. But with NAMA buying the worst of these, this would imply that discounts of greater than 50 per cent, per-haps considerably so, would be justified under this 'long-term

* See chapter 4.

economic value' approach. Paying current market price would protect the taxpayer fully. But current prices are likely to be distressed and this approach would be pointless as the whole point of the exercise is to beef up bank balance sheets damaged precisely because of currently low market values of the assets underlying their loan books. Such an approach means the taxpayer will end up having to assist the bank by capital injection. Or the bank could be allowed to fail. Which makes it crucial to conduct a transparent assessment of each bank and how 'systemically' important it is.

Davy stockbroker have estimated that as property prices recover from current crisis-ridden lows, the taxpayer could end up profiting by up to €6 billion. In an *Irish Times* article in early May, Alan Ahearne stated that NAMA's assets and liabilities would 'roughly match'. But to ensure this will require low discounts, forcing the taxpayer to take up the burden of recapitalizing the banks in the form of acquiring more shares in the banks. On the other hand, in that case, if bank shares do recover in value – not an impossible outcome – the taxpayer could conceivably benefit. Economists differ on this, with those like Brian Lucey and Constantin Gurdgiev warning that losses on NAMA's assets could amount to tens of billions of euro, while those like Rossa White argue that this overstates the risk.

There was an intriguing possibility that, in Ireland's case, NAMA could, hand in glove with other arms of government, turn no-hoper properties into thriving ones. ESRI research (Karen Mayer, 2009) has shown how the construction of the Luas line pushed up property prices along its route by 15 per cent. Although not directly relevant to NAMA, the study underpins the difference infrastructure, planning and amenities can make to property. Had Sean Dunne made his application for his building earlier and had it been granted, the history of that investment – and possibly the Irish banking sector – might have turned out somewhat differently.

Renowned economists like George Soros, Paul Romer, Joe

Stiglitz and Willem Buiter have all argued against the type of approach taken by NAMA. From their perspective – the commanding heights of international academia and finance – their solution is a better one: instead of purchasing bad assets, purchase all the good ones and create a 'good bank' that can get credit flowing quickly again. The secured deposits of the bad banks would be guaranteed by the state, but not unsecured debt such as the subordinated debt. For economies like the UK or US, where the banking system is a smaller component of the economy, wealth less concentrated in property, and confidence in the banking system less a matter of life and death to those countries' ability to borrow on international markets, this approach is absolutely correct. But for a country like Ireland with a rapidly growing population and vast potential to increase the real value of land with careful planning, urbanization and public transport roll-out, NAMA could still work. Also allowing banks to fail poses greater risks for small countries like Iceland than for large countries like the US, from which Soros, Romer, Stiglitz and Buiter derive much of their world view. This underlines the case for a systemic reform of our property laws. Crisis-driven solutions that are uncoordinated with one another could yet be NAMA's undoing. So could the mechanism chosen to value each asset acquired. At the time of writing the broad approach – adjusting asset prices for 'long-term economic value' – has been set out. How this is applied to each individual asset, and what prices will result, will make or break NAMA. In total, however, long-term economic value is expected to exceed current market value by €7 billion at the time of writing.

Crucial, too, will be Brian Lenihan's commitment to imposing a levy on banks to compensate for any properties that don't break even. This idea is not even contained in the legislation and rests on the honour of the minister.

Is NAMA the best way forward for solving Ireland's banking crisis? One might put it this way: given Ireland's unique circumstances, it is probably the worst possible solution apart from all the others. The IMF has proposed the state conducting a swap of mortgage-backed securities with government bonds. This gives the banks access to better quality capital, but has the advantage that ultimately the shareholders of the banks bear the risk. The approach taken by the government on the suggestion of Patrick Honohan is a compromise between this ideal solution proposed by the IMF and what the government proposed in July.

By the time this book is published, these issues will hopefully have been put to bed in the form of passed legislation. Clarity on the pricing of NAMA assets and cast-iron guarantees in relation to protecting taxpayers for losses on asset sales will be critical.

If the government gets this project wrong, the words 'BaNAMA Republic' will enter the lexicon of Irish political life. And they will stay there for ever. But getting NAMA right inevitably will have a significant side-effect: forcing the government to come in on the other side with capital injection to compensate for lower than anticipated loan prices will require a dramatic change to Ireland's banking system.

Wunch of Bankers?

By the summer of 2009 the Irish public was heading for the nation's bankers like a lynch mob. Given what had occurred at Anglo-Irish Bank, who could really blame those holding the noose? But this was in a country that seven years earlier had been screaming at banks to lend them more money. The title of one bestselling book, *Banksters*, captured the public mood accurately. But when US politician and chairman of the House Committee on Financial Services Barney Frank investigated the Fed's role in the acquisition of Merrill Lynch by Bank of America – one of the side-shows in the grand circus of America's recession – his conclusion was an interesting one. 'I cannot find a villain,' he reported back to his committee.

With their high pay and huge bonuses, bankers were excellent scapegoats for the crisis, and hammering them was a great way of selling newspapers. But were all bankers like those at Anglo-Irish Bank? Did they really act totally irresponsibly? Or, like Pavlov's dog, did they merely respond to the incentives of their masters, doing whatever it took to get a juicy bone? Put another way, who, apart from a few commentators, was warning the banks about what they were doing before 2007? Sure, plenty were willing to jump on the bandwagon of recrimination once the downturn became inevitable. Like minor generals in a Latin American country they would replace the picture of the old dictator with that of the new one within ten seconds of a coup. But however necessary for optical reasons, who really believes the departure of the old generals of Irish banking will be enough to cure the system, or that there was no more systemic reason for banking failure? And are central banks and regulators the only people we can blame? Did they, perhaps, come under pressure from political quarters to give free reign to lending growth? And even if the regulator gave commercial banks the freedom to be greedy and stupid, they didn't force them to be so. Why have other banking systems survived the crisis, and what can we learn from them?

The scapegoating exercise of 2009 ignores a simple fact about the banking system: no matter how ethical or unethical those at the top are, their incentives are hard-wired for failure. It's a problem that mirrors the difficulties faced by politicians in managing budgets: everyone knows what the right thing to do is, but they also know they'll be punished for doing it.

In bad times banks suffer falls in the prices of their assets, reducing the value of capital and, in turn, what they can lend. In good times the reverse occurs. Like Charlie McCreevy and the national budget, when the banks have the money they give it to us, and when they don't they take it back. Just when we need it most. The accounting practice of marking-to-market, introduced in response to the Enron crisis of 2001, reinforces the problem by allowing balance sheet valuations to reflect the exuberance or despair of investors with the attention span of a fly.

Regulators need to devise incentive systems that force banks into counter, rather than pro, cyclical behaviour, building up extra capital in good times. Under the presidency of Sweden, a country which successfully resolved a savage banking crisis in the early 1990s, the EU Council of Finance Ministers has agreed to a series of measures that will in time achieve this, including changes to accounting practices to make asset valuations less prone to wild swings. In the US this has already happened, the Financial Accounting Standards Board giving companies greater latitude in how they establish the fair value of assets. A short-term concern about this should be entered here: these very changes, good as they are in the longer term, are a significant factor behind the apparently good performance of US banks. In some cases, Citigroup for instance, they were probably responsible for profits rather than losses being reported. This is another good reason why the performance of the US banking sector in 2009 needs to be treated with extreme caution. Nonetheless, accounting changes like this are a good move in the long term.

Meanwhile, the Committee of European Banking Supervisors published draft guidelines on 'liquidity buffers' in July 2009. These will, if implemented, require banks to hold a month's worth of quickly convertible assets in reserve during good times, in case of bad times.

In addition to regulatory and accounting pressures, internal bank management practices often undermine the banking system's long-term health. Irish banks' practice of recruiting staff at an early age and grooming them up a long and multi-layered ladder is an intangible but arguably huge contributor to the crisis. Like the failure of our financial regulator, the career emphasis on ascending a hierarchical ladder makes it more important for bankers to be acquiescent and politically shrewd than it does for them to be competent and tough. At the very top levels of banking, recruitment from outside the bank is normal practice. But strong leadership at the top needs to be complemented by expertise and strong advice from middle management. And once bankers get to the top, the incentives faced by bank managers also need to be changed.

The logic of bank bonuses is not only sound in theory, but in a dynamic and competitive market for banking executives, bonuses are essential. Hugely volatile profits, thin margins and highly mobile staff mean that firms have to balance staff costs, by holding salary levels fixed, with the need to incentivize high performers to stay. The large bonuses of bankers there don't reflect any exceptional greed on their part as a class of people, but deeply ingrained characteristics of the industry. In more stable industries such as manufacturing, profitability is more steady. For that reason bonuses tend to be a much smaller part of remuneration.

However great they are for generating indignant headlines, it isn't the bonuses themselves that are the problem but their size, the reasons for which they are given out, and, related to that, the obsession in modern banking – reflecting an obsession in Anglo-Saxon capitalism more generally – with short-term profitability as opposed to long-term profitability and stability.

What is most remarkable about the bonuses paid to Irish chief executives of major financial institutions in 2007 is this: they were paid in a year in which the proportion of the loan books of Irish banks exceeded any reasonable or even sane level. The largest bonus paid that year – €2 million to Anglo-Irish Bank's David Drumm – was paid to a bank that had the previous year maintained an enormous 94 per cent of its loan book in property of one form or other (see table 6 in Appendix I). But as most annual reports of banks will tell you, CEOs are rewarded on the basis of the current year's financial performance, not on the long-term stability of the bank's loan book. And therein lies the first problem with bonuses: with those under them brought up in hier-archical structures and cultures, and with a bonus culture emphasizing the achievement of annual or quarterly profits, anyone in a bank pointing to the mounting over-reliance of the economy – and thereby the banking system – on an overvalued property market was liable to have their concerns brushed aside.

The second problem with bonuses is that when measured as a share of the total remuneration package (as distinct from their actual amount) they are actually too small. A glance at the salaries of CEOs shows that even if none of them received a bonus, the lowest salary any of them would have received was €694,000. In America or the UK where shareholders are more vigilant and firing bank CEOs is not unknown, there are sticks as well as carrots. In Ireland, firing anyone for irresponsibility is unheard of. In that regime, the salary levels for Irish bank CEOs represent a system of carrots without the stick. To those who say that several CEOs were eventually fired it must be responded that a good remuneration culture is one that prevents their decisions from wreaking havoc on the economy before they are fired. The head of the UK's Financial Services Authority has joined the discussion, arguing that the debate over bonuses is an irrelevant side show. This is not quite correct. In September 2009 the G20 took probably the right step in limiting the size of overall bonus payments paid by banks, but not individual bonuses. This will limit the damage done to banking by an excessive amount of money being chased by too many bankers, but will allow indi-vidual bankers of excellence to be properly rewarded. Bank remuneration committees will be required to adopt a more trans-parent approach to how much is being paid. Bonus payments will also have to be more linked than before to measures of risk, as well as measures of profitability.

The third problem with bonuses is that they are paid annually. Given the short-term time horizon of bank shareholders, this is logical. But with the rules of the game about to change in favour of a more stable and longer-term approach to measuring capital adequacy and asset values, bank bonuses need to change accordingly.

Unlike in the UK, in Ireland there has been no comprehensive review of banking practices that led to the current crisis. As the day of reckoning for NAMA was drawing closer in the autumn of 2009, calls for such a review were getting louder. Both the government's adviser on expenditure cuts Colm McCarthy and Green Party finance spokesperson Dan Boyle issued clear calls for such a review. In the UK, where the banking crisis was less serious than in Ireland, such a review has already occurred.

Sir David Walker, a sixty-eight-year-old British banker of the old school, led a comprehensive study of corporate governance in large financial institutions. As outrage mounted in the UK over bumper bonuses, Sir David identified a range of problems with banking governance that would get heads nodding in agreement in Ireland. His views are a clear rebuttal to those who think the banking crisis is just about bonuses or regulation. In perhaps its most important sentence, the report states that 'principal deficiencies in BOFI [Banks and Other Financial Institutions] boards related much more to patterns of behaviour than to organization' (Sir David Walker, July 2009).

It's a quote that gives rise to an intriguing thought. If patterns of behaviour are, as he suggests, a factor in what went wrong with the world's financial system this past decade, in what ways did they change for the worse, and how do we change them back?

12

Goodbye Yellow Brick Road II: Society

The tendency of contemporary liberal democracies to fall prey to excessive individualism is perhaps their greatest long-term vulnerability.

FRANCIS FUKUYAMA, *THE GREAT DISRUPTION*

Old Europe's Last Laugh

The attitude of the US Republican Party to Europe was probably best summed up in Donald Rumsfeld's description of French and German objections to the US invasion of Iraq. 'That's old Europe,' he said, dismissively contrasting those countries with more US-friendly countries in Eastern Europe. In a simplistic way it underlined a very different way of looking at the world, not just in matters of the Middle East. Unlike in the 1980s, European objections to US military actions no longer stemmed from ideological grounds, or anti-US sentiment. Perhaps because of their long history, Europeans are simply more concerned with stability. Americans liked to characterize the French as

251

'cheese-eating surrender monkeys' and Europeans as passive appeasers. But a short course in European history would teach any American student that Europeans have probably killed more people and invaded more places than all the other cultures of the world put together. Perhaps because of its history of conflict, most recently in the Second World War, the European political mindset understands the importance of stability and moderation. Since the 1970s the pendulum of world philosophical outlook spent three decades swinging from one extreme of totalitarian socialism and the rights of the state to another extreme of individualism. Neither has worked. At the threshold of the twenty-first century, Europe – old Europe – seems to offer a weary world a third way: a stable central position where the pendulum can stay at rest, in equilibrium.

A major driver of the EU's push to improve banking regulation, French Finance Minister Christine Lagarde has slammed the American and British system of giving out huge bonuses. In an interview with the *Financial Times* she described as 'an absolute disgrace' the slide back to big payouts by big banks. French banks are already following her lead by dropping immediate bonus payments and spreading future payments over a long time frame. Germany's Chancellor Angela Merkel has also attacked the excesses of bankers in New York and London. At a party meeting of the Bavarian Christian Social Union, she warned that neither Wall Street nor the City of London would again be allowed to 'dictate how money should be made only to let others pick up the tab'. The courage and clarity of these two women is hopeful given their growing power.* More to the point, the ideals for which both women stand – referred to as Christian democracy in Germany and Republicanism in France – are very similar.†

During a lunch with Madame Lagarde that I attended in

* Angela Merkel won Germany's general election of September 2009.
† Their different titles merely reflect differing attitudes to the role of religion in politics.

Dublin in 2007 at which the Irish economy was discussed,[*] she conveyed a belief that the state has a role in stabilizing the economy against both the volatility in the economic cycle and the sudden changes that justified reforms can inflict on those affected.[†] However misguided in matters of taxation and bureaucracy, the French – and also German – approach to economic management in relation to financial supervision and monetary policy is one with much to offer the world. The difficulty with the French view, however, is its contradictory hostility to the role of faith in politics.

The evidence is, the world is hungry for change. Barack Obama's defeat of John McCain in the 2008 US presidential election was a decisive rejection of the idea of untrammelled free markets. Not that Obama's party was guiltless when it came to the global crisis. Through Carter's and Clinton's promotion of sub-prime mortgages, and through Greenspan's loose interest rate regime and Republican partiality to donations from Wall Street, both sides of America's political divide have played a sorry part in bringing us to where we are. In fairness, it was George Bush who made the first attempt to reverse the sub-prime crisis – and was opposed by Democrat Congressman Barney Frank. But when in September 2008 John McCain stated that the fundamentals of the US economy were in good condition, he was showing a naive tendency to believe that all was well that was very much more at home with Republicans. Ideologically, the party of George Bush junior was psychologically unable to confront the idea that the new world order created by George Bush senior was unsustainable.

Obama's election promises a new start. But is it enough? Perhaps the most accurate criticism of his proposals came from David Hirschmann of the US Chamber of Commerce. 'While the

---

* She was then Trade Minister.
† The context was an exchange we had over the impact of agricultural reforms proposed under the Doha round of World Trade Organization negotiations which I was covering at the time as Economics Editor of the *Irish Times*.

administration has made several positive recommendations,' said Hirschmann, who heads the chamber's Centre for Capital Markets, 'we're concerned that, overall, the proposal simply adds to the layering of the system without addressing the underlying and fundamental problems . . . We can't simply insert new regulatory agencies and hope that we've covered our bases.' As John McCain showed in the Lincoln Savings and Loan scandal in the 1980s, regulatory bodies, however strong, are no match for determined lobbyists. As Obama put it himself when announcing his reforms, the real challenge for America, Ireland and the world is to get all those involved in its financial markets to be active in the fight against 'a culture of irresponsibility that took root from Wall Street to Washington to Main Street'.

This crisis cannot be prevented by top-down measures alone. This crisis is as much about philosophies and people as it is about policy. For no matter how weak regulatory structures were, a strong value system would at least have led the individuals in those agencies to apply more rigour than they did. But Alan Greenspan is right. As investments between strangers were growing apace, the ethics and trust needed to get people who didn't know one another to continue transacting was being eroded. The process of financial disintermediation also changed banking from a long-term partnership with a tradition of service to local communities into a financial one-night stand. Perhaps financial regulators and central banks weren't at fault. Perhaps they merely retained faith in the values of those they were regulating. But the sheer cynicism and greed of people like Andrew Lahde* show that we are now up against a problem that policymakers alone can't solve.

A Very American Crisis

America is more than just a country. It represents in many ways the philosophical triumph of individualist values over collectivist

* See quotation at the start of chapter 3.

values, the culmination of a struggle that began in the eighteenth century. The growth in neo-liberal values in America since the late 1980s is the ultimate expression of what its founding fathers wanted: the freedom for individuals to pursue their own happiness untrammelled by any defined religious values or collectivist moral structure. Under George W. Bush, America's foreign policy appeared to take direct inspiration from this idea. With profound consequences for Europe and the world, the post-war model of multilateralism – the approach that created global institutions like GATT (now the WTO), the United Nations, the World Bank and Bretton Woods to try to stabilize global political and economic affairs – was abandoned. Just as capitalism was going global in the late 1990s, the new international structures of governance in areas like financial regulation and environmental protection remained uncreated or incomplete. Such global institutions as do exist – the Bank of International Settlements, for example – are confined to issuing guidelines that depend on national bodies for their interpretation and implementation (in Europe, the De La Rosiere report signals the beginnings of a change in this policy, but Europe is not the world). This lack of global financial governance is a key reason why shocks produced in the US economy travelled so rapidly around the world economy.

But perhaps the individualism of America's culture may be just as relevant to the current crisis as the individualism of its foreign policies. For decades US consumers have had one of the world's lowest savings ratios in the world and have been consuming more than they produce. This they funded by selling assets to the rest of the world – in effect mortgaging their future for the sake of consumption today. As they did so, the US Federal Reserve – its central bank – maintained interest rates at levels that spurred Americans to borrow even more.

As more and more Americans were able to borrow at low interest rates to sustain the increasingly glamorous lifestyles their media told them to aspire to, they also found that as well as being able to, they had no choice but to. In contrast with the rising living standards of a minority of Americans, there was a growing divide in the US between the highly skilled and professional and other workers. The phenomenon, known as Skills Biased Technological Change, is a complex one.* But Andrew Lahde's quote does a lot of justice to a situation of huge disparities in opportunity for advancement created by the contrast between the enormous educational opportunities and access to technology for the offspring of the wealthy on the one hand and the invisible but powerful barriers of race, background and lack of access to social networks facing the poor on the other. In a society where the onus of 'making it' is so much greater, this put huge pressure on individuals to strive for ownership of homes they really couldn't afford. This is a key reason why the Clinton administration facilitated the introduction of the now infamous sub-prime mortgages, to deal with the problem of homes becoming unaffordable to a growing minority of poorer Americans. Barack Obama is one highly intelligent American who has overcome those barriers. His challenge now is to help millions more Americans to climb that ladder without having to mortgage their children's future.

The individualism of America has also had another profound impact on its economy, and on Ireland's economy, given our choice of American-style suburban development. Just as Los Angeles' sprawl militates against public transport, so American individualism makes them culturally and temperamentally disposed towards a culture not just of car ownership but high car usage. Hence America's economy is built on a technology that is increasingly inefficient and costly as fossil fuels approach peak

---

* The idea behind it is that workers with a greater literacy in information technology benefited disproportionately from US growth during the 1990s, causing income inequality to increase as unequal access to third-level education became a stronger driver of income differences (Acemoglu, 1998).

production. It is no coincidence that the crisis in the US economy occurred as the price of oil rose above $130 per barrel.

As well as cultural individualism and its various implications for urban living and America's carbon footprint, there are social dimensions to America's economic problems. Family breakdown and inner-city communities that suffer from crime and alienation, from a lack of equal opportunities for schooling, and from a decline in trust and neighbourliness, have made many urban areas of America undesirable places to live in a way many Europeans cannot fathom. In many areas of America the collapse in house prices was the result of a breakdown in the social order. Many who could not afford to escape were nonetheless desperate to do so. Their counterparts in Europe might have had similar or even lower incomes, but greater social cohesion in most large European urban centres means they are less likely to take extreme financial risks to move into better neighbourhoods. In America, those desperate to escape failed neighbourhoods that had become utterly devoid of society would clutch at any straws being held out to them by an often unscrupulous sub-prime mortgage market, a market from which the George Baileys had long vanished. Investors around the world, remote from the realities of the US housing market and in a bad position to assess the value of what they were about to buy into, were also becoming increasingly individualistic. The declining ethics in the US property market and the phenomenon of poor or low-income Americans being sold mortgages that the seller knew were unaffordable, and a shortening of time horizons and a growing emphasis on the share price of an institution as the measure of its success, increased the pressure for quick profits at anyone's expense, even at the expense of the financial stability of the institutions concerned.

In Ireland, too, there is a link between the house price boom-bust cycle and the decline of social values. Many women who wished to stay at home were forced to work because of the pressure high property prices put on the family budget, and because of Ireland's policy of tax individualization. In mainland Europe cheap, high-quality and densified accommodation suitable for families is available in a secure rented market in a way that supports a balance between work and family life. In Ireland, tens of thousands of Irish women who don't wish to go are forced into the workplace to fund the cost of a mortgage because the alternative – well-designed, secure and family-friendly apartment living – does not exist here.

This insidious impact of bad planning, monetary madness and a discriminatory income tax system means that a large number of the 300,000 women who joined the workforce between 1997 and 2008 (the female workforce went in this period from 551,400 to 852,100) did not want to do so. The social consequences of this are a topic for another book. But it has to be noted that not only has our atomizing society damaged our economy, our economy has atomized our society even more.

The End of History, and Other Fairy Stories

The link between American society and America's economic malaise is a problem not just of human importance. America is in many ways the highest expression of a philosophical trend that began in the late seventeenth century known as the Enlightenment. Our current age, in which the role of religion has been separated from society, is in many ways the culmination of that process. It has resulted in a system of political economy where it is now forbidden to advance the idea that religious morality has any role in good governance. Simply create good government, democratic institutions and free markets, so the theory goes, and society will function fine.

In many ways a positive, several aspects of the Enlightenment were, however, deeply flawed – for a start, Adam Smith's belief that the common welfare was best ensured by the separate pursuit of individuals of their own self-interest. John Nash and other economists would disprove this in the twentieth century (and so in our own country, through coordination between important economic groups each comprising their own short-term interest in pursuit of a higher objective, did our system of social partnership). Secondly, although it did not lead to the abandonment of morality (in some ways it made morality more genuine and less rule-oriented), the trend away from a belief in literal and absolute beliefs weakened the ability to say no to financial temptation. At the same time more and more spheres of human endeavour ceased to be undertaken within the realm of kinship and community and became marketable commodities. Two hundred years ago clothes were made and mended within the family; this is now unheard of. A hundred years ago all meals were cooked within the family or community; increasingly, eating is undertaken in restaurants and cafés. Twenty years ago childcare was the preserve of the family; now the crèche is increasingly substituting as a marketable costed service for something that was done naturally out of ties of love and duty. Perhaps, as discussed above, this is because families have no choice. Increasingly, man is becoming a being whose activities can be priced. Sociologist Robert Puttnam has shown us the metrics of this slow conversion in which material values are replacing moral values, and sensuality and selfishness are replacing spirituality. As the urban poor of America were suffering economic dislocation, so many middle-class Americans were suffering a dislocation of a different kind.

In the latter half of the last century of the last millennium, the idea of enlightened self-interested individuals doing their own thing appeared to have eternally triumphed. But perhaps this was because the only alternative, state socialism, was eternally discredited. Now new alternatives have emerged, but how appealing are they? Chinese capitalism is impressive, but how consistent is it with democracy and human rights? Two hundred years after the

Enlightenment it seems we must look for a philosophical alternative to pure individualism. The stability of our economic system, the fragility of our global environment and the appalling persistence of world poverty belie the belief that history is a story of inevitable progress. Certainly much progress has been made in the last three hundred years. But the 'Whig' view of history – the idea that every turn taken by history is by definition the correct one – is long overdue for abandonment.

But where might we have missed the right turn? By the 1950s Europe and the US, thanks to Marshall Aid and the New Deal, had rediscovered the social cohesion and harmony that the industrial revolution and its long aftermath had disrupted. Partly due to left-wing militancy born from a succession of economic crises and high inflation eroding workers' real incomes, the stable social contract of the 1950s and 1960s broke down into polarized conflict during the 1970s. In Europe the centre ground gave way to extremes of left and right. In the US the centre fought against a resurgent Republican right and lost. Eventually neo-liberal ideas replaced centrist Christian Democratic ideals. This was partly the fault of the politicians to whom those Christian Democratic ideals had been entrusted, politicians like Edward Heath in the UK or the leaders of Italy's Christian Democratic Party who were either too weak or corrupt to renew those ideals and apply them to more challenging times. At the same time those who opposed neo-liberalism did so either from the point of view of a discredited and defunct ideology, or out of fear of losing some vested interest. Either way, neo-liberalism has had no credible intellectual opposition since the 1960s. Simultaneously a process of moral individualism – pursued, ironically, by a political left which in Europe strongly advocated collectivism – helped to undermine the role of the traditional nuclear family and the role of religion. Although not intending to, the left's agenda of secularism worked hand in glove with the libertarian agenda of the free market right to create the self-centred model of economic growth that has now come grinding to a halt.

The time has now come to acknowledge that the victory of neo-liberalism is a false dawn. No economic system can survive devoid of a moral structure. The most basic economic transactions require a degree of faith that the other party will honour their commitments. That the shoes being bought won't fall apart within a day of wearing them. That the tin of beans does not contain some toxic ingredient. That the contract being signed with the bank, which most of us are far too busy to read, does not oblige us to pay unfair or hidden charges. That the mortgage being sold is affordable. Capitalism can only work if it is moderated by trust. And trust in good behaviour requires not only institutions that define what 'good' is, but also institutions that transmit a belief in the intrinsic truth of that good. For centuries, Western man has had the Church, the community and the family to perform this function. Is it really an accident that the unravelling of modern capitalism is happening after three decades during which these institutions were so seriously weakened?

Change We Can Believe In

Barack Obama has been elected, and this portends enormous hope for the future in terms of a more stable and better regulated economic and financial system on our planet. In his own country, Obama aims to make college more affordable and access to primary and secondary education more equal, and to introduce healthcare, pensions and minimum wage reforms.

The current crisis needs all of this. But it needs more besides. The collapse of the nuclear family, rising individualism, rising rates of suicide and depression, violent crime, drug abuse and sexual assault, although not economic in character, are indicative of deeper problems that do affect economics. Thirty years ago the sight of a child being assaulted would have prompted any adult walking past to intervene. That was before communities, with their obligations of kinship and neighbourliness, were replaced by more synthetic and transient social groupings. For many of us, our workplaces are replacing our communities as the places where we form the deepest relationships. But these are fundamentally beholden to professional and financial obligations and relationships rather than to the bonds of friendship and love that characterize kinship and community. We will realize, possibly too late, that our social environment is as important as our physical environment and that its degradation by cultural and moral pollution poses hazards that are just as grave for our future as sub-prime mortgages and CO_2 emissions.

US writers like Max Weber, and in more modern times Francis Fukuyama, have attributed the rise of capitalism in the US and UK to the strong Protestant ethos in those countries. Fukuyama has warned that as the strict religious observance that was once the norm of Protestantism was abandoned, so the ethical and moral restraints that regulated the profit motive loosened. In *Bowling Alone*, Robert Puttnam provided clear evidence that it was happening, in spite of a rise in evangelical Christianity. This is perhaps because some strands of such Christianity do not necessarily advocate moderation when it comes to material acquisition, but can in fact encourage such acquisition as a sign of providence. Either that or because they seem more concerned with offering religious justifications for recent trends in US foreign policy than in providing personal moral structure.

Here too, however, the signs are hopeful. One of the reasons for the dominance of social and foreign policy themes in much of America's evangelical Christianity is the fact that, before Barack Obama, US Democrats were wary of recognizing any role for religious values in politics. As a result the Republicans gained sole ownership of religious values and used them only to underpin support for policy objectives in the areas of social or foreign – rather than economic – policy. Of course, the role of religion cannot be constrained from influencing such topics in a free and democratic society. But while taking positions that many religious people will oppose, when he spoke the words 'We know that faith and values . . . can be the foundation of a new project of American renewal',* Obama made a revolutionary acceptance of the role of religion in politics. Together with the ground-breaking alliance between the Democratic presidential campaign and evangelists like Rick Warren,† he is fundamentally challenging the idea that politics can succeed without religion.

Neither was religion found wanting during the current recession. Some days after meeting Obama in Rome, Pope Benedict XVI published the Vatican's response to the global economic crisis. At the most crucial juncture possible *Caritatis in Veritate* has begun the process of reconnecting the worlds of morality and economics. Pointing to the crude materialism of the 1990s, it argues that the free market is only as good or bad as the morality of those involved in it. It makes the sensible and obvious suggestion that regulatory structures need the same international reach as the financial markets they are trying to police, and that the price of human economic activity is not the same as the value of the human person.

It doesn't argue for a third way between capitalism and socialism. To do so is to miss the point entirely about what has gone wrong with economics. Unless individuals are strongly motivated by a deep sense of right and wrong and are immune from corruption, even the strongest state management of the economy can only replace socialist corruption with capitalist corruption. And at least in capitalism the bursting of bubbles and the threat of competitors act as final checks and balances to corruption. The socialist states of Eastern Europe had no such system of checks and balances; had they not collapsed under public pressure in the

---

* Barack Obama, *Change We Can Believe In*, 2008.
† Jim Wallis, *The Great Awakening*, 2008.

late 1980s they would have continued to subject hundreds of millions of people to decades of tyrannical misery. And, as shown in chapter 3 with the Lincoln Savings and Loan scandal, neither can the most elaborate regulation of the free market be effective if the individuals being regulated are devoid of a moral structure, or if the people doing the regulation – or, worse still, the politicians appointing them – are morally weak.

If a sustainable alternative to the current unsustainable trajectory on which mankind finds itself is to be found, it cannot come from government alone. We have absorbed the fallacy that humanity can only be improved by government acting from the top down. Governments are like architects: the quality of what they can build is only as strong as the quality of the bricks and timber they are working with; if the bricks are crumbly and the timber rotten, their work is in vain. The twentieth century saw several failed attempts to improve the human condition by pursuing secular political philosophies that saw government as the only useful instrument in improving the human condition. Like-minded religious institutions must now begin a great work of moral and ethical renewal in Western society, working on the ground to improve and repair the values and family structures that underpin the ethics of individuals who make up our economic system. Likewise, well-meaning politicians across all parties must renew their efforts to improve government from the top down. Hopefully the two forces will meet in the middle; the hope of a better world depends upon it.

Until they do, Ireland's immediate challenge is to spend the next seven years rebuilding its own economic model.

V

Project 2016: Reclaim the Republic

13

2010–2016: A Seven-Year Strategy

A man without a plan, is not a man.

FRIEDRICH NIETZSCHE

Right now, as things stand, the Irish government is headed for economic and political failure. It is a failure that is entirely avoidable if the government would simply do something that most other countries, and all of the successful Nordic countries, have done: formulate an economic strategy. There is, according to some in government, no time for planning. With endless crisis meetings and gigantic issues from NAMA to An Bord Snip to financial regulation to be resolved, strategy, they say, is a luxury we can't afford. When describing to me the pain that would be inflicted on the Irish people by the April 2009 budget a few weeks before it happened, one adviser told me that 'we'll just have to make the necessary cuts and tax increases, regardless of the political impact they have'. This adviser is a deservedly respected figure in government circles. But the fact that painful choices need to be made makes it even more important to have a careful and ordered strategy.

The badly thought-out April 2009 budget has already back-fired, worsening the government's revenue take. Fianna Fáil's vote plummeted to its lowest point since 1927. At the time of writing the government's majority has already been pared down to zero by the loss of two Sligo TDs, Jimmy Devins and Eamon Scanlon, over the removal of cancer services for Sligo hospital. Under circumstances of instability, an election could plunge the country into an even more serious crisis. The collapse of the Fine Gael/Labour government in 1982 over the taxation of children's shoes delayed Ireland's recovery by five years. This happened because a reform of insignificant size (in terms of saving money) but huge political sensitivity put politicians off any cuts at all. There is currently a dominant and cohesive party in government, but as opposition parties appear to move further away from each other in policy approach, the chance of logjam and political breakdown after the next election grows stronger.

For this reason, the path to recovery must be trodden carefully. Political strategy is as important as economic strategy. The hap-hazard removal of medical cards from senior citizens shows how not to do things. On economic grounds the move was justified entirely. But, just like former Justice Minister Michael McDowell's fatal error over stamp duty in 2006, getting the method of transition and communication right is equally crucial. In the case of medical card holders, account needed to be taken of how elderly citizens had taken the government at its word in 2002 when the cards were introduced. Having abandoned med-ical insurance, they would have found it highly expensive to re-enter the insurance market. Of course the cards should never have been extended as widely as possible. But having been taken on faith, a transitionary arrangement needed to be set in place. The government has to date no economic strategy for planning and roll-out of policy.

The resignation of Devins and Scanlon shows how decades of inability to plan are now catching up with us at the wrong time. Yes, the government is right to argue that, on its own, the population of Sligo town is too small to justify having its own cancer services. But when added to that of Donegal, Leitrim, Sligo county and north Roscommon and north Mayo, the population of the North-West does justify them. If targeted in 2002 for a big enough slice of the population growth about to hit the country, and made the focus of transport hubs in the North-West, and if spatial planning and transport policy had been linked strategically to the roll-out of health policy, Sligo's population could have grown by tens of thousands in the ensuing six years. With an earlier and more efficient roll-out of transport it would have become a quick commute away for around a quarter of a million people. Cohesive planning from 2002 could have avoided the ludicrous situation we have now: there are no specialist health services in the northern half of the Republic. What passes currently for economic planning, the National Economic and Social Development Organization, is good on theory and research but devoid of expertise on strategy and implementation and overly reliant on academic perspectives.

Devastating though they are, the examples above are just a foretaste of what is to come: a tragic situation where an economic recovery that is more than possible comes a cropper because of avoidable political mistakes. As the scale of correction intensifies and as the necessity of a bank bail-out raises the emotional stakes of welfare cuts and tax increases, the government can no longer afford the risk of advice that is economically justified but politically inept.

In 2016 Ireland will celebrate the hundredth anniversary of the 1916 Rising. From 2010 included, there are seven years until that event. Seven years to clean out the stables and steer us back to where we need to be: a high-tech economy with Irish as well as multinational parts leading Europe in international services exports and providing a growing population with jobs and prosperity. It can be done. But it must be done strategically.

A Strategy in Four Parts and Seven Years

There are five main elements to Ireland's recovery: restoring cost competitiveness, rescuing the banking sector, controlling public spending, tax reform and building the smart economy. Achieving the latter is a medium- to long-term goal. As it was dealt with in chapter 9, here we will focus on the first four, and they're not just laid down in any old order: for good reasons, a successful strategy will follow a logical sequence. That doesn't mean that one part of that strategy must finish before another begins. In some cases there must be overlap. But maximizing political success demands that some strategies begin earlier than others. If signalled in 2010, for instance, an irreversible plan to reduce the cost of living by lowering state fees and charges can, even if not completed until some years after, convince the electorate of the case for reducing some welfare payments. Likewise, announcing an irreversible and radical programme of public sector reform is a must before introducing new taxes. The most urgent problem facing the economy – reducing costs – is not just necessary for these political reasons, it will also alleviate pressures on those who need help the most and the fastest: our exporters. Like the request made before take-off on a plane that in the event of oxygen masks dropping down adults should fix theirs first before helping others, our exporters must first be in a position to create jobs before they can help us.

Priority No. 1: Reducing the Cost of the State Sector, 2010–2012

Even if the full range of prices, fees, charges and taxes that need to be reduced cannot all be reduced by 2010, that year must see the government make a cast-iron pre-commitment to a schedule of targeted reductions of any cost burden the state inflicts on the rest of us.

As the most exposed economy to the US and UK in the Euro Zone, Ireland's business cost levels are bleeding us of jobs and business in a way that can't wait any longer for a cure. Some would say the banking sector is the most pressing priority. In terms of timing, they are right. But strategically speaking, it isn't. Before securing a flow of credit to business, everything has to be done to ensure its viability. Ensuring viability of business has to go hand in hand with providing credit to it, but strategically the former is more important than the latter.

Tens of thousands of workers in the private sector have lost their jobs because of high electricity prices, high rents, high rates and a plethora of state charges and professional fees influenced by state regulation. The more the non-traded sector is reformed, the more businesses can switch from the red back into the black, taking pressure off the banking system for working capital and pressure off the exchequer via slower rises in unemployment.

Finance Minister Brian Lenihan showed a clear grasp of the need for general price falls in the economy when I interviewed him for this book back in July 2009. 'We have to do an adjustment because we were living beyond our means,' he told me, 'and that adjustment means that the price of doing business here, the return on the different factors of production whether it's the return on capital, the return on labour in the form of income, the return on property in the form of rent, all of this has to fall.' What is less understood by government, as I've already argued, is how the state is largely responsible for most of these price increases.

The first and last of the five elements mentioned above are the two sides to our productivity. They're equally important, but one is a long-term objective that needs years if not one or two decades to achieve. The other is within the government's immediate grasp. Electricity prices, VAT rates, land prices, commercial rents, professional fees, local authority rates and a whole host of other costs currently killing business are within the immediate control of government. With a stroke of a pen, they can be reduced. Politicians will tell us that doing so 'isn't that simple'. Oh, but it is that simple. Even if they cannot understand the urgency of this action for economic reasons, perhaps they can reflect on the trauma inflicted on the government by the 2009 elections. Four years after Eddie Hobbs' *Rip-Off Republic,** our traumatized politicians need to rapidly adjust their mindsets as to their idea of what voters will not tolerate. Until now, reform was dangerous for politicians. It would cause vested interests to revolt. But now politicians need to be more fearful of the majority. The Celtic Tiger has awoken a sleeping tiger; the citizenry of Ireland is silent and acquiescent no longer. The fact that the government's September electricity price cut still leaves us with the second highest prices in Europe, and the fact that despite a 90 per cent cut in UK gas prices our regulator has permitted a fall of just 12 per cent, shows how so far the action taken is totally inadequate.

Fine Gael's document 'Rebuilding Ireland: A New Era for the Irish Economy' shows the scale of the vision that needs to be adopted. It recommends the creation of a new state industrial holding company to drastically restructure and reshape the way our semi-state companies feed into the economy. ESB, Eirgrid, An Post, Bord Gais, Bord na Mona, Coillte and Metropolitan Area Networks will be consolidated and reformed. As well as allowing costs and prices to be driven down, the approach will put the 'fat pipes' essential to the creation of jobs in sectors like cloud computing at the disposal of a proper state innovation policy. Aspects of the policy are wrong. It does not include transport companies like Dublin Bus and Iarnrod Eireann. It also needs to change how it proposes to make massive investments in

---

* The *Rip-Off Republic* TV series ran in the early autumn of 2005 – an exposé of high prices in Ireland by consumer rights advocate Eddie Hobbs.

state-of-the-art broadband and clean energy. Its proposal to raise bonds with commercial investors and the public is laudable, as is the idea of raising money from the European Investment Bank. But the proposal to tap into the National Pensions Reserve Fund is not. Given the chronic overexposure of Ireland's pension funds, not to mention the tax base to the domestic economy, exposing the state pension fund even more to it is like divorcing your first cousin so you can marry your sister. The document also needs to quantify how those bonds would be repaid. Revenues would ultimately have to be raised by charges on businesses and consumers. As the whole point of the policy must be to reduce the cost of these inputs, that point needs to be made clear.

Fine Gael are also right to identify the need to privatize An Bord Gais and ESB International, and equally right to acknowledge that the manner of Eircom's privatization was disastrous and it should not be afraid to argue for a reversal of that policy on a temporary basis to roll out broadband property.

Where Fine Gael need to go much further is in recognizing the need for drastic reform in other areas. Local authorities, for instance, must be cut down in size and expanded greatly in catchment area. Local authority financing must be reformed to take the burden off job creators in business. And, perhaps above all, land prices must finally be controlled by a modified implementation of the Kenny report. The fact that Tom Parlon, former Irish Farmers Association president, former junior minister with responsibility for the Office of Public Works (OPW) and current president of the Construction Industry Federation, has dropped his long-standing opposition to the idea of controlling land prices is a sign from above.

Fine Gael having no stomach to take the initiative on this, the government should in 2010 begin work on reforming our whole system of land and planning. Where Fine Gael have shown a willingness for reform is in relation to local authority reform. Together with reform of the National Spatial Strategy, the development of a new national densification strategy for the seven cities identified in chapter 10, a major review of how we use space and land should be concluded by 2012 to be put to the electorate. This timeline would, as Bertie Ahern suggested should happen in 2002, allow the people to express their views on land reform in a referendum by 2012. It would be ten years late, but better late than never. It would also allow policy errors like decentralization and the spatial strategy to be buried on the tenth anniversary of their creation.

Work also needs to begin on overhauling and strengthening competition law and regulation. This area is too vast and complex to be the subject of a chapter in this book. But a comprehensive review of market power is needed in Ireland. Competitive considerations also need to loom large in any review of planning. Rip-off Ireland is far more a story of consumers unable to get to competing shops – because town planners refused to give them planning permission – than a story of conspiracy by retailers.

It is also a story of high costs imposed on the private sector by the public sector. Public transport, healthcare charges, educational charges, airport charges and taxes, parking and clamping charges – all of which feed directly or indirectly (via wage pressures) into business costs – need to be drastically reduced.

What better way for the current government to precommit itself – and to precommit future governments – to eliminating public sector waste than to withdraw in one fell swoop the funds that allow it to continue? There is none. For immediate competitiveness, for political and for strategic reasons, the costs the state sector imposes on business must be swiftly and savagely removed.

Of course, however sound Fine Gael's instincts on this are, political realities will make that party baulk at what needs to be done. This issue is addressed in the next chapter.

A final reason why cost reductions are a number one priority is that the third priority, controlling public spending, relies upon it politically. Ireland's spending on social welfare is unsustainably high. But cutting social welfare rates – a reduction of 5 per cent in welfare payments together with a reduction in child benefit – is advocated in An Bord Snip as a way of saving €1.3 billion. But the state's role in giving us in Ireland such a high cost of living would make any cuts in welfare highly unjust, unless they were preceded by a reduction in those costs. Take, for instance, a packet of cigarettes. Thanks to the highest state taxes in Europe the excise duty burden on a packet of twenty cigarettes in Ireland, €4.30, exceeds the tax-inclusive price in many EU states. The same is true for Ireland's VAT rate of 21.5 per cent and various charges in transport, education and health. The point is that unlike taxes on luxury goods or income, these are taxes on things the poor cannot avoid paying for. So cutting welfare before reducing the highest state charges and taxes is grossly unjust. The former must precede the latter.

Priority No. 2: Rescuing the Banking Sector, 2010–2016

The banking sector has been dealt with in chapter 11. The political importance of how our banks are rescued deserves a mention here. The irresponsible actions of a minority of bankers, the inevitable – however justifiable – rises in interest rates and the prospect of taxpayer exposure to billions of euros in liabilities arising from NAMA's work greatly complicates the government's political ability to deal with our public finances. The sight of banks being bailed out to the tune of billions of euros while social welfare allowances are cut and hospital services cut back could produce a backlash that makes protests over medical cards seem mild.

There are, therefore, economic reasons why an all-party approach to the banking crisis should be taken. So crucial is the importance of banking to the economy, and so potentially disruptive to other vital areas of government policy is the rescuing of the sector, that this must be above and beyond the cut and thrust of normal political debate. One of the reasons Sweden's financial crisis was dealt with so well was the existence of an all-party consensus on how to handle the banks. Finance Minister Brian Lenihan expressed disappointment to me that such an approach does not exist here. 'We do not have all-party agreement on banking in this country,' he said. 'I can assure you I have sought it time and time again. The opposition parties have insisted on playing politics with this and it is rooted in ignorance.'

Opposition parties might – understandably – retort that this is a mess of Fianna Fáil's making and that Fianna Fáil had better clean it up. There are two responses to that. Firstly, having gone along with government forecasts on the state of the economy in 2007, opposition parties effectively endorsed the economic regime we currently have and would be in exactly the same position as Fianna Fáil is in now. Secondly, our banking mess is so great that although it will hopefully take only one economic cycle to achieve, it could take longer. Even if it is resolved by 2016, any temporary advantage the opposition gets now from attacking the government will become a headache if that opposition suddenly finds itself in government. Opposition parties should realize that unless it collapses before NAMA is made legal, the government has the opportunity to precommit future governments to its plan of action. In theory a different government could overturn NAMA, but once set in train, the burden of international reputation and domestic legal obligations will make NAMA very hard to radically alter. For that reason opposition parties would be wiser to adopt an all-party approach. The Finance Minister's offer to select Fine Gael and Labour nominees to the board of NAMA is a final opportunity for them to do so.

The government, for its part, has responded to several suggestions by amending draft legislation in ways that will improve its operation. Banks will share a portion of the risk associated with NAMA by receiving part of the payment for loans in the form of subordinated debt. This reduces the chances of loss to the taxpayer. A variant of this idea was proposed by the new central bank governor Patrick Honohan before taking up his position (see chapter 11). It also outlaws any lobbying in relation to NAMA.

Priority No. 3: Public Spending Control, 2010–2013

With among the highest marginal income tax rates[*] in the EU, the highest property tax[†] and the highest rates of VAT, not to mention the highest excise duties, Ireland is now overtaxed. The collapse in tax revenues after April 2009 shows that taxation is now crippling the economy. The severe backlash against tax rises in the April 2009 elections also shows how taxation is dividing society in a way that, unless dealt with now, may permanently rupture the cohesion on which our society is based. Simply put, the public sector has presumed too much in our willingness to absorb its insatiable demand for funding. It must either drastically reform or lose the backing of the citizens it is there to serve.

If it is broadly right in its approach to the microeconomy, Fine Gael is dangerously awry on macroeconomic issues. In fact, as its former leader Garrett Fitzgerald told me, its failure to confront the realities of the macroeconomic situation in its 2007 election manifesto was a betrayal of its solemn moral and constitutional duty to provide opposition. Events since then show that it has learned nothing. Although greeted with jubilation, the 34 per cent it received in the 2009 local elections was, in a time of unprecedented dissatisfaction with the government, below its all-time high of 39 per cent.[‡] An opinion poll taken in the *Sunday Independent*[§] showed that 55 per cent of voters did not want an election because they didn't think it would improve matters. They were right. When George Lee ruled out a reversal of

[*] When income levies, health levies and PRSI are taken into account.
[†] In the form of stamp duty.
[‡] Attained in the 1982 general election.
[§] 8 August 2009.

benchmarking pay awards a few days before his election victory, he was merely enunciating Fine Gael policy as determined by its finance spokesperson Richard Bruton. Fine Gael will only cut pay levels in the public sector above €100,000, enough to yield only €81 million a year.

Yet research conducted by ESRI suggests that public service pay remains, even after the pensions levy of January 2009, 12.5 per cent above private sector levels. Restoring parity at all pay points – some would say cuts should go further and put secure public sector salaries 10 per cent below private sector salaries – would yield at least €1.5 billion a year in net terms to the exchequer. Clearly a preferable alternative to cutting social welfare or raising primary school sizes, a reversal of benchmarking is an obvious priority step for the government to take. Ironically, such a cut would reverse the extent of benchmarking pay rises made in 2002, rises that Fine Gael opposed but are now too timid to reverse.

Even more ironically, the government that introduced and initially defended them is now not ruling out reversing them. As Brian Lenihan told me in interview, 'I'm ruling nothing out in terms of where we go on public expenditure, I'm ruling nothing out in terms of how we make the necessary savings.'

As Lenihan understands, and as Fine Gael do not seem to, two thirds of state spending involves transfer payments, salaries to public servants or welfare payments to social welfare recipients. The idea of ruling out any adjustment for public servants means that you have to have either an even bigger adjustment for social welfare recipients or you have to abolish state programmes. An Bord Snip was prevented for political reasons from examining cuts in public sector pay. But that didn't stop it recommending a new benchmarking exercise. Taking note of the ESRI research showing that – allowing for pensions – public servants were on average paid 12.5 per cent more than private sector workers, it called for such an exercise to recommend public sector pay cuts if needed. Even former Irish Congress of Trade Unions General

Secretary Peter Cassells says that when trade unions participated in social partnership negotiations in the 1980s they accepted that a competitive economy required a situation where secure public service employment was not better rewarded than equivalent private sector employment. But, eyeing public sector votes, Fine Gael is not embracing this principle. If it gets into government on this strategy – and it might – it is merely sowing the seeds of economic decay, and for an emaciation of its own traditional voting base, some years from now.

Fine Gael's position on the Stability Pact is also questionable. The perception that the party puts the country first put the wind behind its back in June 2009. But this advantage was eroded when it called for the five-year stability and growth programme – agreed with the EU Commission to stabilize public finances by 2013 – to be renegotiated.

According to Fine Gael, we should try and consolidate our public finances over a longer time period. Clearly, the party has learned nothing from its history in government during the 1980s when economic recovery was delayed because of a failure to act on public spending. Former Fine Gael Finance Minister Alan Dukes has acknowledged that the fiscal correction of the mid-1980s should have been implemented more quickly than it was. Between 1987 and 1989 Dukes supported Fianna Fáil Finance Minister Ray MacSharry's swift and decisive correction in public finances. MacSharry's feat – reducing state spending by 10 per cent of GDP in just two years – shows what can be done in a short space of time.

Fine Gael's policy of a long-drawn-out process of consolidation would certainly suit its desire to coalesce with the Labour Party. But as Brian Lenihan makes clear, it would inflict a fatal cost on our international credibility. 'The cost of money for Ireland will become prohibitive and it won't be sustainable in our own terms irrespective of what analysis we share with our colleagues and the commission . . . the quicker the approach to the correction the better, and we are starting off on a far more affluent basis this time.'

Lenihan is right, because it is absolutely crucial that Ireland's international reputation is upheld abroad. As bond market expert Donal O'Mahony has pointed out, 'the decline in Irish sovereign debt yield spreads – the premium paid on our borrowing costs from their mid-March 2009 peaks – has saved the exchequer in the region of seven hundred million euros in annual debt serving costs. Yet current spreads remain significantly wider than those implied by our AA credit rating thus betraying residual market unease regarding Ireland's economic and budgetary outlook'.

That unease is costing us enough to build several hospitals. Those who want to delay the correction will cost us even more.

Weighing advice from experts like O'Mahony, it is clear that Ireland must stick to its agreed deadline for fiscal correction. We must keep our promises and go further so that real benefits of tough action taken now can accrue to ordinary people before 2016.

But Lenihan is also right for a different reason: starting as we are from a position of far greater affluence and lower debt than in the 1980s, swifter action will have a lesser social impact than would have been the case in the 1980s. And with far more aggressive international competitors snapping at our heels than existed in the 1980s, we need to move much faster now.

Between July 2008 and April 2009 the government achieved a correction in our budget of around 5 per cent of GDP – half of what MacSharry achieved in two years. Its composition has been entirely wrong – by raising taxes rather than substantially cutting spending (which continues to increase), the government has cost the economy jobs and confidence – but the scale is still impressive. And hopeful. The challenge now is to achieve a symmetric 5 per cent reduction in public sector expenditure, starting with pay levels over €40,000 a year.

There is also a political reason for prioritizing not only control of public spending before reshaping the tax base, but also for prioritizing public pay reductions within the various other parts of spending reductions that need to occur.

Reshaping the tax base – as proposed by the Commission on Taxation[*] – will involve introducing highly charged taxes such as a property tax, a carbon tax and perhaps a wealth tax. In particular the property tax, linked as it is to funding local government, could cause explosive resentment at the inefficiency of our local government structures. Consolidating the number of local authorities and curbing their excesses is the price that must be paid before implementing any such taxes. And as no one trusts commitments on reform, that price must be paid first before any new taxes are implemented.

Within the overall drive to cut spending, An Bord Snip achieved notional savings of €5.3 billion per annum without even touching public sector pay. To meet its commitments under the stability and growth pact, which the government should stick to regardless of what Fine Gael says, it need only reduce spending by €4 billion per annum. A comprehensive reversal of benchmarking will achieve at least €1.5 billion of that in net savings. This must be implemented before any of the other measures. The argument for this is best expressed by Alan Barrett of the Economic and Social Research Institute. When I asked him what sequence of public spending reductions the ESRI would like to see, this is what he said: 'The ESRI's preference would be to see cuts in public sector pay . . . The income levy did go some way towards reducing the size of the gap. The levy averaged out at 7.5 per cent, the gap was 20 per cent, so we would still be of the view that there is still some way to go in closing the gap. We would prefer to see those wage cuts in the public sector as opposed to public services cuts which would have more damaging effects on the public more broadly.' Even those who don't share his economic viewpoint will see that, politically, his point is unarguable.

* See Appendix III

The sight of the government imposing welfare cuts and cuts in public services while leaving untouched a situation where public servants earn on average 12.5 per cent more than private sector workers would sound the death knell for any government foolish enough to pursue such a policy.

Finally, reform of public services more generally has to come before any implementation of the report of the Commission for Taxation. For instance, the recommendation for the introduction of a property tax will only be supportable if everything has been done to rationalize what it is funding: local government. The Ireland of the hundred governments – a reference to the 129 local authorities, town councils, borough councils and regional authorities – has to go. An Bord Snip does make welcome recommendations to reduce the number of local authorities from twenty-nine to twenty-two. For reasons other than fiscal ones the recommendation doesn't go far enough (see below), but it is a good idea of what the public needs to see if it is going to accept new forms of local taxation.

The public will also want to see public servants subject to the same kind of efficiencies as they are. Closed shops must be replaced by open recruitment at all levels of the public sector. As this has been introduced only to be stymied by resistance, it must be enforced by way of quota. Effective appraisal systems and bonus payments must be introduced to the public sector. Not the system to date, where everyone gets a bonus, but where bonuses are reserved for the top 10 or 20 per cent. Expensive and outdated differentials between largely redundant grades of management must be done away with, along with the salary increments that go with them. Public servants who either do not wish to or cannot cope with change should be excluded from promotion beyond a certain level. Promotion should henceforth be reserved for those who are willing to be appraised, to take risks and to risk punishment or sacking for incompetence. The option of the traditional secure form of employment should be kept as a respected but lower-profile option for the remainder. Finally, the myth of the generalist public servant performing wonders has been laid bare. Some generalists have performed their jobs in the public service to an excellent standard, but that reflects their own brilliance rather than their educational background. Expert opinion in economies, accountancy, human resource management, engineering and science and many more disciplines now needs to be brought into our public service by direct recruitment from outside. Only then can policy management reach the excellent standards needed to run the country to Scandinavian levels of efficiency.

Priority No. 4: Reshaping the Tax Base, 2012–2016

The final priority is to reshape the tax base. Some taxes – stamp duty and income levies – do not require a government report to justify action. At the earliest opportunity, they should be abolished.

Putting the entire tax base on a firmer footing for the future demands more care. The terrible mistakes of tax policy have been dealt with in chapter 5. The Minister for Finance recognizes that the priority is not to increase the burden of taxation – a strategy which has backfired – but to make it more sophisticated. 'I see little scope for increases in the general burden of taxation,' he said. 'There may be some limited scope in terms of carbon tax or household levy but the overall scope from substantial revenue-raising increases in the budget later this year is very, very limited.'

The worry here is that, due to the pressures of fiscal adjustment, tax changes will occur in a vacuum from other policy initiatives. As argued above, property taxes need to come after, not before, local authority reform.

Although the Commission on Taxation did not recommend it be changed, the individualization of tax bands must be reversed. Introduced at the behest of the Progressive Democrats, this retrograde and discriminatory tax penalizes mothers who wish to stay at home by forcing a family with a single income to pay up to €6,240 more* in tax than a double-income couple. A typical example of an economic policy that understands the price of everything and the value of nothing, this regime does the reverse of what the state should be doing: giving monetary recognition to the huge contribution made to society by full-time mothers.

It is also pernicious that at a time of mass unemployment the state is forcing women who don't want to work into the workplace, displacing other men and women who do but consequently cannot.

One specific measure that needs to be made by government is a clear definition of what it means by a fair distribution of income. As Revenue Commissioner figures show, Ireland's top earners pay an extraordinarily high share of income tax while the bottom 40 per cent pay virtually nothing. Yet trade unions responded to increases in the marginal tax with delight, stating that this was fair because the rich were being made to pay more. But if the top 3 per cent of earners already pay one third of income tax, isn't this way too much? And if one third pay almost nothing, isn't that too little? However you are inclined to answer, we should write down and stick to a schedule that describes a benchmark in terms of fairness. The unequal distribution of pre-tax incomes is a separate matter that needs to be dealt with by looking at other aspects of policy: inequal access to education, wealth transfers by inheritance, social snobbery and lack of social mobility within certain urban areas. But an eat-the-rich policy on taxation will simply do what our banking system did to bright entrepreneurs like John Collison, drive them away to America or somewhere else where their job-creating skills will be lost to us for ever. A hard lesson we must learn in the twenty-first century is that begrudgery is a disease we can't afford any more. It must finally be eradicated.

* Based on 2007 tax codes. The figure is taken from the study 'Tax Individualization: Time for a Critical Rethink', Iona Institute, 2007.

Finally, the government needs to ensure that whatever tax system is put in place is property-indexed. The tax system should avoid bringing taxpayers into higher bands of tax simply because inflation has pushed up their wages, house prices or their business turnover. The most efficient and modern tax systems index tax rates, and so should Ireland. It would also send an important signal to taxpayers, that future Finance Ministers will not patronize them by assuming they are too stupid to understand stealth taxation.

Economic Management: An Idea Whose Time Has Come

The lack of cohesion between different arms of Irish economic policy is both breathtaking and frightening. Fifty years after London obtained one, we still don't have a system of integrated ticketing for urban public transport. The absence of integrated public transport across the entire country could be seen as a valid reason why this is so. But rolling out such a system in areas of Dublin and Cork where sufficient public transport networks do exist will at least create a precedent – and public political pressure – to do what almost every other country in the EU does: provide comprehensive public transport roll-out on a national basis. Our attempts to roll out twenty-first-century infrastructure are constantly blocked and delayed by land-pricing mechanisms and local authority structures designed in and for the nineteenth century. We don't even have a strategy for regional economic or urban development. And even if we did, the chances of joining it up in any cohesive way with other arms of government policy are slim: An Bord Snip recommendations to cut the number of local authorities would still leave our capital, the driver of growth in the whole country, with four separate steering wheels.

Policy formation as it now stands is a collection of isolated, uncoordinated processes driven more by the demands of social partners than by a central, credible economic plan. Such plans as exist – those of the National Economic and Social Council (NESC), the National Economic and Social Forum (NESF) and the National Economic and Social Development Office (NESDO) – are strong in academic skills but too biased to the left and lacking in practical policy insight.

Social partnership is in a process of slow decline. If it is to be abolished, so be it. But whether it should or shouldn't be abolished should at least be considered carefully, decided upon, and communicated. There is too much drift in public policy, and too little strategy. If partnership is to be redesigned, it must be designed to be dominated by the majority of citizens and to strongly represent the most modern, productive and progressive parts of the economy.

There should also be a comprehensive review of the statistics we need to monitor the progress of the economy. The Central Statistics Office has made good strides with the Measuring Ireland's Progress series, but a much more comprehensive dashboard of indicators – particularly on competitiveness, on sectoral trends in labour markets, and on the responsiveness of our tax and state spending to the economic cycle – will be needed to steer Ireland Inc. back to safety. And, as Garrett Fitzgerald has advocated, we need a council of wise men and women, drawn equally from academic and non-academic economic traditions (that is, theoretical as well as applied), to guide and comment on the evolution of economic policies.

There are also fundamental political changes that need to occur. These are the subject of the final chapter.

14

Civil War, RIP

I am concerned about the fact that the political system
of the country is ill equipped to put the country first.
FINANCE MINISTER BRIAN LENIHAN TD, JULY 2009

War is Over If You Want It

It was my privilege, when writing this book, to be granted
interviews with many important people at the centre of Irish
economic and political life. I have opened this final chapter with
the man most preoccupied with our current crisis, Brian Lenihan,
the Finance Minister at the time of writing. After ten years of
cheering on and re-electing a government as it was making
chronic economic mistakes, the electorate has suddenly turned
on the very people who are trying to clean up the mess. Fianna
Fáil was never more popular than in 2006 when it was presiding
over disastrous rises in borrowing and spending. And it was
never less popular in its history than when making strenuous
efforts to do the right thing: in September 2009 an opinion

287

poll* showed support for Lenihan's party at 17 per cent – around one third of the heights enjoyed in 2006 and its all-time lowest level. By default rather than acclaim, Fine Gael enjoyed 34 per cent of the vote. In most European countries it is normal for an opposition party to enjoy a substantial lead over the government in times of crisis. Ireland is just getting used to the idea that Fianna Fáil is no longer the most popular party in the country. The real winner of the poll is Ireland's Labour Party. On 24 per cent, it at last appears to be normalizing support for the left, which in Ireland has been traditionally low.

For outsiders, the two main parties are hard to tell apart. Fine Gael has always seemed to have brains. Fianna Fáil has always seemed to have political brawn. But the legacy of the civil war politics has kept them apart. Like former leader Dr Garrett Fitzgerald with Fine Gael, Brian Lenihan is also candid about his party's past failings. 'I recall after Charles Haughey was elected leader of Fianna Fáil he made an address to the nation, in 1980, in which he said that we were living beyond our means and then he failed to take action about it and the economy drifted for a number of years and I was among those within Fianna Fáil who were unhappy at his failure to take action at that stage.'

From their separate parties and from across Ireland's old civil war divide, Fitzgerald and Lenihan – scions of perhaps Ireland's two oldest political clans – are now saying more or less the same thing. Lenihan honestly acknowledges his party's difficulty in confronting tough decisions. Fitzgerald acknowledges the failings of his own party in opposition. Explaining his decision to enter politics by joining Fine Gael, George Lee said he wanted to respond to the failure of Fianna Fáil to govern properly. But as far as their respective preparations for the coming economic disaster were concerned, there was – as Fitzgerald's quote from the beginning of chapter 6 makes clear – no alternative to Fianna Fáil in

* TSN/MRBI poll in *Irish Times*, 3 September 2009.

2007. It has been stated before, but it bears repetition: it isn't just Fianna Fáil that has failed the country, it is the entire political system. Lock, stock and barrel.

In their heart of hearts, our party leaders know that our electoral system is broken, our systems of local governance are defunct and our political dialogue is immature and bankrupt to the point of parody. They know too that our land laws belong in the mists of medieval time, that our social partnership system needs drastic reform and that our tradition of deference to vested interests has ruined public finances and broken our banking system. But they daren't say it. They daren't say it because of the power our seismically sensitive electoral system gives those who benefit from silence. And by refusing to coalesce, Fine Gael and Fianna Fáil prevent each other and the country from realizing exactly what it needs: a cohesive majority government strong enough at last to implement the interests of the Irish people – the long-term collective interests – over the short-term partisan interests of our current power brokers. This would also allow the left to regroup and consolidate to the point of being able to provide a stable left-dominated government, where at present there exists only a loose constellation of fragmented and mainly small parties.

But, slowly, things are changing. From the levels in the 1980s, the percentage support commanded by Fianna Fáil and Fine Gael put together has gradually but inexorably declined to levels of around 51 per cent in the September 2009 elections. From the comfort zone of post-colonial adolescence, Ireland's political system appears to be starting out on a dramatic journey of transition. But to what?

If the trend decline in support for the two main parties in the Dáil continues, they will command at some election in the future, possibly the near future, combined support of less than 50 per cent. Like the apple falling on Newton's head, the realization will finally dawn: there is only one stable cohesive two-party coalition that can meet the country's needs, a joint government comprising Fianna Fáil and Fine Gael. A closure, if you will, of the ancient clannish cleavage that has warped our governance these past eighty years. The question is, can that realization come in time to avert a disaster that could happen were an election to be called? Although an alternative government exists – Fine Gael and Labour – how cohesive would it be? Such coalitions work well in conditions like the mid-1990s, where problems can be solved by opening state coffers. These are not such times. This is not to suggest that the left could not provide an equally good government. But not yet. Until support for the left congeals around a single party with the support of at least one fifth of the electorate, it cannot provide that combination of numerical stability and cohesion of values. If that changes, then good luck to the left. Until it does, we must look elsewhere for strong government in stormy conditions.

There are several signs that the mutual antipathy between Fianna Fáil and Fine Gael is waning, or at least becoming less emotional. In June 2009 Garrett Fitzgerald asked Fine Gael voters to support Fianna Fáil's candidate for the European elections. In the local elections many Fianna Fáil voters switched directly to Fine Gael. The Irish people still support the objective of a United Ireland. They still support the Irish language. And, surprisingly, they are more reluctant than the media would believe to abandon their Church: religious attendance has revived thanks to the recession, and in spite of scandals. But some traditions are more questionable.

A Lesson from Recent History

The political birth of the Celtic Tiger can be traced to the collaboration, across the party political divide, of two men. Shortly after becoming the new Fine Gael leader in the spring of 2007, Alan Dukes gave a speech in the Dublin suburb of Tallaght.

Dukes had been Finance Minister between 1983 and 1986 and had, under the duress of realpolitik, been forced to attempt a budgetary correction by raising taxes and cutting spending. The approach failed, but the blame was not his. Thanks to Fine Gael's flawed decision to enter government with Labour – a decision that was equally bad for the latter – it was a government that was destined to fail. And if seven years later a similar combination was to appear successful it was only because of the fair fiscal winds at its back.

With Fine Gael reduced from seventy to fifty-one seats and seen as responsible for the state of the country's economy, Dukes correctly perceived that his party had some obligation to put things right. Beyond all expectations, that is what he did.

On the other side of the divide, Fianna Fáil had won an election, but not a majority, on the promise of opposing any cuts in health and social welfare spending. The logical conclusion of its position was that the cutbacks that were so badly needed, and which the outgoing government had planned but failed to agree on, would be scrapped in favour of a Latin American reflation of the economy. With unemployment running at around 20 per cent and government debt at 120 per cent, the country was teetering on the brink of insolvency. An experiment of the kind envisaged by Fianna Fáil's self-proclaimed mandate would have pushed it over the edge.

As Finance Minister, Ray MacSharry was working to convince his leader Charles Haughey to change tack. Five years earlier Fianna Fáil had scrabbled together a majority with backbenchers and TDs from the ultra left. The inherent instability that resulted paralysed the government and its inconsistency caused it to collapse. But now everything had changed.

In his Tallaght speech, Alan Dukes offered to support the government from the backbenches on condition that it address the country's finances. Although a social democrat of centre-left orientation, Dukes was an economist who understood that the choices were hard. Either consolidate now on Irish terms, with some prospect of preserving a social democratic project at some point in the future, or watch the IMF destroy that prospect for ever.

It was sixty-five years since the civil war had ruptured the two parties. For two brief years that division was suspended, and in that time a 10 per cent reduction in public spending was achieved. What followed has been described in detail in chapter 5, but it is no exaggeration to say that those two short years saved Ireland from a disastrous fate. And more. The growth in population – of one million persons, one third of the initial population – the doubling in real incomes, the flourishing of a vibrant and young population able to make a future in Ireland for the first time in two centuries, and the rebirth of pride and culture and sense of place that Ireland has achieved – all of these things owe their parentage to these two years, during which these two people played perhaps the central role. The recession will knock this country back a couple of years, for sure. But it cannot take away more than a fraction of what has been achieved since then. Nor will it. But a great deal still depends on what happens next.

Under Enda Kenny, Fine Gael has become less hostile to Republican values and more mindful of the need not to alienate conservative core voters that could otherwise switch to Fianna Fáil. Fianna Fáil has moved a long way from its past incarnations. But for as long as both parties refuse to contemplate government with each other, and with only parties on the left to appeal for transfers since the PDs disappeared, both Fianna Fáil and Fine Gael are like greyhounds on a racetrack with lead weights behind their left ear. If the tax increases in the budgets of October 2008 and April 2009 prove anything, it is that economically disastrous policies will still be implemented if they are deemed politically expedient. Fine Gael's refusal to accept the need to reverse benchmarking pay increases shows the same. Its need to win three out of five seats in a constituency like Dublin South explains it. With the PDs gone and with the only non-Fianna Fáil candidates on the left, the primal battle with the ancient enemy can only be won with left-wing transfers.

Brian Lenihan illustrated how this very consideration paralysed government in the early 1980s. 'My own father was a member of that administration,' he told me, 'so naturally I discussed it with him and the impression I found was that Mr Haughey was afraid of the electoral system and was afraid of the fact that he would lose so much support, and in some respects he was right because he postponed action in 1980, then in 1981 Garrett Fitzgerald took office and began to take action, then they lost action, they lost government in early 1982, and by the time Garrett Fitzgerald came back into office later in 1982 he found it impossible to obtain Labour agreement to the kind of decisive action that was needed.'

Is it a coincidence that the 1980s crisis emerged at a time when there was no smaller party – a party not trying to catch all votes from left to right – to challenge the right of the state to keep increasing public spending? Surely not. Now, over two decades later, we are back in the same situation. With the PDs gone, Fianna Fáil and Fine Gael can no longer outdo each other by courting PD votes, only by courting votes from the left. This point is not made against the left, but rather against the lack of balance in the system: however they may be described by some as being of the right, Fianna Fáil and Fine Gael are essentially pragmatic parties of the centre.

But what if the primal struggle were to end? What if both parties were to think outside the box, and join forces? When Fianna Fáil did finally grasp the nettle of action in 1987, Fine Gael's agreement to cooperate was instrumental. Lenihan again: 'I think what Alan Dukes did in 1987 was very good from a national point of view . . . many older Fine Gael figures like Peter Sutherland and Garrett Fitzgerald have endorsed the strategy taken by the government.'

The reference to Fitzgerald and Sutherland is key. Twenty years ago, neither would have dared to endorse any policy from a Fianna Fáil government. On a whole host of issues the two parties are now closer than ever before. Both are united on Ireland's role in Europe as defined by the Lisbon referendum, and on achieving national reunification by constitutional means. By contrast, the divergences between the Labour Party and Fine Gael are growing. Fine Gael wants to privatize non-essential state assets, Labour is opposed to this. Fine Gael wants to suspend public pay rises and increments, Labour is opposed to this. Fine Gael wants sweeping reforms to the public sector, reforms that would get the trade unions who fund Labour up in arms. Fine Gael want 15,000 public sector redundancies. Labour want no such thing. Fine Gael stops short of reversing benchmarking pay increases. Its policy agenda doesn't go far enough to cure the public finances. But it goes far enough to alienate much of Labour's traditional vote.

If anything, Fianna Fáil is closer to the Labour Party. And therein lies a huge risk for Fine Gael. The risk is that while being too far away from Labour for comfort, the efforts Fine Gael has made to position itself for government with Labour will destroy its credibility with its core voters. These include refusing to reverse the 2002 benchmarking pay rises it so strongly opposed, opposing the 2013 deadline for consolidating the country's finances and calling for yet more tax increases on higher earners, when even its social democratic former leader Garrett Fitzgerald has called instead for income taxes to be increased on the 38 per cent of lower-income earners who currently pay little or none.

In summary, Fine Gael risks falling between two stools. It could – it is indeed likely to – win the next election. In fact it stands a chance of replacing Fianna Fáil as the largest party in the Dáil for the first time in eighty years. But Irish politics has changed. In the mid-1990s Ruairi Quinn understood that in coalition with Fine Gael it would be essential for Labour's left flank to be guarded. The introduction of Democratic Left was instrumental in preventing that government being destabilized from outside, 1980s style. As we approach the second decade of the new millennium Labour faces far more aggressive competition on its left. Although not as strong as a few years ago, Sinn Fein is far more robust now than in the 1990s. And there is the Socialist Party. And the People before Profit Alliance. And unlike Democratic Left, these are not groups that can be easily accommodated in government.

The key difference between the 1990s and now is not political but economic. Even if the economy recovers, so damaged is the tax base that it will take five years before any kind of tax buoyancy is likely to emerge. In the 1990s tax revenues were plentiful. The government could increase spending to please Labour and Democratic Left, cut taxes to please Fine Gael and still meet the Maastricht deficit criterion of keeping deficits below 3 per cent of GDP. Such luxuries do not await a Fine Gael/Labour government in the near future. And even if the economy recovers in the medium term, tax revenues will take longer to follow suit, depriving Labour and Fine Gael of the weapon they used in the 1990s to paper over ideological cracks – money. At the same time, Fine Gael's up-and-coming frontbenchers are more to the right than ever before. The prospects of stability in such a combination have never been worse. And they will deteriorate, not improve, with time.

Options and Scenarios

George Lee's stunning performance aside, Fine Gael's ability to form a cabinet of experienced ministers grows more difficult with every year it spends out of government. By the time of the next election, three decades will have elapsed since it was last democratically elected to government. On 34 per cent of the vote it would be likely to win around sixty-five seats in the Dáil. Even if it surges to a level closer to 40 per cent, coalition with a smaller party would realistically mean Sinn Fein – anathema to a hard-core but important minority of its supporters. But 34 per cent represents a likely mid-term peak. With the economy set to improve, Fine Gael's vote may yet fall back to the high twenties, and Fianna Fáil's may yet rise back above 30 per cent.

The prospects for government with Labour are also complicated by the fact that the fiscal weather for the next five years is, for the left, cold. In government with Fine Gael, Labour could find its core vote emaciated, particularly given the relatively old nature of its parliamentary base.

There are alternatives open to Fine Gael besides the Labour Party. There are also alternatives open to the Labour Party besides Fine Gael. For Labour the alternative is to pursue a tactical alliance with Sinn Fein of the kind pursued with Democratic Left in the 1990s. It would mean abandoning Labour's antipathy towards nationalist ideals and rediscovering its Republican roots in the tradition of James Connolly. But there's no harm in that for Labour.

On the other hand, were history to repeat itself in the form of a Labour/Fianna Fáil coalition – an unlikely event – Fine Gael would be given a huge opportunity to consolidate its position as the largest party in the country. This would be strongly in the interests of its younger TDs who are more ideologically traditional and can afford to wait longer for government. Older frontbenchers, on the other hand, might not favour this option which could rule them out of ever serving in government. This outcome is unlikely in that for Labour it could involve a loss of credibility. For Fianna Fáil it would involve paying a high price for Labour to accept such a loss.

Should Fianna Fáil lose a substantial number of seats as implied by June 2009 election results and the September poll, it might be impossible for Labour to justify going into government with it even if its leadership were to contemplate the option. No mandate would exist for it. A coalition with Labour based on

Labour's agenda could be justified, depending on how well Labour does. But this is highly unlikely to be accepted by Fianna Fáil.

There is another scenario, one that takes us back to the Tallaght strategy and the question of the civil war. Should Fine Gael outseat Fianna Fáil, Fianna Fáil might see the advantage of pursuing a Tallaght strategy-style tactic of supporting a minority Fine Gael government. Ideological tension would be likely to be lessened, compared to either a Labour/Fine Gael or Labour/Fianna Fáil arrangement. And given Fianna Fáil's need to redeem itself with the electorate, this would also be appropriate for electoral reasons. For the left it would be an excellent opportunity to attract what remains of the left-wing vote that still goes to Fine Gael or Fianna Fáil.

It looks impossible at present. But then many impossible things have come to pass on this island. If once mortal enemies like Sinn Fein and the DUP can govern together, why can't Fine Gael and Fianna Fáil? The statistical odds are not as low as they seem. In my interview with Garrett Fitzgerald, he confirmed, albeit in qualified terms, that the latest set of election results confirms a downward trend for both parties: 'Note that 2009 results are the results of European elections and as such may somewhat overstate the decline in support for Fine Gael and Fianna Fáil. This notwithstanding, support for both these parties in joint terms was lower in the 2009 European election than in the 2004 European election, suggesting that, on a like for like basis, the former election indicates a fall in joint support for the two largest parties that would reflect itself in a general election, albeit less severely.'

The steady decline in the two parties' combined support levels, and the increasing disinclination of voters to preserve civil war loyalties – only about a third of those under twenty-five really care which party gets into power, as shown in table 4 (see Appendix I) – suggests that coalition between the parties may be inevitable in the near future. But such a coalition is arguably necessary now. If necessary now and inevitable in future, there is a strong case for contemplating it immediately, especially if it can potentially rescue the country from disaster.

Fitzgerald warns that such a government could present its own disasters. 'We don't have a big enough left in Ireland. Firstly you need a government but then you need an opposition with a real possibility of getting into government because without that governments become lazy, inefficient and possibly even corrupt, if they have too big a majority and there is no way of getting rid of them.' Right now, he would be right. But the glacial melt in support for the two parties weakens the consideration, as does the fact that such a coalition would drive some Fianna Fáil supporters towards Sinn Fein and some Fine Gael supporters towards Labour. Growth in the left would under such a coalition be assured. The question is whether it would be growth in a consolidated or a fragmented left.

Alternatively, the two parties could merge. But what kind of party would they produce? It was an Irish philosopher, Edmund Burke, who invented conservatism as a political value system. And Ireland is a conservative country. Yet it is the only country in Europe without an avowedly conservative party. The left describe the two main parties as conservative, but this is only true in a 'small c' sense of the word. Ideologically, both parties have to date steered clear of espousing a thought-out philosophy in European terms. There is no Irish 'right' to speak of at present. What some on the left regard as the 'right' is really just a cautious mentality towards change. A dynamic one-nation conservatism – in the continental European sense rather than the British or American sense – could resonate with our political culture strongly, and in several ways.

Firstly, it would be different from the neo-liberalism of the US Republican Party. More open to the social market economy, it would reflect the values of the German, Dutch and Belgian

Christian Democratic parties. Those values are more consistent with a responsible role for the state in planning and guiding important aspects of policy, like land use, planning, transport and regulation. They are hostile to the short-term free-for-all that has characterized the world economy of late.

It also offers an approach to something which even the most right-wing economist must accept is holding Ireland back. As school league table results make clear, Ireland is a land of huge inequality of opportunity, an inequality conferred by unequal access to schooling. That unequal opportunity is reinforced by massive differences in inherited wealth and differing access to social networks. Like Liberals, Christian Democrats believe in an inequality that reflects merit and achievement. Unlike them, they accept the need for a lower bound to that inequality, as well as the need for a well-defined and fair and stable social contract, one particularly characterized by equity, i.e. equal access to education, basic access to quick and decent healthcare, and a process of socialization that removes obstacles to social mobility. None of these three things exist in Ireland.

There are two further meanings to the words 'one nation'. A union between Fianna Fáil and Fine Gael would finally lay to rest a split that has long outlived its usefulness. In its own way, the split between Labour and Sinn Fein replicates on the left the split between Fine Gael and Fianna Fáil on the right and a merger between those two parties would complete a transition in Irish politics that has arguably been a long time coming, a ninety-degree rotation in the axis along which Irish politics is organized from one that separates nationalists and non-nationalists on either side to one that separates right from left.

Finally, the 'one nation' description would begin perhaps the most important political project of the century: the reunification of the island of Ireland. As a Republican party, Fianna Fáil faces obstacles in achieving a reunited Ireland. Firstly, its political image resonates poorly with many unionists in the north.

Secondly, its economic record of late blunts its ability to deliver the key message about a united Ireland: its undoubted economic advantages, the recession notwithstanding.

A point needs to be made here in relation to both Fianna Fáil and Fine Gael's existing identities and the obstacles they might place in the way of unity. Fianna Fáil sees itself as a Republican party in the nationalist sense of the word. But any objection to unifying with a 'less nationalist' Fine Gael should meet with three responses. Firstly, it was Fine Gael that founded the Irish Republic in 1949. Secondly, a joined party could assert the mission of a united Ireland far more effectively than either party can separately. Thirdly, as far as Republicanism goes, Fianna Fáil needs to reconcile its understanding of that word with the more common understanding of it as government of the people by the people and for the people. Its recent spell in government renders that meaning of the word a little too ironic for it to be used with any effect.

As for Fine Gael objections, it might argue that it is on the cusp of power and should not now reconcile itself with an old enemy. But Fine Gael should not be deluded either by its June 2009 performance or the September 2009 opinion poll results. Not only is its current rating 34 per cent below its all-time high of 39 per cent, in 1982, the satisfaction rating of its leader is also far lower, and in net terms negative,* than back then. The electorate may use Fine Gael to register a strong protest against the government, but come a general election the competence and leadership displayed by parties will weigh heavily with voters. The electorate is certainly in no mood to elect Fianna Fáil into power at the next election, but were changes to occur in the faces that party presents, voters might swing back to it on the grounds of its more experienced personalities. Had Fine Gael based its

---

* According to the aforementioned poll (see previous footnote), significantly more voters disapprove than approve of Enda Kenny's leadership style.

election manifesto on principle in 2007 it would now be in a strong position to consolidate what it thinks it achieved in 2009. But it isn't. Doubts about Fine Gael's resolve on policy matters will not go away, and Garrett Fitzgerald himself says that Fianna Fáil could yet recover. 'Fianna Fáil is a very efficient organization,' he warns, 'and I am sure they will in time recover some of the ground lost. If the government manages to stay in power the position in two or three years' time may be quite different.'

Whether he's right or wrong, one thing seems certain: like no time since the 1940s, the civil war party system is in serious decline. Fianna Fáil is certainly in dire trouble. If offered competence and strong and decisive policies by one of the two civil war parties, the public will choose it. But they are not fools. If both parties show a lack of resolve and an indecision when confronting unavoidable issues such as public spending or land reform, the public will continue to turn away from them. Until the left consolidates, this drift will be a drift into a fractious void of contentious and squabbling small parties. Just when it needs strong and stable government like never before in its history, Ireland could become ungovernable.

Political Reform

As chapter 6 argued, party politics aside, the time has come to realize that even if it served us well in the past, our political system is now unfit for purpose. Under social partnership, single transferable voting has become a dictatorship of insiders and vested interests. The civil war party system has accentuated this, allowing lobby groups to drive a wedge between parties that ought to be cooperating in the national interest.

Our Oireachtas needs reform. The Senate is a potentially good forum, but needs to be given more power, to act as a check and balance against the kind of reckless spending binges pre-election budgets have inflicted on the economy by at least being able to control the size if not the composition of budgets, and their impact on debt. And it should have the power to bring our financial regulators and public sector to book. To be given such powers it must be reformed so that its franchise is universal. To conform with a proper separation of powers, its electoral term must overlap with, rather than coincide with, the Dáil. If elected two years before the Dáil, its exercise of any powers in relation to budgetary matters will not be unduly swayed by a general election. In fact, if elected in mid-term its majority is less likely to be in the gift of government.

There is also a need for electoral reform. Proportional representation is a good basis for democracy, but the single transferable vote has failed the Irish people spectacularly. A list system, whereby voters can elect the party, could be blended with a direct mandate, whereby they can elect a personality, to give the best of both worlds: politicians who are locally responsible but also nationally minded and well educated enough for cabinet responsibility.

The removal of the multi-seat constituency will also stabilize Irish politics and policymaking. How, after all, can we expect sensible and cohesive policies from any Irish government when ministers must watch their constituency backs at every twist and turn? Is it any wonder that no one from successful private sector organizations wants to enter a political system where you need to fear your friends more than your enemies? Garrett Fitzgerald is scathing about the impact of the multi-seat constituency on policymaking and on the type of politicians that get elected. 'It means that ministers are under pressure and a lot of time is wasted on constituency work. This is happening in an already clientelist society. The kind of people who get elected are those who most respond to clientelist pressures and it is obvious that our whole society is vulnerable to an electoral system manned by people who are chosen on a clientelist basis and whose orientation is towards meeting local and public pressures and who do not have the education, the formation and the experience of taking wise policy decisions.'

He is absolutely right. When we look back on the last decade, half of it a period of utter disaster, there is a growing temptation to blame Bertie Ahern for all that went wrong in Ireland's economy. We forget that we elected him three times in a row. We forget that his flaws – an anti-intellectual resentment against smarter colleagues who might as ministers have prevented many of the mistakes made – and all the damage they did were the product of a deeply unequal social contract and a chaotic and dysfunctional system that forces Irish politicians to choose between the shabbiest of compromise or the most devastating career failure.

It is time to stop knocking Ireland. It is time to stop blaming this or that sector for what has gone wrong. It is time to accept responsibility, collectively, morally and politically, for what has gone wrong. As voters and citizens we now need to rise up and return the Irish nation to its rightful owners. As I write the final sentences of this book there are seven years left to the centennial celebrations of the 1916 Rising. We must use them to undertake a collective national project: creating a real Republic.

Appendices

I: Tables

Table 1: Irish and Euro Zone inflation

	1996	1997	1998	1999	2000	2001	2002	2003	Cumulative percentage point difference 1996–2003
Ireland	+1.6	+1.5	+2.4	+1.6	+5.6	+4.9	+4.6	+3.5	
Clothing & Footwear	*–6.8*	*–5.3*	*–6.3*	*–4.9*	*–2.8*	*–4.3*	*–4.0*	*–3.5*	
Health	*+3.3*	*+5.4*	*+5.7*	*+7.1*	*+7.5*	*+10.0*	*+7.7*	*+6.0*	
Euro Zone	+2.2	+1.6	+1.1	+1.1	+2.1	+2.3	+2.2	+2.1	
	–0.6	–0.1	+1.3	+0.5	+3.5	+2.6	+2.4	+1.4	+11.0

Source: Eurostat, Central Statistics Office

Table 2: From Tiger to something else

	1997	2004 (end year)	2008
Export growth	17.50%	7.5%	−1%
Investment growth	18.90%	9.60%	−15.5%
GDP growth	11.50%	4.50%	−2.80%
Private Sector Credit	circa 100bn	200bn	400bn
Construction employment	110,000	206,000	268,000
Percentage total	*8.0%*	*11.2%*	*13.6%*

Table 3: Budgetary history and projections

	1997	2004	2008	2012
Gross government spending	23.7 billion	45.7 billion	68 billion	76 billion
Debt / GDP level	64.30%	29.40%	25%	79.70%
Gross spending as % share of GDP	39.80%	36.20%	42.40%	49%

Source: Department of Finance, April 2009 Budget, EU Commission, Spring 2009 forecasts (Colm McCarthy)

Table 4: Declining party loyalty: how much does it matter to you which party wins the election?

Age range	…a great deal	…somewhat	…very little	…not at all	…don't know
All	34.1	26.6	18.2	14.4	6.7
18–19	16.7	20.6	24.2	21.1	17.4
20–24	24.9	26.9	19	15.6	13.5
25–34	31.3	27.9	18.6	15.7	6.2
35–44	35.1	27.9	17.7	15.1	3.8
45–54	37.3	27.3	17.9	13.1	4.1
55–64	39.8	25.6	18.1	12.4	3.8
65+	41	24.8	16.2	12.1	5.4

Table 5: A comparison of price trends for traded and non-traded sectors

	Consumer Price Index (Base Dec 2006=100)	Percentage change	Jan-05	May-09
All items	92.3	102.4		10.9%
Health	93.5	111.8	NT	19.6%
Hairdressing	89.3	108.8	NT	21.8%
Insurance	99	119.8	NT	21.0%
Clothing and footwear	88.3	83.2	T	−5.8%
Computers	139.7	56.2	T	−59.8%
Furnishings and household	99.7	94.3	T	−5.4%

Table 6: Salaries and bonuses for CEOs of Irish banks in 2007

	Annual Salary (euro)	Annual Bonus (euro)	Share of property/ mortgages on Loan Book	Description in Annual Report of reason for bonuses
Brian Goggin, Bank of Ireland	1,155,000	323,000	70%	Earnings per share growth
Eugene Sheehy, AIB	916,000	850,000	59%	Specific performance-related objectives
David Drumm, Anglo-Irish Bank	956,000	2,000,000	94% in 2006	Paid once financial results for the year independently audited
Michael Fingleton, Nationwide Building Society	812,000	1,400,000		'Bonuses are recognized to the extent that the Society has a present obligation to its employees'
Denis Casey, Irish Life and Permanent	694,000	617,000	93.76%	Related to the achievement of 'additional stretching performance targets'

Source: Annual Reports of Financial Institutions

II: National Asset Management Agency (NAMA)

Basics of NAMA

As of 16 September, the Irish government proposes to purchase from five financial institutions (AIB, Bank of Ireland, Anglo-Irish Bank, Irish Nationwide and the Educational Building Society) property loans with a book value of €77 billion (which includes €9 billion in rolled-up interest payments, so €68 billion of original loan value) for €54 billion. The original value of the properties against which these loans were secured is estimated at €88 billion, but due to the collapse in the property market their current market value is estimated by NAMA to be €47 billion. The €54 billion will be paid to the banks in the form of bonds which they can then use as collateral to borrow from the ECB and, in theory, on-lend to the rest of the economy. This higher valuation is based on the assumption that the 'long-term economic value' of these properties is higher than their current value, which the government argues is artificially low due to the distressed state of the economy.

Thus the government is paying €7 billion more for these loans than the collateral for them is currently worth. The argument for doing so is to remove from the Balance Sheet of banks loans which are bad and uncertain and therefore mitigate against the banks increasing lending (given the need, as discussed in chapter 2, to ensure an adequate asset base to support further lending). The government says that if property prices appreciate by 10 per cent in the coming decade then the taxpayer will – assuming it can sell off all the properties underlying the loans – fully recoup the €7 billion overpayment. To provide some degree of cushioning against property prices not recovering as expected, €2.7 billion worth of the bonds is payable in subordinated bonds, the payment of which is conditional upon the properties achieving their expected 'long-term economic value'. This change was introduced after Professor Patrick Honohan, who was subsequently appointed Central Bank Governor, recommended that the banks should bear some of the risk that properties might fail to attain long-term economic values. It was also supported by the Green Party. It aims to protect the taxpayer to some degree by introducing risk sharing between the taxpayer and banks, as does the Minister for Finance's promise, if kept, to introduce an additional levy on banks to cover any further shortfall in the values obtained by NAMA for properties when finally sold.

The fact that those borrowers who took out these loans to the banks will still have to repay – in theory – creates the possibility of the taxpayer making a profit. However, the proposal has been widely criticized – nationally and internationally – and remains controversial.

The Green Party have obtained some modifications of the plan, including the sharing of the risk that properties sold might fail to attain long-term economic values and also a requirement that all directors of institutions participating in NAMA will be required to step down, a 'social dividend' from NAMA – namely that some of the properties taken over will be used for health and education purposes – and that a fixed percentage of loans issued will be lent to small and medium-sized interests. At a 'preferendum' held by members of the Green Party, there was significantly stronger support for a modified NAMA than for alternative proposals forwarded by the Fine Gael, Labour and Sinn Fein opposition parties (see below).

Criticisms of NAMA

Although it gives banks greater freedom to lend, the NAMA approach does not guarantee that they will. On the other hand, the extent to which lending should increase in the economy is a question that perhaps needs separate consideration from NAMA. NAMA may be a necessary but insufficient condition for lending in the economy to increase; other necessary conditions – improved competitiveness, consumer confidence and a stabilized or falling tax burden – may need to complement NAMA in this regard and their present absence does not necessarily mean that NAMA is not a necessary precondition.

It is also argued that the taxpayer faces a large risk if properties do not sell for their long-term economic value. There is a risk that a proportion of the properties could decline in value – the logic behind the valuations is not clear – or that the loans they underly may be non-performing.

Although higher than current market values, the valuation of the properties is not high enough to prevent the need to further recapitalize the banks. NCB stockbrokers have suggested a further 7.5 billion of taxpayers' money will be needed to recapitalize the banks. This higher debt will add further to the cost of government borrowing.

There is also a funding issue. The bonds required to purchase the loans must themselves be borrowed by government and hence interest must be repaid. Even aside from whether their principal value is repaid, sufficient interest from the borrowers who took out the loans being purchased by government is needed to make sure the government can cover its funding costs.

NAMA is also criticized for being a state agency that lacks the expertise of managing and selling such assets. Some (leading financier Dermot Desmond, for example) have argued that instead of buying the loans outright the state should merely guarantee bonds that the banks would issue themselves. Those banks and their shareholders would then face the risk of the properties not reaching full value and would therefore, it is argued, be better incentivized to maximize the return/minimize the losses from them.

The issue of phantom equity has arisen. In theory the developers lose the deposit they raised before buying the loan: the €68 billion original value of loans corresponds to €88 billion original value in the property acquired, implying a significant deposit. However, some developers may have borrowed in order to stump up these deposits.

Alternatives to NAMA

Fine Gael's 'Good bank bad bank' solution Pointing to France, Fine Gael has advocated the establishment of a good bank. Under this system a wholesale bank, a 'National Recovery Bank' would be set up by government to lend to banks who would on-lend to the economy. Fine Gael propose an initial injection of €2 billion which, it argues, could leverage €20 billion worth of new lending. The recovery bank would purchase the good loans from banks and encourage them to ask their bondholders to swap debt for equity, to raise equity capital privately and to sell off distressed loans. Banks themselves will continue to manage the other assets on their loan books (Fine Gael argues they have better expertise in doing so). This, they argue, will minimize the loss to the taxpayer. Instead, bank shareholders and subordinated debt holders will face the risk. The government has criticized Fine Gael's approach by saying it would expose the property market to 'firesale' property prices. The government also maintains that, because subordinated debt holders could in theory lose their investment, this would damage Ireland's credibility abroad and make it more difficult for Irish financial institutions to raise capital (Fine Gael has responded by arguing that in the case of several troubled banks such as Bayern LandesBank (December 2008) the EU Commission instructed several banks not to pay interest on subordinated bonds, thereby giving non-payment an official seal of approval).

Labour and Sinn Fein's approach of Nationalization Labour and Sinn Fein have advocated nationalization of the banks. Pointing to Sweden's successful resolution of its banking crisis of the early 1990s, they say temporary national ownership of the banks can give the taxpayer an opportunity to purchase the banks at low prices. Shareholders and bond-holders would then suffer the losses justified by the risk they took. The approach has been criticized on the basis that, unlike Sweden, Ireland is in the euro and therefore not in a position to reflate its economy by lowering the value of its currency, a factor which helped Sweden's policy to work (the effect of inflation on debt is the reverse of the effect of deflation on debt discussed in chapter 2). Also objections have been raised on the grounds that Ireland's culture of public ownership is not as transparent or effective as in Sweden.

Dermot Desmond's proposal In the final days of the NAMA debate, financier Dermot Desmond proposed in the Irish Times (Friday 11 September) that the state should guarantee any bonds issued by banks, but leave them to manage their existing loans themselves. The state would charge a fee for this guarantee and force banks availing of it to establish 'Delinquent Asset Management' subsidiary companies which would hold all the assets that would otherwise be bought by NAMA. It would also require banks to pay no dividends to ordinary shareholders and prevent the acquisition of overseas assets by banks, thus encouraging them to lend to Irish interests instead. Desmond has argued that this arrangement would allow liquidity into the banking system but prevent a situation in which politicians and public servants could interfere in the valuation of loans. He also argues that as banks would retain responsibility to manage their bad loans, they would be better incentivized to maximize their value/minimize their loss. Desmond's proposal has been criticized for being made too late to have any impact on national debate.

III: Proposals contained in the Report of the Commission for Taxation

A comprehensive list of recommendations in the report, published in September 2009, is beyond the scope of this book. However, some key recommendations were:

- To broaden the base of taxation away from the over-reliance on property-related tax revenues that built up in recent years.
- To retain the 12.5 per cent rate of corporation tax.
- The integration of pay-related social insurance, health levies and income levies (introduced in October 2008 and increased in April 2009) into an integrated rate of income tax.
- No increase in the average rate of income tax, but the possible introduction of a higher third rate of income tax.
- The integration of tax and social welfare systems, but not the introduction of a refundable tax credit.
- To discontinue the tax relief on trade union subscriptions.
- To abolish stamp duty and replace it with an annual property tax to apply to residential housing units to fund local government, as well as water charges.
- The introduction of carbon taxes based on a standardized measure of CO_2 in tandem with the replacement of Vehicle Registration Tax over ten years and the latter's replacement with a tax on car usage. Also the introduction of a scrappage scheme focused on encouraging car owners to switch to electric and low carbon emitting vehicles.
- A review of 'tax expenditures' – transfers of public moneys achieved by reducing tax obligations rather than by direct expenditure – should be reviewed.
- In relation to enterprise, the Commission recommend, *inter alia*
  - A continuation of research and development tax credits and tax deductions for capital spending on scientific research
  - A discontinuation of income tax relief for farm land leasing, milk quota purchase and stock relief for farming and payments to the National Co-operative Farm Relief Services Ltd
  - Discontinuation of tax exemption for patent royalties
- In relation to tax incentives for retirement savings, the Commission recommended, *inter alia*
  - Replacing current tax relief by a matching exchequer contribution of €1 for each €1.60 contributed by the taxpayer (effectively 38

per cent relief), but for the first five years this would be a €1 for €1 euro matching contribution (effectively 50 per cent relief). This is in line with the principle of replacing 'tax expenditures' (see above) with direct spending

o A lump sum of up to €200,000 withdrawable on retirement tax free with the balance withdrawn taxable at the standard rate

IV: Key proposals contained in the Report of the Special Group on Public Service

Department	Full-year savings (€ million)
Agriculture, Fisheries & Food	305
Arts, Sports & Tourism	105
Communications, Energy & Natural Resources	66
Community, Rural & Gaeltacht Affairs	151
Defence	53
Education & Science	746
Enterprise, Trade & Employment	238
Environment, Heritage & Local Government	130
Finance Group of Votes	83
Foreign Affairs	42
Health & Children	1230
Houses of the Oireachtas Commission	8
Justice Group of Votes	136
National Treasury Management Agency	5
Social & Family Affairs	1848
Taoiseach's Group of Votes	18
Transport	127
Other	21
TOTAL SAVINGS	**5312**

Some of the significant measures in terms of their sizeability and/or controversy include the proposals to (amount saved in brackets where relevant):

- (Agriculture, Fisheries & Food) Discontinue REPS schemes (€80 million) and reduce spending on the Disadvantaged Area Compensatory Scheme (€66 million)
- (Education & Science) Staffing reductions in primary and post-primary (various measures €180 million), reduction in number of Special Needs assistance (€60 million) and English language support teachers (€25 million)
- (Health & Children) Reduce HSE staffing (€300 million), invite tenders by open competition to provide services under the GMS (€370 million), revise income guidelines to basic rate of social welfare (jobseekers allowance) to remove all existing non-medical allowances (€100 million), means test for home care packages (€28 million)
- (Social & Family Affairs) General reduction in rate of 5 per cent (€850 million), reduce by 20 per cent the child benefit rate (€513 million)
- Abolish the Department of Community, Rural & Gaeltacht Affairs
- Discontinue the Irish Film Board

Bibliography

Acemoglu, D., 'Why Do New Technologies Complement Skills?', *Quarterly Journal of Economics*, Vol. 113:4, President and Fellows of Harvard College and the M.I.T., November 1998.

Annual Competitiveness Report, National Competitiveness Council, Dublin, 2008.

Annual Report, 2003, 'Competitiveness Challenge', National Competitiveness Council, December 2003.

Kelly, E., *Benchmarking, Social Partnership and Higher Remuneration: Wage Setting Institutions and the Public-Private Sector Wage Gap in Ireland*, 2008.

McCarthy, C., *Expenditure Control and Fiscal Consolidation*, 2009.

National Employment Survey, 2007, Central Statistics Office, Cork, 2009.

O'Brien, F., *Assessment of Public Sector Pensions Liabilities*.

Overseas Travel statistics, *May 2009*, Central Statistics Office, Cork, 2009.

Puttnam, R., *Bowling Alone*, Simon and Schuster, 2001.

Quarterly National Household Survey, First Quarter 2009, Quarterly National Household Survey, Central Statistics Office, Cork, June, 2009.

Report of the Special Group on Public Service Numbers and Expenditure Programmes, Special Group on Public Service Numbers and Expenditure Programmes, Dublin, July, 2009.

Soros, G., *The Crash of 2008 and What it Means*, Public Affairs, 2009.

Statement on Prices and Costs, National Competitiveness Council, September, 2004.

Tett, G., *Fool's Gold*, Little Brown, 2009.

Wiesmann, G., 'German Industrial Orders Surge'. *Financial Times*, 8 July 2009.

Woodward, B., *Maestro: Greenspan's Fed and the American Boom.* Simon and Schuster, 2001.

Index